The Jacobean Kirk, 1567–1625

For my parents and in memory of Farquhar Macarthur

The Jacobean Kirk, 1567–1625

Sovereignty, Polity and Liturgy

ALAN R. MacDONALD

Ashgate

Aldershot • Brookfield USA • Singapore • Sydney

© Alan R. MacDonald, 1998

Published by
Ashgate Publishing Limited
Gower House
Croft Road
Aldershot
Hants
GU11 3HR
England

Ashgate Publishing Company
Old Post Road
Brookfield
Vermont 05036–9704
USA

The author has asserted their moral right under the Copyright, Designs and Patents Act, 1988, to be identified as the author of this work.

British Library Cataloguing in Publication Data

MacDonald, Alan
   The Jacobean Kirk, 1567–1625: Sovereignty, Polity and
   Liturgy. (St Andrews Studies in Reformation History)
   1. Reformation—Scotland.   2. Scotland—Church history—16th
   century.   3. Scotland—Church history—17th century.
   I. Title.
   274.1'1'06

Library of Congress Cataloging-in-Publication Data

MacDonald, Alan R., 1969–
   The Jacobean Kirk, 1567–1625: sovereignty, polity, and liturgy/
   Alan R. MacDonald.
      p.   cm. (St Andrews Studies in Reformation History)
   Includes bibliographical references and index.
   ISBN 1-85928-373-X (alk. paper)
   1. Church of Scotland—History—16th century.   2. Scotland—Church
   history—16th century.   3. Church of Scotland—History—17th
   century.   4. Scotland—Church history—17th century.   5. Scotland—
   History—James VI, 1567–1625.   I. Title.   II. Series.
   BX9071.M24 1998
   285'.2411'09031—dc21   98–19314
                                                              CIP

ISBN 1 85928 373 X

This book is printed on acid free paper

Typeset in Sabon by Manton Typesetters, 5–7 Eastfield Road, Louth, Lincolnshire, LN11 7AJ and printed in Great Britain by MPG Books Ltd, Bodmin, Cornwall

Contents

List of maps   ix

Acknowledgements   xi

Conventions and abbreviations   xiii

Introduction   1

1   The formative years, 1567–85   6

2   Compromise and conflict, 1586–92   30

3   An untidy tumble towards crisis, 1592–96   50

4   The road to consensus, 1597–1602   74

5   The regal union and the collapse of consensus, 1603–1606   101

6   The new autocracy, 1606–10   124

7   New polity, new liturgy, 1610–25   148

8   Conclusion   171

Appendix: Maps   189

Bibliography   197

Index   205

St Andrews Studies in Reformation History

*The Shaping of a Community: The Rise and Reformation of the
English Parish c. 1400–1560*
Beat Kümin

*Seminary or University? The Genevan Academy and
Reformed Higher Education, 1560–1620*
Karin Maag

Marian Protestantism: Six Studies
Andrew Pettegree

Protestant History and Identity in Sixteenth-Century Europe
(2 volumes) edited by Bruce Gordon

*Antifraternalism and Anticlericalism in the German Reformation:
Johann Eberlin von Günzburg and the Campaign against the Friars*
Geoffrey Dipple

*Reformations Old and New: Essays on the Socio-Economic
Impact of Religious Change c. 1470–1630*
edited by Beat Kümin

Piety and the People: Religious Printing in French, 1511–1551
Francis M. Higman

The Reformation in Eastern and Central Europe
edited by Karin Maag

John Foxe and the English Reformation
edited by David Loades

The Reformation and the Book
Jean-François Gilmont, edited and translated by Karin Maag

The Magnificent Ride: The First Reformation in Hussite Bohemia
Thomas A. Fudge

Kepler's Tübingen: Stimulus to a Theological Mathematics
Charlotte Methuen

'Practical Divinity': The Works and Life of Revd Richard Greenham
Kenneth L. Parker and Eric J. Carlson

*Belief and Practice in Reformation England: A Tribute to
Patrick Collinson by his Students*
edited by Susan Wabuda and Caroline Litzenberger

*Frontiers of the Reformation: Dissidence and Orthodoxy
in Sixteenth-Century Europe*
Auke Jelsma

List of maps

1 Ecclesiastical organisation immediately before the
   Reformation   190

2 Proposed dioceses of superintendents in 1560   191

3 Actual dioceses of superintendents and commissioners after
   1560   192

4 Diocesan structure resulting from Concordat of Leith, 1572   193

5 The 13 'model' presbyteries and the planned national system
   of presbyteries and synods of 1581   194

6 Provinces of commissioners of visitation in 1586   195

7 Presbyteries in 1593 and 1606   196

The maps in the Appendix come from the *Atlas of Scottish History to 1707*, eds P.G.B. McNeill and H.L. MacQueen (Scottish Medievalists and Department of Geography, University of Edinburgh, 1996), (Maps 1, 4 and 6) and *An Historical Atlas of Scotland c. 400–c. 1600*, eds P.G.B. McNeill and R. Nicholson (Scottish Medievalists, 1975), (Maps 2, 3, 5 and 7). They are reproduced with permission of the Atlas Committee of the Scottish Medievalists and with the permission of their individual authors: D.E.R. Watt (Map 1); P. McNeill (Maps 2, 3, 5 and 7); and J. Kirk (Maps 4 and 6).

Acknowledgements

The genesis of this book was a doctoral thesis at the University of Edinburgh and I owe particular thanks to my former PhD supervisor, Michael Lynch. When I was an undergraduate, his teaching awoke in me both an interest in ecclesiastical history and the desire to question every preconception I had or would come across. After I embarked on research, his encouragement and advice were always appreciated, as was his sometimes frustrating ability to come up with an awkward question just when I thought I had the whole thing sorted out. I am also very grateful to my second supervisor, Jane Dawson, for complementing Michael so well by not asking awkward questions and by providing very much appreciated reassurance over equally appreciated lunches. I am now allowed to mention Roger Mason, my external examiner, who has provided help and advice and a great deal of food for thought in the course of numerous discussions of the two kingdoms theory. We continue to disagree profoundly and very amicably.

Chris Smout is due a good measure of gratitude for deciding to employ an ecclesiastical historian to look at woodland history, thus broadening my horizons, keeping the wolf from our door for 18 months and providing much pleasure in a new and fascinating area of research. In my next guise as a parliamentary historian, Keith Brown's forbearance while I finished this book has been greatly appreciated. Equally tolerant and long-suffering have been the editors of the *St Andrews Studies in Reformation History* series, who have helped an inexperienced author through the editorial maze and have taken every excuse for every delay in their stride.

There are numerous other people to whom my thanks must go and to name them all would be impossible but I will do my best to name as many as I can. One cannot begin to understand the sixteenth century in Scotland without drinking from the well of John Durkan. He is generous with references, and conversations with him always prove there is something new to ask of the evidence as well as increasing one's stock of corny jokes. The support and knowledge of colleagues and friends in the world of Scottish historical studies have been invaluable. Particular thanks are due to Sharon Adams, Julian Goodare, Ruth Grant, Ronnie Lee, Andrew MacKillop, Robin Macpherson, Diana Newton, Wayne Pearce, Fiona Watson, Vaughan Wells and Jenny Wormald with whom I have had many long and fruitful discussions. I must also thank Doris Williamson, departmental secretary at Scottish History in Edinburgh, who must have appeared in more Scottish historical acknowledgements than almost any other, and deservedly so. Her cheery help on innumerable occasions, even before I left home to come to Edinburgh in 1987, will not be forgotten, nor will the advice of Owen Dudley-Edwards to read Scott's *The Fortunes of Nigel*. The usual caveat must, of course, be added, that all of the interpretations, conclusions and, most of all, mistakes in this book are entirely my own responsibility.

My parents have provided rest, physical labour on the croft and a sense of proportion for which I am very grateful indeed. They and my parents-in-law have often given me sanctuary from James VI and the ministers, thus averting insanity. I am grateful, too, to my brother and his wife for providing accommodation and distracting trips to test matches at Lord's on research visits to London.

The staff of the Scottish Record Office and the National Library of Scotland in Edinburgh, the Public Record Office in London and the University Libraries at Edinburgh, Glasgow and St Andrews were all helpful, efficient and friendly. To all of them, both up front and behind the scenes, my thanks. I am grateful for the help of the Carnegie Trust for the Universities of Scotland, which provided the financial support for three years of full-time postgraduate study. Without that, none of this would have been possible.

Finally, my greatest debt is owed to my wife, proofreader and critic – the *sine qua non* of this book – Janet Foggie who has read the whole text and provided innumerable invaluable comments and suggestions. I can only apologise for being too obsessed with the Kirk and James VI to pay sufficient attention to the Dominicans, the cats or the hoovering on so many occasions. Without her support and help, given unfailingly even when her own work should have taken priority, this task would have been unimaginably more difficult.

Alan R. MacDonald

Conventions and abbreviations

Before 1 January 1600, the year turned on 25 March, a fact which has led to many instances of misdating. All dates are given here in post-1600 style, therefore 9 February 1596 *is* 1596, not 1597. The letters *u*, *v* and *w* were used interchangeably in the period concerned and have been regularised according to modern usage. The letters 'yogh' and 'thorn' have been given as 'y' and 'th' throughout. It should also be noted that the 'quh' prefix was equivalent to the modern 'wh', reflecting the greater aspiration which Scots still give that letter combination. In Scots, plurals and possessives were formed in '-is', past participles in '-it' and present participles in '-and'. Proper names have normally been modernised.

A number of Scots words have been retained because of their current use: caution = security/bail; escheat = confiscation of property for crime or debt; horning/putting to the horn = outlawing/proclaiming as an outlaw; leet = shortlist; outwith = outside or beyond; sederunt = attendance list; tack = fixed-term lease; teind = tithe; Court of Session = the highest civil court in Scotland, its judges are known as 'Lords of Session' or 'Senators of the College of Justice'. Unusual words within quotations have been explained where it is thought necessary. If any have been missed, readers are referred to M. Robinson's *The Concise Scots Dictionary* (Aberdeen, 1985) or the *Dictionary of the Older Scottish Tongue*, eds W.A. Craigie et al. (Oxford, Aberdeen and Edinburgh, 1937–).

All money is given in £ Scots which began the period at a ratio of £1 sterling to £4 Scots and ended it at £1 sterling to £12 Scots. The merk was two-thirds of £ Scots.

The following abbreviations have been used in footnotes:

Aberdeen Presbytery	Register of the presbytery of Aberdeen, SRO, CH2/1/1.
APS	*The Acts of the Parliaments of Scotland*, eds T. Thomson and C. Innes, 12 vols (Edinburgh, 1815–75).
Balfour, *Works*	Haig, J., ed., *The Historical Works of Sir James Balfour*, 4 vols (Edinburgh, 1824–25).

BUK   *Acts and Proceedings of the General As-
                                 sembly of the Kirk of Scotland*, ed. T.
                                 Thomson, 3 vols (Bannatyne Club,
                                 1839–45).

Calderwood, *History*   *History of the Church of Scotland by
                                 Mr David Calderwood*, ed. T. Thomson,
                                 8 vols (Wodrow Society, 1842–49).

CSP Scot   *Calendar of the State Papers Relating
                                 to Scotland and Mary, Queen of Scots,
                                 1547–1603*, eds J. Bain et al., 13 vols
                                 (Edinburgh, 1898–1969).

Dalkeith Presbytery   Register of the presbytery of Dalkeith,
                                 SRO, CH2/424/1.

Deer Presbytery   Register of the presbytery of Deer, SRO,
                                 CH2/89/1/1–2.

Dunblane Presbytery   Register of the Presbytery of Dunblane,
                                 SRO, CH2/723/1.

Ecclesiastical Letters   *Original Letters Relating to the Ecclesi-
                                 astical Affairs of Scotland*, ed. B. Botfield,
                                 2 vols (Bannatyne Club, 1851).

Edinburgh Presbytery   Register of the presbytery of Edinburgh,
                                 SRO, CH2/121/1–3.

Ellon Presbytery   Register of the presbytery of Ellon, SRO,
                                 CH2/146/1–2.

Forbes, *Records*   J. Forbes, *Certaine Records Touching
                                 the Estate of the Kirk in the Years
                                 MDCV & MDCVI*, ed. D. Laing
                                 (Wodrow Society, 1846).

Glasgow Presbytery   Register of the presbytery of Glasgow,
                                 SRO, CH2/171/1–2 (microfilm).

Haddington Presbytery   Register of the presbytery of
                                 Haddington, SRO, CH2/185/1–3.

HKJVI   *The Historie and Life of King James the
                                 Sext*, ed. T. Thomson (Bannatyne Club,
                                 1825).

Jedburgh Presbytery   Register of the presbytery of Jedburgh,
                                 SRO, CH2/198/1–2.

Letters and State Papers   *Letters and State Papers During the
                                 Reign of James the Sixth*, ed. J.
                                 Maidment (Abbotsford Club, 1838).

Linlithgow presbytery   Register of the presbytery of Linlithgow,
                                 SRO, CH2/242/1–2.

Lothian Synod	*The Records of the Synod of Lothian and Tweeddale*, ed. J. Kirk (Stair Society, 1977).
Melrose Presbytery	Register of the presbytery of Melrose, SRO, CH2/327/1.
Melville, *Diary*	*The Autobiography and Diary of Mr James Melville*, ed. R. Pitcairn (Wodrow Society, 1843).
Moysie, *Memoirs*	*Memoirs of the Affairs of Scotland by David Moysie, MDLXXVII–MDCIII*, ed. J. Dennistoun (Bannatyne Club, 1830).
NLS	National Library of Scotland, Edinburgh.
Paisley Presbytery	Register of the presbytery of Paisley, SRO, CH2/294/1.
Peebles Presbytery	Register of the presbytery of Peebles, SRO, CH2/295/1/1–2.
Perth Presbytery	Register of the presbytery of Perth, SRO, CH2/299/1.
PRO	Public Record Office, London.
Row, *History*	J. Row, *History of the Kirk of Scotland from the Year 1558 to August 1637*, ed. D. Laing (Wodrow Society, 1842).
RPC	*The Register of the Privy Council of Scotland*, eds J.H. Burton et al., 14 vols (Edinburgh, 1877–98).
RSCHS	*Records of the Scottish Church History Society.*
'Ryseing and Usurpation'	'The ryseing and usurpation of our pretended bishops', NLS. Advocates Manuscripts, 34.2.11.
St Andrews Presbytery	Register of the Presbytery of St Andrews, St Andrews University MS 23.
Scot, *Apologetical Narration*	W. Scot, *An Apologetical Narration of the State and Government of the Kirk of Scotland since the Reformation*, D. Laing (Wodrow Society, 1846).
Scott, *Fasti*	Scott, H., ed., *Fasti Ecclesiae Scoticanae*, revised edn, 8 vols (Edinburgh, 1915–).
Scots Peerage	*The Scots Peerage*, ed. J. Balfour Paul, 9 vols (Edinburgh, 1904–14).

SHR	*Scottish Historical Review*
Spottiswoode, *History*	*History of the Church of Scotland ... by the Right Rev. John Spottiswoode,* eds M. Russell and M. Napier, 3 vols (Spottiswoode Society, 1847–51).
SRO	Scottish Record Office, Edinburgh.
Stirling Presb. Recs	*Stirling Presbytery Records, 1581–1587,* ed. J. Kirk (Scottish History Society, 1981).
Stirling Presbytery	Register of the presbytery of Stirling, SRO, CH2/722/1–4 (microfilm).
Watt, *Fasti*	*Fasti Ecclesiae Scoticanae Medii Aevi ad Annum 1638,* ed. D.E.R. Watt (Scottish Record Society, 1969).
Wodrow Miscellany	Laing, D., ed., *The Miscellany of the Wodrow Society* (Wodrow Society, 1844).

Introduction

In recent years, a number of historians have discussed aspects of the Jacobean Kirk in varying depth and detail. Yet there has, hitherto, been no single study dedicated to the ecclesiastical history of the reign of James VI, with the exception of a short essay by the late Professor Gordon Donaldson and a chapter in his volume of the *Edinburgh History of Scotland*.[1] The reign is a difficult one to deal with for reasons of length. Fifty-five years on the throne was longer than any of his predecessors and an adult reign of a few months short of 40 years was surpassed only by William the Lion (1165–1214). It encompassed major changes in the history of Scotland and of Britain, most notable being the regal union of 1603. For ecclesiastical historians, the personal reign, beginning in November 1585, has fallen victim to the fact that it drops neatly between two of Scotland's biggest historiographical stools – the Reformation of 1560 and the Covenanting Revolution of 1638. Too often it is dealt with briefly in discussions of the aftermath of the former or of the roots of the latter and, as a result, it has been subsumed within other agendas without receiving detailed attention in its own right.[2] The prodigious amount of work carried out by Maurice Lee on various aspects of the secular politics of the reign of James VI has done much to fill the gap in the study of that facet of Jacobean Scotland but no comparable work has been devoted to the Kirk. Accordingly, the PhD thesis upon which this book is based and, to a lesser extent, the book itself, have been written as if they were an exploration of *terra incognita*, using an unashamedly empiricist approach because the groundwork was still required for much of the period.[3] It is hoped that this has

---

[1] G. Donaldson, 'The Scottish Church 1567–1625', in ed., A.G.R. Smith, *The Reign of James VI and I* (Aylesbury, 1973); G. Donaldson, *Scotland: James V–James VII* (Edinburgh, 1971), ch. 11.

[2] G. Donaldson, *The Scottish Reformation* (Cambridge, 1960), covers the period as a brief postscript and W.R. Foster, *The Church before the Covenants* (Edinburgh, 1975), traces the history of the Kirk before 1638 by starting in 1596. Uncut pages covering the period *c.* 1585–*c.* 1610 were found in many basic printed primary sources in more than one major library.

[3] M. Lee, *Great Britain's Solomon: King James VI and I in his Three Kingdoms* (Urbana, 1990); *Government by Pen: Scotland under James VI and I* (Urbana, 1980); *John Maitland of Thirlestane and the Foundation of the Stewart Despotism in Scotland* (Princetown, 1959); A.R. MacDonald, 'Ecclesiastical Politics in Scotland, 1586–1610' (unpublished Edinburgh PhD dissertation, 1995). This forms the basis of Chapters 2–6 of the book, dealing with the core 26 years of the reign, which are covered here in more detail because it is the poorest served in terms of secondary literature.

revealed much which would otherwise not have come to light had the preconceptions of some rather superficial recent historiography been carried into the research.

The study of ecclesiastical politics cannot reasonably be argued to be more or less important than any other field of historical investigation in this, or any other, period. Simply because the so-called 'traditionalist agenda', which 'identified the centrality of the Kirk–State controversy', is not as widely accepted as it once was does not mean that any study of such themes is 'pushing against the frontiers of dead history', nor is it merely a 'foot-note checking exercise'.[4] Far from being dead, the history of the Reformed Kirk, its relationship with the state and its internal relationships, remain crucial, not least because so many mistaken notions concerning basic aspects of that history require revision in the light of a reassessment of the evidence. Each generation of historians questions and modifies what has gone before – that is the very vitality of the discipline. Because there are no answers to satisfy the perceptions of every age, new answers, and indeed new questions, continually emerge. A recent observation on Reformation historiography in general is an important lesson: 'the past couple of decades in Reformation historiography have seen substantial changes in interpretation of the phenomenon. There has been a conscious attempt to transcend the rigidities of confessional historiography, in which one's interpretation of the Reformation was closely tied to the self-justification of one's own religious creed'.[5]

This is perhaps more true of Scotland than of anywhere else in Europe. Here can be found sectarianism between Catholics and Protestants and even between different presbyterian, let alone Protestant, denominations. Questions of ecclesiastical politics in the sixteenth and seventeenth centuries have, down the intervening centuries, remained intensely important. As a result, Scotland lags behind in the decline of 'confessional historiography'. To borrow a term from sports journalism, too many Scottish ecclesiastical historians are and have been 'fans with typewriters', unstintingly justifying the present through the past, their writings peppered with partisan value judgements.

This tradition can be traced back to the period of study when James Melville, Archbishop Spottiswoode, David Calderwood, William Scot, John Row and numerous others tried to provide their world with the truth, as they saw it, of James VI's ecclesiastical policies and the Kirk's

---

[4] A.I. Macinnes, 'Early Modern Scotland: the Current State of Play', *SHR*, 73 (1994), 30–46, at 31–2.

[5] R. Scribner, 'Introduction' in *The Reformation in National Context*, eds R. Scribner et al. (Cambridge, 1994), 2.

reaction to them.[6] This polemical history was carried on through the seventeenth-century religious controversies, emerging, notably, in the prodigious collections and works of Robert Wodrow in the early eighteenth century. As well as writing on the more immediate concerns of late seventeenth- and early eighteenth-century Scotland, Wodrow amassed a huge collection of material on the history of the Kirk, much of which was published in the nineteenth century.[7] The later eighteenth century saw the advent of the Scottish Enlightenment, providing a new perspective on the historical process. Gone was the cyclical view of human existence and in came the notion of progress from barbarism to civilisation. Yet the standard narrative sources were already established as the basis of the ecclesiastical aspects of histories of Scotland. Whether a writer extolled notions of ancient Scottish 'liberty', demonstrated in presbyterianism, or disapproved of certain ministers' opposition to the state, it was to the perspectives of Calderwood and Spottiswoode that they turned. They expressed the views of those writers in terms of civilisation, refinement and moderation and placed the Reformation into the framework of a progression towards liberty.[8]

The firmest roots of the modern tradition, equally faithful to the views of the early narrative historians, were established in the nineteenth century when Thomas McCrie revived 'assertive presbyterian historiography' in his *Life of John Knox* and *Life of Andrew Melville*. The titles themselves reveal that they were, fundamentally, Protestant hagiographies, the latter reflecting a desire to find a 'successor' to Knox even though there was no obvious candidate.[9] The controversy surrounding the 'Disruption' of 1843, leading to the formation of the Free

---

[6] An excellent survey of the near contemporary historiography can be found in D.G. Mullan, *Episcopacy in Scotland, the History of an Idea 1560–1638* (Edinburgh, 1986), ch. 8.

[7] The NLS possesses the 'Wodrow Manuscripts', the largest collection of manuscripts of Scottish sixteenth- and seventeenth-century ecclesiastical history, while the library of the University of Glasgow has more of his papers. A selection of the biographical material which he collected was published as W.K. Tweedie, ed., *Select Biographies*, 2 vols (Wodrow Society, 1845–47) and R. Lippe, ed., *Selections from Wodrow's Biographical Collections*, (New Spalding Club, 1890). See also C. Kidd, *Subverting Scotland's Past: Scottish Whig Historians and the Creation of an Anglo-British Identity, 1689–c. 1830* (Cambridge, 1993), ch. 4

[8] See D. Hume, *The History of Great Britain*, 2 vols (London, 1757), i, 61; W. Robertson, *The History of Scotland During the Reigns of Queen Mary and King James VI* (London, 1794), 431, 443; Kidd, *Subverting Scotland's Past*, ch. 8.

[9] T. McCrie, *Life of John Knox* (Edinburgh, 1811) and *Life of Andrew Melville* (Edinburgh, 1819; 2nd edn 1824). There is no evidence that Melville was the 'leader' of the Kirk. In his era, nobody had the role which had been accorded to Knox by the Kirk of the 1560s. Kidd, *Subverting Scotland's Past*, 201.

Church of Scotland, caused an explosion of publication. The old arguments of the sixteenth and seventeenth centuries over state control were dusted off, given a new relevance and a vigorous airing. Scores of narrative histories and collections of documents were published by interested parties in a bizarre war of words in which centuries-old writings were resurrected, not for use as historical source material but as contemporary propaganda, to support or oppose attempts to change the Kirk's relationship with the crown.

If the works of J. Hill Burton and P. Hume Brown are a guide to the late nineteenth- and early twentieth-century approach, two historiographical 'camps' remained firmly entrenched.[10] In recent years those favouring an 'episcopalian' interpretation and their 'presbyterian' counterparts have continued to fight out what must be one of the longest-running historiographical battles, and their works receive frequent attention in the following pages.[11] The accusation may be levelled that this book is, in some respects, merely another volley of fire in that battle. It is, however, intended to be a request for the two armies to come out of their trenches and look again at the Kirk in the reign of James VI. The approach adopted here is primarily an institutional one yet the records of the institutions of the Kirk are not the dry, laconic minutes of modern committees but a rich seam of political and religious opinion, revealing action and reaction and possessing a striking immediacy. This is the first study to be based on an examination of all the surviving records of presbyteries and synods from the reign of James VI. It is an exploration of the important ecclesiastical political issues of the time through analysis of shifting patterns of opinion rather than concentration on the notion of fixed clerical 'parties' and ideologies. That notion has its origins in generations of historians taking at face value the partisan accounts written in the early seventeenth century. Few attempts have been made to look behind and beyond their polemical frames of reference which required a two-dimensional contrast between the 'good guys' and the 'bad guys'. This has done much to obscure the more complex reality.[12]

---

[10] The Wodrow and Spottiswoode Societies were established and the records of general assemblies and the *Histories* of Calderwood, Spottiswoode and Knox were published. J. Hill Burton, *The History of Scotland*, 8 vols (Edinburgh, 1873), vols v–vi; P. Hume Brown, *History of Scotland to the Present Time*, 3 vols (Cambridge 1905), vol. ii.

[11] For a review of recent work in this area, see G. Hewitt, 'Reformation to Revolution', in eds, I. Donnachie and C. Whatley, *The Manufacture of Scottish History* (Edinburgh, 1992), 16–30.

[12] See below, esp. Chapter 8, for a discussion of the notion of 'parties' in the Kirk in the light of the evidence presented here.

Scotland, in the latter half of the sixteenth century and the first quarter of the seventeenth, underwent radical change. Large-scale magnate violence was reduced to a level unknown for generations. Economic instability, characterised by severe price inflation, was almost endemic, although the economy did begin to settle down after *c.* 1600. Government in all spheres was intensifying – Parliament was legislating on more and more aspects of people's lives and taxation reached unprecedented levels.[13] In this period too, Scotland lost the personal presence of the king, a factor which cannot be overestimated in any assessment of the nature of royal government under James VI. In spite of the incidence of numerous minorities, the accessibility of the monarch when he or she was an adult, or of the regent during one of the minorities, had been a marked feature of the Scottish constitution. The succession of James VI to the thrones of England and Ireland in 1603 was to change this irrevocably. Power structures within government were reorientated and access to the king's ear became much more limited. Individuals, such as the Earl of Dunbar, who were prepared to make the tiring journey to court a number of times in any year became very powerful indeed. These changes at the centre of power in the state inevitably impinged upon the Kirk which was interested in keeping close contact with secular authority through its own power structures which linked the centre to the localities over a broad sweep of the realm. As the only institution, other than the crown, which had any claims to being national, the king's desire to control the Kirk is hardly surprising.

Finally, one major caveat must be observed. The word 'Scotland' must be assumed not to cover the north and west Highlands. The system of kirk session, presbytery and synod did not penetrate the *Gaidhealtachd* in any significant way during the reign of James VI and record material for the Kirk in that area is severely lacking. Few ministers from that part of the kingdom participated in general assemblies, let alone in the ecclesiastical politics of the period.[14]

---

[13] K.M. Brown, *Bloodfeud in Scotland, 1573–1625* (Edinburgh, 1986); T.M. Devine and S.G.E. Lythe, 'The Economy of Scotland under James VI: a Revision Article', *SHR*, 50 (1971), 91–106; J. Goodare, 'Parliament and Society in Scotland, 1560–1603 (unpublished Edinburgh PhD dissertation, 1989); and by the same author, 'Parliamentary Taxation in Scotland, 1560–1603', *SHR*, 68 (1989), 23–52; see *APS*, vols i–iv, the first two covering the period 1124–1567, the next two 1567–1625.

[14] J. Kirk, 'The Kirk in the Highlands at the Reformation', in his *Patterns of Reform: Continuity and Change in the Reformation Kirk* (Edinburgh, 1989), ch. 8; J. Dawson, 'Calvinism and the *Gaidhealtachd* in Scotland', in eds, A. Pettegree et al., *Calvinism in Europe, 1540–1620* (Cambridge, 1994), 231–53. Although these works challenge received wisdom, hidebound by a literate culture, about the extent of the penetration of the Reformation into the predominantly oral *Gaidhealtachd*, they do not challenge the perception of a lack of institutional ecclesiastical penetration.

CHAPTER ONE

The formative years, 1567–85

On 29 July 1567, Charles James Stewart, only 13 months old, was crowned as James VI, King of Scots in the Kirk of the Holy Rood in Stirling. The ceremony, performed by a pre-Reformation bishop who had conformed to Protestantism and two superintendents, Reformed regional overseers, with a sermon delivered by the parish minister of Edinburgh, John Knox, epitomised the state of flux in which the Kirk found itself. A few weeks previously Mary, Queen of Scots, had been imprisoned by nobles opposed to her marriage to the Earl of Bothwell and, a few days before the coronation, some of those nobles forced her abdication in favour of her son, appointing her half-brother, James Stewart, Earl of Moray, as regent. Within less then a year, she escaped from captivity in Lochleven Castle, confronted the forces nominally supporting her son and fled to England after defeat at Langside near Glasgow. Between the summer of 1568 and 1573, Scotland would be riven by a civil war between the Queen's Party, fighting for her restoration, and the King's Party. Amidst this civil turmoil, the Kirk, precariously established in law since the Reformation Parliament of August 1560, undertook a second attempt at giving itself a firm footing in Scotland.

In the Regent Moray, it had the closest thing to a 'godly prince' it would ever see. In spite of the political and military difficulties which the new regime faced, 'church and government were working together in a way that had not previously been possible'.[1] The Kirk experienced an unprecedented, and never to be repeated, level of state sympathy and support. The first General Assembly after Mary's imprisonment requested ratification of the acts of the Reformation Parliament, the patrimony of the pre-Reformation Kirk, the vetting of schoolmasters and college regents, punishment of Darnley's murderers and a test oath for all in public office. The Privy Council, on the very day it formally accepted Mary's abdication, endorsed them, although with reservations about the financial requests.[2] On 15 December, Parliament met and, immediately after ratifying Mary's abdication and Moray's regency, restated and ratified the legislation of the Reformation Parliament abrogating papal power, outlawing the mass and adopting a Protestant

---

[1] M.H.B. Sanderson, *Ayrshire and the Reformation: People and Change, 1490–1600* (East Linton, 1997), 124.
[2] *BUK*, i, 107–10; *RPC*, i, 531–3, 534–6.

confession of faith. It also recognised the Kirk's right to examine all presentees to benefices, restricted public office to Protestants and acknowledged the Kirk's exclusive jurisdiction in preaching, discipline and administration of the sacraments.[3] Over the next two years, the government showed remarkable favour to the Kirk, purging Aberdeen University of its Catholic staff in 1569, giving judgements before the Privy Council in favour of Protestant benefice holders and proceeding against recusant Catholic clergy. The thirds of benefices, a settlement of 1562 whereby one-third of all pre-Reformation ecclesiastical livings was shared between Kirk and crown, were given entirely to the Kirk, the crown receiving only the surplus. It has even been claimed that Moray tried to restore the Kirk's entire pre-Reformation patrimony, only to be thwarted by Parliament.[4] This was the toughest request which the Kirk could make; it would never be granted and would remain a source of tension for decades to come.

In January 1570, Moray was assassinated by a junior member of the foremost Marian family, James Hamilton of Bothwellhaugh. For six months the King's Party reeled and the Kirk lamented the loss of their protector. Moray was not replaced for six months. The new regent was the Earl of Lennox, the king's paternal grandfather, appointed on English advice on the back of a brief English invasion on behalf of the King's Party. This regency lasted only 14 months, Lennox being killed in a raid on Stirling by the Queen's Party in September 1571. He was quickly replaced by the Earl of Mar whose regency ended with his assassination in October 1572. Scotland's last regent, James Douglas, Earl of Morton, had signed the first bond of the Lords of the Congregation in 1557 and attended the first General Assembly after Mary's deposition. Much had changed since he had conspired to make Scotland Protestant and the Kirk would find this head of a godly state to be an uncomfortable bedfellow.

With the King's Party struggling after Moray's death, continuing political instability meant that the Kirk made little progress. By the time Mar was in power, however, only Edinburgh Castle remained in the hands of the Queen's Party and the Kirk could once more attract the state's attention in furthering its aims. Other than endowment, the foremost issue in this period, and for a considerable period afterwards, concerned how the Kirk should be governed. In 1560, attempts were made to establish a new administrative system, based upon the *First Book of Discipline*, written by six Johns: Douglas, Knox, Row, Spottiswoode, Willock and Winram. As far as oversight was concerned,

---

[3] *APS*, iii, 14–24.
[4] *RPC*, i, 673, 675, 680–81, 685–6, ii, 40–41; Spottiswoode, *History*, ii, 83.

'superintendents' were to be appointed to oversee ten streamlined 'provinces' or 'dioceses' each containing about 100 parishes, replacing the 13 medieval dioceses.[5] The return of a Catholic monarch in August 1561, the conformity to Protestantism of three pre-Reformation bishops and, above all, the failure of the Kirk to secure all the property of its Catholic predecessor, meant that this remarkably tidy system was never more than half-formed, attempts to appoint further superintendents in 1563 failing (see Maps 1, 2 and 3 in the Appendix). To fill in the gaps of oversight, 'commissioners' were appointed for areas which had neither superintendents nor conforming bishops.

The debate about whether this system was essentially episcopal or essentially collective is a complex one, far more complex than anyone at the time could ever have realised.[6] From the beginning of a legal Protestant Kirk in Scotland, individuals were given power far in excess of the moderation of ecclesiastical courts. They received presentations to benefices, examined presentees and gave them collation. They had exclusive rights to visit the parishes in their areas of oversight, they held courts in the principal towns of their provinces with appellate jurisdiction over parochial kirk sessions and they were constant moderators of the provincial synods with power to nominate commissioners to general assemblies.[7] Yet they were not bishops in the English style. They were not given residences and they did not administer diocesan property. They were responsible to the General Assembly which could suspend or deprive them and they did not sit in Parliament or exercise any *ex officio* civil jurisdiction. Ultimate authority lay with the General Assembly but a dogmatic desire for parity of ministers was as absent from the Kirk of the 1560s as was enthusiasm for lordly bishops.

When a 'godly' state was achieved, the opportunity arose to rectify anomalies and regularise the system of oversight. The Kirk hoped that reform would come in conjunction with the restoration of its patrimony; indeed in 1569, the General Assembly requested to be allowed to appoint more superintendents and asked for financial provision in

---

[5] *The First Book of Discipline*, ed. J.K. Cameron (Edinburgh, 1972), 115–28.

[6] The late Gordon Donaldson argued for episcopacy in his *The Scottish Reformation* (Cambridge, 1960), esp. ch. 5, and '"The example of Denmark" in the Scottish Reformation', in his *Scottish Church History* (Edinburgh, 1985), 60–70, while James Kirk emphasises superintendents' 'subordination to … their fellow ministers' in 'The Superintendent: Myth and Reality' in his *Patterns of Reform* (Edinburgh, 1989), 154–231, at 231 and, in the same work, '"The Polities of the Best Reformed Kirks": Scottish Achievements and English Aspirations in Church Government after the Reformation', 334–67 where he argues that the Kirk was, from the outset, essentially presbyterian in that it had a graded series of courts (341).

[7] Donaldson, *Scottish Reformation*, ch. 5.

a list of articles submitted to the privy council.[8] The Kirk, meanwhile, had to try to make the patchwork of oversight work. Between 1567 and 1572, it regularly examined those with powers of visitation, admonishing the Reformed bishops, superintendents and commissioners of visitation for failing to carry out their jobs properly and exhorting them to diligence. In December 1567, the Bishop of Orkney was deprived of all ecclesiastical function for having performed the marriage of Mary and Bothwell and the superintendent of Fife was admonished for failing to visit his kirks. In the following year, it was found that John Knox, as commissioner for Ayrshire, had yet to do his visitation, while in 1570, the commissioner for Ross was provided with assistance because he had no Gaelic.[9] Efforts were made to ensure that the supervision of the Kirk was being carried out by filling vacant parishes, encouraging those in post and seeing that parochial discipline was maintained.

The issue of oversight shifted to centre stage in August 1571 when 'Mr John Douglas, rector of the Universitie of Sanct Andrewes, was presented to the bishoprick of St Andrewes' by the crown after the previous incumbent, John Hamilton, a Catholic and a Marian, had been executed for treason by the King's Party.[10] The appointment of a kinsman of the Earl of Morton was the first presentation to an episcopal see since the deposition of Mary. The General Assembly complained to Parliament that benefices should not be given to anyone who was not approved by the Kirk and John Winram, superintendent of Fife and Strathearn, warned the new archbishop not to vote in Parliament until he had been admitted by the Kirk, on pain of excommunication. The Earl of Morton commanded him to vote on pain of treason! There ensued a tussle between the Kirk and the crown with John Erskine of Dun, superintendent of Angus and the Mearns, writing to the regent in November, protesting that all benefices should have cure of souls and should not be given out like pensions. The crown's reply noted that there was a basic problem caused by the unsettled nature of ecclesiastical polity.[11] In December, Archbishop Douglas got into a dispute with the collector of the thirds of benefices in Fife over revenues which, Douglas claimed, pertained to his see. Douglas and Superintendent Winram went to Leith where the King's Party was based, Edinburgh still being in the hands of the Queen's Party, to meet the Privy Council to resolve the dispute. As the result of similar problems elsewhere, all

---

[8] *BUK*, i, 145–6.
[9] *BUK*, i, 112, 114, 130, 175.
[10] Calderwood, *History*, iii, 135.
[11] Calderwood, *History*, iii, 135–8, 156–62, 164.

five superintendents were called to this meeting.[12] The issue required much thought, so the meeting was postponed until January.

A General Assembly at Leith on 12 January appointed commissioners to negotiate a settlement of oversight and endowment with the crown. The Kirk sent two superintendents, John Winram and John Erskine of Dun, three provincial commissioners, Andrew Hay, David Lindsay and Robert Pont, and one parish minister John Craig, while the Privy Council's six negotiators were headed by the Earl of Morton. In a 'quiet' meeting, the 'Concordat of Leith' was drawn up, in which it was agreed that the medieval dioceses would be retained (see Map 4 in the Appendix), that the 'most qualified' ministers should be presented to vacant sees and that bishops should have spiritual jurisdiction. They would be compelled to hold a parish and to have a 'chapter' of at least six to advise them regarding their oversight. They were to be subject to the General Assembly *in spiritualibus* and to the crown *in temporalibus* and would be permitted to exercise no more ecclesiastical power than the superintendents. As well as discussing reform of the episcopate, it was agreed that those presented to monastic prelacies should be examined by a bishop or superintendent 'concerning their qualifications and aptness to give voice for the Church in parliament'. It was also agreed that all benefices of cure which had been appropriated to prelacies in the past should be given to ministers and that specific sums from some of the monastic benefices would be used to pay for the royal household.[13] In the Concordat of Leith, the crown and the Kirk met half-way. Its terms suggested that much of the revenue from the pre-Reformation prelacies would fall to the Kirk, thus allowing the expansion and better endowment of the ministry. The Kirk had, apparently, secured episcopal revenues while maintaining the principles of oversight established for the superintendents. The fact that the crown retained rights of appointment to vacant sees was hardly a radical departure from the system of superintendents. The *First Book of Discipline* gave the crown the right to appoint them initially, and subsequent requests for the appointment of further superintendents were directed to the Privy Council.[14]

The Concordat was not binding on the Kirk until it was approved by a General Assembly. The next one, in March at St Andrews, established a committee, including Archbishop Douglas, to discuss the agreement but other actions of the Assembly suggest that it was already recognised

---

[12] Calderwood, *History*, iii, 165; *RPC*, ii, 90, 101, 103. Superintendents were equally capable of nepotism – the collector of thirds in Fife was one Robert Winram.

[13] *BUK*, i, 208–36; *RPC*, ii, 106–13; Spottiswoode, *History*, ii, 170–71; advices from Scotland, 26 Feb. 1572, *CSP Scot*, iv, no. 149.

[14] *First Book of Discipline*, 123–5; *BUK*, 145–6.

as effective. John Winram, superintendent of Fife and Strathearn, demitted the office of 'superintendentrie which he had in the diocese of Sanct Andrewes' and was ordered, along with the superintendents of Lothian and of Angus and the Mearns 'to use his awin jurisdictioun as of befoir in the provinces not yet subject to the Archbishoprik of Sanct Androes'. Although they were not abolished, it has been suggested that the 'introduction' of episcopacy was 'responsible for eclipsing the work of superintendents' and thus disrupting a workable system.[15] At the following assembly, at Perth in August, Douglas was granted full authority of visitation in his diocese and Winram was styled 'superintendent of Strathearn'. This Assembly formally approved the Concordat of Leith as an interim settlement: it was explicitly intended to operate until the king reached his majority. Precisely what 'farder and more perfyte ordour' they would seek 'as occasion sall serve' is not clear. It may have been in relation to endowment, since only the benefices under prelacies, not the lands, had been granted to the Kirk. It is hard to sustain an argument that this was a Kirk hostile to episcopacy. There were certainly strong misgivings about hierarchical and diocesan titles such as archbishop, archdeacon, dean, chapter and chancellor which were described as 'slanderous and offensive' and tainted with 'papistry'. Yet the solution was merely to find new names for these positions which were 'more agreeable to Gods word'.[16] That some efforts were indeed made in this direction is indicated by the Kirk's determination to call those with archiepiscopal sees merely the 'bishops' of St Andrews and Glasgow. John Knox's opinions about episcopacy are a source of controversy. He allegedly refused to inaugurate Douglas as archbishop after the Leith conference but he wrote to the assembly in August enjoining it to admit bishops according to the Concordat. Although not enthusiastic for over-mighty bishops, he was not opposed to a lucrative system in which the crown and the Kirk shared responsibility for bishops with limited powers.[17]

The Kirk's acceptance of the Leith settlement is indicated in the separate and senior place given to bishops in the sederunts of general assemblies, in the precedence they took over superintendents in their powers of oversight, visitation and admission to benefices, and in the

---

[15] *BUK*, i, 238, 239, 242; Kirk, *Patterns of Reform*, 228.

[16] *BUK*, i, 243–6; Spottiswoode, *History*, ii, 172; Kirk, *Patterns of Reform*, 341 where the author put undue emphasis on the desire to 'jettison' names, implying that offices too were to be abolished.

[17] Calderwood, *History*, iii, 206; *BUK*, i, 247–9; Melville, *Diary*, 31–2 suggests that Knox was opposed to bishops in principle. This, and Calderwood's record of his refusal to inaugurate Douglas are not contemporary and should be set beside his contemporary endorsement of the Leith settlement.

Assembly's request, in 1574, for the dioceses which remained vacant to be filled. In 1573, new bishops were provided to Glasgow and Dunkeld and they, along with the superintendents and commissioners of visitation, continued to be examined, admonished and exhorted to better service.[18] Since the provinces under the charge of John Erskine of Dun and John Spottiswoode (Angus and the Mearns, and Lothian respectively) fell within the diocese of St Andrews, they were to be relieved of their duties. Confusion reigned. The Assembly felt it had to ask the regent and the Privy Council about cancelling their superintendency and, in the following year, Winram, Spottiswoode and Erskine of Dun all tried to resign, while Robert Pont demitted office as commissioner for Moray because of the appointment of George Douglas as bishop. In 1575, after the death of John Douglas, Winram's superintendency was again declared to cover Fife.[19] Had the Kirk fully taken on board the Concordat of Leith, the system of commissioners and superintendents should have disappeared. As it was, the mechanisms for oversight became more confused and nobody did his job very well. The Kirk was not anxious 'that the bishops might usurp ecclesiastical functions', only that they would carry out 'the work which it was their duty to perform'.[20] The problem was, they failed in that respect. Bishops, superintendents and commissioners were regularly criticised for failure to carry out visitations or to have done them badly. Pluralism, non-residence, simony and fornication were some of the worst accusations made against them but, to a man, they were lax in their visitations.[21] It became clear that the system of oversight was failing badly. Even the Privy Council acknowledged the problem, noting that the archbishops, bishops, superintendents and commissioners were negligent. Unqualified men had been admitted to the ministry, so the Privy Council ordered the archbishops to see to the examination of all those recently admitted and remove those who did not come up to standard.[22]

Much has been made of Andrew Melville's return to Scotland from Geneva in 1574, both in the educational and ecclesiastical spheres. Some have argued that he wrought great changes in both, others have restricted his innovations to the universities. Too much has been made of the coincidence of the emergence of anti-episcopal sentiment within

---

[18] *RPC*, ii, 223, 301; *BUK*, i, 255–6, 261, 269–70, 283, 286, 300, 305–6, 314–16.

[19] *BUK*, i, 264, 296, 297, 302–3 (the rejection of Spottiswoode's resignation; he was even given the assistance of the minister of Leith), 318.

[20] Donaldson, *Scottish Reformation*, 173.

[21] D.G. Mullan, *Episcopacy in Scotland: the History of an Idea, 1560–1638* (Edinburgh, 1986), 42–3; M. Graham, *The Uses of Reform: 'Godly Discipline' and Popular Behavior in Scotland and Beyond, 1560–1610* (Leiden, 1996), 69, 83.

[22] *RPC*, ii, 349–50.

the Kirk with Melville's return and a more complex, less immediate context has thus been obscured.[23] In March 1574, a committee of the Assembly was established to discuss the 'jurisdiction and policie' of the Kirk with the Privy Council. The thorny problem of which matters lay within whose jurisdiction had been discussed by general assemblies since 1567 but, under Moray, Lennox and Mar, these were attempts by the Kirk and the crown to work out who was competent in such matters as divorce and what were sins, punishable by the Kirk, and crimes, punishable by the civil power. Under Morton, the tone of the discussions changed, with the emergence of a tussle for ultimate authority. Morton has been credited with directing government with an intensity and determination not seen since James V had taxed the Kirk to the full in the 1530s.[24] To this end, in 1574, he tried to maximise the revenue which the crown obtained from the Kirk by reducing drastically the number of parochial charges so that four parishes would be served by one minister. The cost of running the Kirk would plummet and the state might cream off the considerable surplus. This soon prompted complaints and a heavy-handed response from the crown. John Davidson, a regent at St Andrews, wrote a pamphlet against this policy and was summoned before the Privy Council. He refused to appear, arguing that his summons was issued to 'tempt God', declaring that, as Christ had enjoined, if they persecuted him in one city, he would flee to another.[25] For the first time since the Reformation, the state was attempting to direct ecclesiastical policy. As one observer noted in August 1575, Morton was trying to make the Kirk's position *vis-à-vis* the crown, akin to that in England 'which they [the ministers] like not of'.[26]

If Andrew Melville had an important influence in the Kirk, it was because he returned to Scotland when the time was ripe for a showdown with the regent. Melville did not foist an alien idea on to the Kirk,

---

[23] Kirk, *Patterns of Reform*, 353, 355 and '"Melvillian" Reform in the Scottish Universities', in eds, A.A. MacDonald et al., *The Renaissance in Scotland: Studies in Literature, Religion, History and Culture Offered to John Durkan* (Leiden, 1994), 276–300; Donaldson, *Scottish Reformation*, 146–7, 190 where Donaldson described him as 'the presbyterian missionary to Scotland'; G. Donaldson, *Scotland: James V–James VII* (Edinburgh, 1971), 148–50; M. Lynch, *Scotland: a New History* (London, 1991), 226, 228; Mullan, *Episcopacy in Scotland*, 48; T. McCrie, *Life of Andrew Melville*, 2nd edn (Edinburgh, 1824); R. Mason, 'George Buchanan, James VI and the Presbyterians', in ed. R. Mason, *Scots and Britons: Scottish Political Thought and the Union of 1603* (Cambridge, 1994), 112–37, at 122.

[24] *BUK*, i, 127–9, 145–6, 187; Spottiswoode, *History*, ii, 196; Lynch, *Scotland*, 227.

[25] Melville, *Diary*, 28; Calderwood, *History*, ii, 301, 314–26; Spottiswoode, *History*, ii, 195 where he wrote, 'These things lost him the Church'.

[26] Enclosure with letter from Henry Killigrew to Burghley, 19 Aug. 1575, *CSP Scot*, v, no.187.

nor did he merely tinker with a system which was essentially presbyterian. In the autumn of 1574, the Kirk was ready for a fresh look at its administrative structure and Andrew Melville had a role to play in formulating a new one, although there is no evidence to suggest that he took a leading role. In the General Assembly of August 1575, John Durie protested that the regular examination of the bishops should not prejudge the question of whether episcopacy *per se* was lawful. This has been portrayed, by Archbishop Spottiswoode in the seventeenth century and by more recent writers, as evidence that an ideological aversion to episcopacy had been introduced by Melville who put Durie up to his interjection. Yet at this Assembly, fears were also voiced that the 'lang continuance of commissioners in thair offices sould induce some ambition and inconvenience within the Kirk'. It was agreed that they should be changed annually.[27] This was not simply an attack on episcopacy, it was a two-pronged assault on a failed system of oversight.

The Assembly established a committee to look into 'whither ... the bischops, as they are now in the Kirk ... hes thair function of the word of God or not'. They agreed that the title 'bishop' was common to all ministers, out of whom the Kirk could appoint individual visitors. In 1572 the contrast between true and false bishops was drawn, as in England, within the framework of lifelong diocesan episcopacy.[28] Now it was drawn between that notion and a different perspective which emphasised the equality of all clergy as far as authority was concerned. In the following year, these conclusions were 'resolutlie approvit and affirmit'. The Bishop of Glasgow was asked by the moderator to render his 'commission of visitation ... in[to] the hands of the assembly' and he replied that he would, if it 'findeth that the commission ... should endure only from year to year'. The Bishop of Dunblane, asked the same question, was also willing to demit, as was the Bishop of Ross, while the Bishop of Dunkeld was deprived for dilapidation of the revenues of his see. He appealed to Parliament, presumably since the Concordat of Leith gave the crown as well as the Kirk authority over bishops.[29]

Morton's reaction set in train a process which would culminate with the *Second Book of Discipline* which, it is fair to say, 'was largely the product of ecclesiastical dissatisfaction with the Leith agreement'. Morton 'could find no fault' in their deprivation of Bishop Paton of Dunkeld

---

[27] *BUK*, i, 331, 336–7; Spottiswoode, *History*, ii, 200–201; J.H.S. Burleigh, *A Church History of Scotland* (Edinburgh, 1960), 197. Oddly, there was no similar attack on superintendents.

[28] P. Collinson, *The Elizabethan Puritan Movement* (Oxford, 1967), 104–5.

[29] *BUK*, i, 340, 342–3, 348–51, 352–3.

but suggested that a clear 'policie and universal order' should be established. To that end, the assembly appointed a committee to 'advise what answer shall be given to my Lord Regents Grace'.[30] Additionally, it was noted that 'the great and intollerable burden' endured by the bishops, superintendents and commissioners meant that 'good discipline [was] unexercised ... for lack of visitation'. A committee of 56 ministers and lairds was established 'to make a proper ... division of the whole bounds of this realme' and to decide 'how every bounds may be best visited'.[31] The Assembly enacted that the powers of all those burdened with visitation should be more corporate than hitherto and many important matters were assigned to the provincial synods of which the new visitors would be merely moderators. The committee drew up 20 areas, most of which were to include more than one person responsible for visitation. This Assembly closed by appointing ministers and academics to discuss 'the policie and jurisdiction of the Kirk' and report to the next assembly.[32]

Over the next few years, this committee and its successors met, negotiated with the crown and reported back to general assemblies. By the time of the Assembly of October 1577, disagreement was confined to one head, concerning deacons, so it was decided to draw up the 'heids of the Policie and Jurisdictioun of the Kirk' for submission to the regent for final approval.[33] The *Second Book of Discipline* was a departure from the first in its greater emphasis on the independence of the Kirk and on collective ministerial oversight and discipline. It emphasised 'parity', or equality, of ministers and was thus averse to notions of hierarchy or of lifelong authority vested in individuals. Episcopacy, for a combination of reasons headed by the dire failure of the Leith bishops, was unpopular. Even Spottiswoode later noted the 'small respect' given to bishops during the 1570s and the fact that they ceased to attend assemblies.[34] An emergent desire for greater clerical equality has been noted in a number of places a decade or two after the Reformation. What has been described as the development of a professional ethic in the generation of clergy who did not experience pre-Reformation service and were increasingly graduates, may go some way to

---

[30] *BUK*, i, 352; Kirk, *Patterns of Reform*, 361.

[31] *BUK*, i, 353.

[32] *BUK*, i, 357–9, 362–3.

[33] *BUK*, i, 368–72, 397–8; G. Donaldson, 'Lord Chancellor Glamis and Theodore Beza', in his *Scottish Church History*, 120–36.

[34] *The Second Book of Discipline*, ed. J. Kirk (Edinburgh, 1980). Ministers, pastors and bishops were equated (176, 183) and the section on visitation explicitly excluded diocesan episcopacy (196–7); Spottiswoode, *History*, ii, 258. Until 1576, five or six bishops normally attended, thereafter there was never more than two before 1600.

explaining the hostility to episcopacy in Scotland in the mid-1570s.[35] This can be only a partial explanation, as James Kirk has demonstrated in an analysis of those who composed the *Second Book of Discipline*. Of the 23 ministers and academics involved, 18 were either ministers or had been approved for the ministry before 1562 (six had served in the pre-Reformation Kirk) and only two had entered ecclesiastical or academic service after 1570, one of whom was the Archbishop of Glasgow! All but one of those who had negotiated the Leith settlement participated. Gordon Donaldson asserted that, far from having 'wrought a "change of sentiment"' (as Thomas McCrie had argued), 'Melville's influence lay rather in the formation of a party of younger men than in the conversion to his views of men who had previously accepted reformation principles'. McCrie may have been closer to the truth, although the idea that the *Second Book of Discipline* 'was largely Melville's work' is, as James Kirk has argued 'not supported by the facts of history, and its abandonment is long overdue'.[36]

In the spring of 1578, it was reported that the 'Booke of Policie' had been presented to Morton and a day had been appointed for discussion but 'the alteration of the authoritie ... interveinit'. The Assembly sent a delegation to the Privy Council requesting a meeting between commissioners of the Kirk and the Council 'to reason and conferre' on the 'Booke of Discipline or Policy', before Parliament met. In March, Morton had been stripped of the regency by a thinly attended Convention of the Estates and the king was declared to have reached his majority, three months short of his twelfth birthday. Morton, however, soon recovered influence, although he did not regain the regency because the king could not revert to being a minor. It was clear, however, that some powerful men wanted to remove him and would seize any opportunity to do so.[37]

The same Assembly, because of the 'great corruption in the estate of bischops' decided 'that no bischops shalbe electit or made ... befor the nixt generall assemblie ... and that this matter be proponit ... in the nixt assemblie, to be consultit quhat farder ordour salbe tane therin'. The 'nixt assemblie', in June, suspended indefinitely the election of bishops until all corruption was removed from them. They were to submit to the Assembly, being threatened with excommunication if they

[35] E. Cameron, *The European Reformation* (Oxford, 1991), 390–96.

[36] *BUK*, i, 362, 365, 385, 398; Scott, *Fasti, passim*; Burleigh, *Church History of Scotland*, 198; Donaldson, *Scottish Reformation*, 193, yet he admitted that it 'was bound to attract very wide support' (199); McCrie, *Melville*, i, 138; Kirk, *Patterns of Reform*, 355 and his introduction to the *Second Book of Discipline*, 45–57 where he provides details on the book's authors; Mullan, *Episcopacy in Scotland*, 50.

[37] *BUK*, ii, 404–5; *RPC*, ii, 678–9; G.R. Hewitt, *Scotland under Morton, 1572–80* (Edinburgh, 1982), 44–9.

refused.[38] As well as being the result of the long-term failure of the Leith episcopate, it was, in a more immediate sense, a reaction to Morton's attempts to appoint a new archbishop of St Andrews. At the General Assembly of October 1576, it emerged that he had presented Patrick Adamson, his chaplain, to the bishopric after the death of Douglas. Adamson, on Morton's instructions, refused to be drawn on the matter because the Kirk was undecided over polity. The Assembly felt that, because this prejudged the issue, such an answer equally justified the chapter's rejection of the presentation.[39] By the time of the next Assembly, in April 1577, Adamson was summoned for having taken possession of the bishopric and usurped powers of visitation. The Assembly, with some forbearance, suspended judgement until the discussions on polity were concluded but, in 1578, it discovered that Adamson had given collation of a benefice within someone else's area of jurisdiction.[40]

The Kirk had a problem. While it was drawing up a blueprint for a new system of oversight and administration, the crown was carrying on as if nothing had changed. At the Parliament of June 1578, representatives of the Kirk submitted the new polity to the lords of the articles, the committee which drafted legislation, as an 'Act anent the policie of the Kirk', requesting its ratification. The articles argued that, because it was such a complex document, further consideration and discussion were required. Morton offered to ratify parts of it but this was rejected because 'it became the assemblie to collect out of the booke of God a forme of discipline ... to propone it to the prince ... to be confirmed, as a law proceding from God; and it became not the prince to prescrive a policie for the Kirk'.[41] Further meetings between the crown and the Kirk did not take place until December. In the meantime, the crown appointed the Archbishop of Glasgow to the Privy Council. In October, the General Assembly described the 'archbishops' merely as 'commissioners' of visitation and pressed each to submit 'for reformation of the corruption of the state of a bishop in his person'.[42] Predictably, deadlock was reached with the crown. It wanted to carry on with episcopacy according to the Concordat of Leith and it was unhappy about the *Second Book of Discipline*'s strict curtailment of the state's authority in ecclesiastical matters.[43]

---

[38] *BUK*, ii, 405, 408–9.

[39] *BUK*, i, 367. The assembly replied that the same 'ansuer ... sould be given be the chapter to my Lord Regent'.

[40] *BUK*, i, 385, ii, 403–4; Melville, *Diary*, 59.

[41] *APS*, iii, 105; Calderwood, *History*, iii, 413–16.

[42] *RPC*, iii, 36; *BUK*, ii, 420, 423.

[43] Calderwood, *History*, iii, 433–42; *Second Book of Discipline*, 163–72, 213–16.

In spite of failure to agree, the Kirk, despairing of civil ratification of the new polity, began to implement some of its proposals. Since the Reformation, groups of ministers from between ten and 20 parishes had met regularly for the 'exercise' in which they discussed doctrine and underwent mutual self-scrutiny, a much narrower body than the contemporary English exercises or 'prophesyings' which had lay participation.[44] For the better execution of discipline, the *Second Book of Discipline* proposed that the parochial kirk session might be replaced with a 'commoun eldarschip', comprising the ministers and elders from a group of parishes. At the Assembly of July 1579, the ministers of Lothian called for the erection of these elderships, or 'presbyteries', to start the implementation of the new polity. The Assembly resolved that 'the exercise may be judgit a presbyterie' thenceforth and this was implemented in at least one place, for at the assembly of June 1580, the 'Presbyterie of Sanct Andrews' was mentioned. As a result of the state's failure to ratify the *Second Book of Discipline*, it was never fully implemented and four tiers of ecclesiastical courts resulted because kirk sessions persisted.[45]

Although Morton had regained political ascendency, his problems returned in the autumn: 'with the arrival at Leith on 8th September of Esmé Stewart, lord d'Aubigny, there emerged a new challenge to his pre-eminence'.[46] He immediately won the king's affection and received lands and titles, becoming Duke of Lennox, the only aristocrat of that rank. The Kirk was worried about the presence of the king's French-born cousin, for he was given a whole year to conform to Protestantism and special permission to hold a market on a Sunday. It was feared that foreign policy might revert to France after years of 'amity' with England and that the Reformation might be overturned. It was rumoured that he had spoken with the exiled Catholic bishops of Glasgow and Ross before he left France and that he carried money and instructions from the house of Guise, the king's other French relatives, 'in effect with a plean course of papistrie'. In April 1580, the English ambassador, Robert Bowes, was told to encourage the ministers to 'abuse d'Aubigny's credit' because, if he prospered, it 'shall be the instrument to overthrow the religion there'.[47] The arrival of Esmé Stewart led to the development of a very close

---

[44] Collinson, *Elizabethan Puritan Movement*, 195; G.D. Henderson, 'The Exercise', *RSCHS*, 7 (1941), 13–29.

[45] *BUK*, ii, 439, 459; *Second Book of Discipline*, 195, point 2 did envisage 'four sortis' of 'assemblies', but only three within one realm, the fourth being of 'divers nationis' and 199, point 14 contains the proposal that 'thrie or four' parishes should unite in one 'eldership'.

[46] Hewitt, *Scotland under Morton*, 71.

[47] Melville, *Diary*, 76–7; Calderwood, *History*, iii, 457, 460; Spottiswoode, *History*, ii, 266; Burghley and Walsingham to Bowes, 17 April 1580, *CSP Scot*, v, no. 475.

relationship between the English ambassador and the ministers of Edinburgh. Their paranoia over Catholicism meant, however, that they were an eager yet ineffective diplomatic tool. Moreover, their entanglement with the agents of another state in the interests of Morton did nothing to endear them to those who sought to sideline the former regent.

The General Assembly of June 1580 showed just how disconcerted the Kirk was by the influence of Lennox. Its pronouncements against episcopacy were taken a stage further when it was declared that 'the office of a bischop, as it is now usit and commounly takin within this realme' (that is as hierarchical and not simply equal to pastor) is unscriptural, a 'pretendit office' and 'unlawfull in the selfe'. The bishops were ordered to resign and cease their ministry until readmitted by the assembly. All those holding episcopal benefices were summoned to their synods or to the next Assembly. Only the Bishop of Dunblane was present and he agreed to the act. At the next Assembly the bishops of St Andrews, Glasgow and the Isles agreed to 'certain articles and heidis' which the others were to be asked to approve. Their nature can only be guessed at because Patrick Adamson later removed the offending pages from the Assembly's register, having recanted from whatever it was he had agreed to. The Assembly of July 1580 also demanded the ratification of the *Second Book of Discipline* by Parliament and the Privy Council and admonishcd John Craig and John Duncanson, thc king's ministers, for failing to protest strongly enough against the Catholics in Lennox's company.[48]

The ministers continued to apply pressure on the crown to purge itself of Catholicism and to spurn French advances. They 'cryed out continuallie aganis atheastis and papistis ... saying it wald turne to his Majesties ruine and the hurt of the trew professouris'. In the autumn, the ministers of Edinburgh and the synod of Lothian demanded the removal from court of M. Montbirneau, the French ambassador, and complained that Lennox had yet to make a public commitment to Protestantism, now that his year was up.[49] At the beginning of December, John Durie and Walter Balcanquhal, two of the ministers of Edinburgh, spoke out against the French courtiers and their Catholicism and were supported by their colleague, James Lawson. They were summoned before the Privy Council and asked to provide the texts of their sermons; Durie refused and was briefly warded in Edinburgh Castle as an example to others.[50] Lennox had now attained to a

---

[48] *BUK*, ii, 449–62; Melville, *Diary*, 80.

[49] Moysie, *Memoirs*, 26; Bowes to Burghley and Walsingham, 20 Sept. and 6 Oct. 1580, *CSP Scot*, v, nos 597, 608.

[50] Calderwood, *History*, iii, 480; *RPC*, iii, 335.

position of considerable influence and was angered by the ministers' criticisms. It may have been evident that the English ambassador and the ministers were in league in favour of Morton; it has even been surmised that Lennox saw Morton as the engineer of the whole campaign. By December, Lennox had managed to build up an eclectic coalition against Morton. On 31 December, in front of the Privy Council, Captain James Stewart, later to be Earl of Arran, accused Morton of being an accessory to Darnley's murder, an accusation which could have been levelled against almost any prominent noble who had been alive in 1567. He was imprisoned in Edinburgh Castle and then transferred to 'the Lennox stronghold of Dumbarton'.[51]

Perhaps realising that they had yet to do anything material to aid Morton, an English diplomatic offensive was launched. The Prince of Orange, champion of the Dutch Calvinists was enlisted and wrote to James VI warning against favouring France and Rome. The veteran diplomat, Thomas Randolph, was sent by England in an attempt to rescue Morton and to 'deal earnestly with the ministers ... to make them acquainted with the practices of d'Aubigny at Rome and elsewhere'. Attempts were made to mobilise a 'Queen of England's party' in Scotland and orders were given for raising English troops to invade on behalf of Morton if necessary. A Convention of the Estates then voted £40 000 to defend the realm against invasion. It was addressed by Randolph who delivered an intemperate invective against Lennox, threatening that England would restore Morton if they would not. Twice before, in 1559 and in 1573, the English had intervened decisively in Scottish politics. This time it was too late.[52] Confident of his control of the realm, Lennox had Morton brought to Edinburgh in May for trial. He was convicted by a packed jury of 'airt, pairt, foir knowledge and conceling' of the conspiracy to murder Darnley. On the following day he was beheaded.[53] The Kirk had not loved Morton but, as was the case with Darnley in 1567 and as would be the case with John Maitland of Thirlestane in 1595, his death made him their champion, a transformation which was undoubtedly enhanced by their hatred of his replacement.[54]

---

[51] Hewitt, *Scotland under Morton*, 76–7, 188; Calderwood, *History*, iii, 481.

[52] Private Memo for Thomas Randolph, Jan., Walsingham to Hunsdon, Feb., Randolph's dealing with the Earl of Angus, all 1581, *CSP Scot*, v, nos 635, 722, 737; Moysie, *Memoirs*, 29; *APS*, iii, 189–90; Cameron, *European Reformation*, 376–81; H.G. Koenigsberger et al., *Europe in the Sixteenth Century*, 2nd edn (London, 1989), 317–19. Philip II had made peace with the Sultan so Dutch Calvinists feared international meltdown if Scotland fell to France.

[53] Hewitt, *Scotland under Morton*, 199–200. 'Art & part' = (Scottish Law), party to devising and executing a crime.

[54] Melville, *Diary*, 117–18.

Aware of and alarmed by the growing dominance of Lennox, the Kirk continued to press for his public conformity to Protestantism. To that end, a kirk session was established in the king's household and, soon after Morton's arrest, the 'Negative Confession' was drawn up and presented to the royal household for all to subscribe. Although they all did so, it did nothing to reduce the Kirk's suspicions of Lennox who again declared his adherence to Protestantism in December.[55] The General Assembly of April 1581 formally adopted the *Second Book of Discipline* and reiterated the act against bishops, explaining that, in 1580, they 'meanit haillelie to condemne the estate of bischops as they are now in Scotland'. To further their demise, it was resolved that 600 parishes should be divided into 50 presbyteries with 12 parishes in each and groups of three or more presbyteries would make up provinces or synods. A list of 53 was actually drawn up and it was resolved to establish 13 pilot presbyteries (see Map 5 in the Appendix).[56]

The Kirk's unease with the Lennox regime was exacerbated in the autumn when it emerged that Robert Montgomery, minister of Stirling, had been presented to the archiepiscopal see of Glasgow. Montgomery's association with Lennox had already created friction in the newly erected presbytery of Stirling.[57] By the time of the Assembly, the king had charged the ministers of Glasgow to accept Montgomery and ordered the Assembly to stay all proceedings against him as Archbishop of Glasgow. It therefore dealt with accusations which pertained only to his ministry, including the bizarre allegation that he advocated female circumcision. He was asked if he would remain minister of Stirling and, when he said he would rather not, he was told to remain there and the presbytery of Stirling was ordered to investigate his life and conduct. A delegation was sent to the Privy Council demanding that nothing should be done by the crown in relation to the see of Glasgow until the Kirk's process against Montgomery was complete. The presbytery of Stirling then embarked on a long case against him, eventually suspending him from the ministry in the following March, for neglecting his charge. For this, the presbytery was summoned to the Privy Council, as were the presbytery of Glasgow and the synod of Lothian. On 12 April, it was declared that the right to present to the archbishopric had fallen to the

---

[55] RPC, iii, 264–5, 431–2; Calderwood, *History*, iii, 501–2; G. Donaldson, *Scottish Historical Documents* (Edinburgh, 1974), 150–53. Its name derives from the fact that it was more a renunciation of Catholicism than a positive Protestant statement.

[56] BUK, ii, 474–5, 480–87; 488–512; Melville, *Diary*, 87. Dalkeith, with records surviving from this period, was not one of them so it must have been an exercise recognised as a presbytery in 1579.

[57] *Stirling Presb. Recs*, 6–10; BUK, ii, 524–9, 533–4, 538, 541–2, 544, 546–7.

crown, the chapter having failed to do so, and Montgomery was duly appointed. In truth, the chapter had resisted his appointment, so the crown circumvented it. Delegates from the Kirk protested that it should be allowed to exercise its discipline freely and that, if it came down to a choice, God rather than man would be obeyed.[58]

The presbytery of Stirling's sentence was confirmed at the Assembly two weeks later. A royal messenger tried to stay all proceedings against Montgomery but the Assembly decided that the charges concerned only his ministry and judged him worthy of deprivation although the messenger managed to extract a stay of doom for two days, after which the deprivation proceeded. Montgomery then promised not to attempt anything further regarding the see of Glasgow and the Assembly ordered the presbytery of Glasgow to monitor events and, if he broke that condition, notify the presbytery of Edinburgh who would proceed to excommunication.[59] A delegation from the Assembly visited the king at the Earl of Arran's house at Kinneil only to be called 'knaves and poltroons' by Arran and Lennox. A few weeks later, John Durie was banished from Edinburgh, having publicly insulted Lennox and criticised the king for accepting a gift of horses from the duc de Guise. Tension escalated, 'the whole Kirk and preachers ... [cried] out upon the Duke and all his faction', and it was feared that some ministers might receive harsh punishment.[60] On 10 June, Montgomery was excommunicated according to the act of the Assembly. Just over two weeks later, an extraordinary Assembly met in Edinburgh to plead for the liberty of Durie and some ministers of Glasgow presbytery who had been imprisoned for opposing Montgomery. The Assembly protested against the crown's exercise of ecclesiastical authority, warning the king that 'in your graces person some men preases to erect a new Paipdome'.[61] At the beginning of July, students at Glasgow University rioted against Montgomery after John Howison was forcibly removed from the moderator's chair of the presbytery, the minister of Glasgow was evicted by the king's guard and the beadle was imprisoned. A Convention of Estates at Perth on 20 July confirmed Montgomery's rights to the property of the bishopric.

A serious confrontation seemed unavoidable but there were many powerful men as keen to see Lennox ousted as were the ministers. At the end of June, an anonymous English agent had written that 'the

---

[58] Calderwood, *History*, iii, 596-7; *RPC*, iii, 474-7.

[59] *Stirling Presb. Recs*, 13-37; *BUK*, ii, 557-9.

[60] Calderwood, *History*, iii, 619-20; John Colville to Randolph, 18 May, advertisements from Scotland, May 1582, and Laird of Carmichael to Walsingham, 1 June, *CSP Scot*, vi, nos 112, 120, 121.

[61] Calderwood, *History*, iii, 621-2; John Davidson's Excommunication of Montgomery, 11 June 1582, *CSP Scot*, vi, no.124; *BUK*, ii, 576-84.

whole barons of the religion are so incensed that they are in a readiness to take arms when any occasion shall be offered'.[62] The Lord High Treasurer, William Ruthven, the Earl of Gowrie, had been part of the faction which ousted Morton. In the summer of 1582, however, he fell out with Lennox. As Treasurer, he was personally liable for crown debts which had risen dramatically under the somewhat spendthrift Lennox.[63] Many, not least those forfeited or sidelined for supporting Morton, felt that Lennox had undue influence over the young king, so a plot was hatched to remove James from his control. On 22 August, the 'Ruthven Raid' took place, in which the king was seized by Mar and Gowrie and taken to Gowrie's castle of Huntingtower near Perth. Lennox was ordered to leave Scotland and Arran was warded, as were two other prominent members of the dominant Stewart faction.[64]

The Kirk was delighted. James Melville described the *coup* as 'a grait relieve to the Kirk', while the General Assembly in October called it 'the lait actione of the Reformatione', seizing the opportunity to submit a long shopping list of requests to the crown.[65] It sought ratification of numerous ecclesiastical rights and privileges, recognition of the new polity and the dissolution of the prelacies, with the money going to finance the Kirk and education. The expulsion of Catholics from Scotland was also requested, as was a 'godly' foreign policy, precluding alliance with Spain or France. The Kirk's euphoria, born out of relief at the removal of Lennox rather than real confidence in the godliness of his replacements, may explain why Gordon Donaldson described the Ruthven lords as 'ultra-protestant', a notion which has been too readily taken up by other historians, although it has recently been moderated, with the lords being ascribed 'presbyterian sympathies'.[66] The best that could be said of them, from the Kirk's point of view, was that they were not hostile, allowing general assemblies to proceed against bishops, and that they let John Durie return to Edinburgh. They would not recognise the *Second Book of Discipline* or commit money to the Kirk. Instead they cautiously approved the system of kirk sessions, synods and the general assembly without mentioning bishops or presbyteries.

[62] Melville, *Dairy*, 131; Anon. to Anon., 22 June 1581, *CSP Scot*, vi, no. 130.

[63] Calderwood, *History*, iii, 632; Donaldson, *Scotland: James V–James VII*, 178.

[64] Calderwood, *History*, iii, 637, 647; *RPC*, iii, 508–9; Moysie, *Memoirs*, 38–9; W.C. Dickinson, *Scotland from the Earliest Times to 1603*, 3rd edn (Oxford, 1977), 372.

[65] Melville, *Dairy*, 134; *BUK*, ii, 594, 600–603.

[66] Donaldson, *Scotland: James V-James VII*, 179; Kirk, *Patterns of Reform*, 364; R. Mitchison, *A History of Scotland* (London, 1970), 147–8; Graham, *Uses of Reform*, 262. See also Burleigh, *Church History of Scotland*, 189 where they were described as 'a group of Protestant Lords', which could have described most noble factions; Mason, 'George Buchanan, James VI and the Presbyterians', 129.

Anti-Catholic the Ruthven leaders certainly were but they were primarily anti-Lennox. Arran was imprisoned at Huntingtower only as long as Lennox was still in Scotland. In October, he was permitted freedom of movement north of the river Earn (which lies just to the south of Perth) and, in November, he was allowed to return to his own residence at Kinneil on the Forth and a four-mile radius thereabout. Gowrie refused to countenance requests from the Kirk for his banishment. During the winter of 1582–83, a French embassy was received, much to the anger of the Kirk, and in the spring of 1583 Colonel William Stewart, warded in Stirling Castle for support of Lennox, was in sufficient favour again to carry the king's consent for the approval of the 'Ruthven Raid' to a Convention of Estates and to go in embassy to England.[67] The Ruthven lords were attempting to form a broad-based coalition after the achievement of their principal goal, the removal of Lennox. Their downfall came because the king's affection for Lennox meant that, in spite of formal undertakings, he did not like the new regime. Also, although attempts were made to bring on board some of those who had been prominent under Lennox, the Earls of Angus and Mar kept a tight hold on power. In early July 1583, James VI removed himself from the Ruthven lords with the help of Colonel Stewart and declared that he had been held against his will. At the end of the month, the Privy Council condemned the 'Ruthven Raid' and summoned eight ministers for their verbal support of the recently ousted government. Angus, Mar and the Master of Glamis fled to Ireland. The ministers refused to condemn the Ruthven regime because the king and Privy Council had approved it, as had the General Assembly. Their viewpoint was judged to be reasonable by some Privy Councillors, so they were allowed to return home after professing obedience to James. This is consistent with the way that lay supporters of the fallen regime were treated, being forgiven if they craved the king's pardon. Further trouble ensued, however. The General Assembly cried out against resurgent Catholicism and backsliders at court, condemned the release of a captured English Jesuit and criticised the king's affection for France.[68]

Patrick Adamson, Archbishop of St Andrews, took advantage of the return to power of a reconfigured Stewart faction now headed by the

---

[67] RPC, iii, 519; Moysie, Memoirs, 40–41, 44; Calderwood, History, iii, 693, 694–7, 699–700, 703; Melville, Diary, 136.

[68] APS, iii, 328; RPC, iii, 575, 585; Calderwood, History, iii, 716, 722–3; Bowes to Walsingham, 31 July, same to same, 22 Aug., same to same, 25 Aug., CSP Scot, nos 582, 608, 609; BUK, ii, 630–32. The ministers were John Christison (Logie), John Durie (Edinburgh), David Ferguson (Dunfermline), Patrick Galloway (Perth), Andrew Hay (Renfrew), James Lawson (Edinburgh), David Lindsay (Leith), Thomas Smeton (Glasgow University).

Earl of Arran. He spoke out against the Ruthven government and ingratiated himself with the crown, quickly becoming one of the principal figures in government.[69] As a result of the Kirk's support for the ousted regime, Arran's government had little affection for the dominant sentiment among the ministry. Accordingly, it revived the episcopal policy of Morton and Lennox. In October, it was put about that Adamson was to go to Europe for his health but many suspected that an embassy to England was planned.[70] In December, he went south to meet John Whitgift, recently elected Archbishop of Canterbury and John Aylmer, Bishop of London. Whitgift had just begun a campaign against puritan clergy, involving the imposition of a subscription to three articles as a 'condition for exercising any ecclesiastical function'. One of those articles stated that 'the Book of Common Prayer and ordering of bishops, priests and deacons' were not contrary to God's word and bound the subscriber to adhere strictly to the Book in all his ministry. Although there was no co-ordinated Anglo-Scottish anti-presbyterian campaign, the idea was stored away by Adamson for later use.[71]

At about the same time, James Lawson and John Durie were hauled before the Privy Council for praising the old regime. Durie was again banished from Edinburgh, this time to Montrose.[72] Tension rose and, in February 1584, Andrew Melville appeared before the Privy Council, accused of making speeches which were 'offensive and sklanderous to the kingis majestie'. He declined the jurisdiction of the Privy Council and was ordered to enter ward in the state prison of Blackness Castle on the Forth within 24 hours. Instead, he fled to England in fear of his life, according to his nephew James.[73] Melville's flight provoked an outburst of protest from the pulpits and the Kirk's relationship with the crown was not helped by the failure of an attempt by the Ruthven faction to regain power in April. The perpetrators, some of whom had returned from exile in Ireland to stage the attempted *coup*, fled to England and the Earl of Gowrie, although not directly involved, was arrested while trying to leave Scotland, tried and executed on 2 May. On the same day, a further four ministers went south, having been

---

[69] Melville, *Diary*, 137; Calderwood, *History*, iii, 716.

[70] Bowes to Walsingham, 26 Oct., *CSP Scot*, vi, no.681.

[71] Calderwood, *History*, iii, 763; Collinson, *Elizabethan Puritan Movement*, 244–5, 276.

[72] *BUK*, ii, 631–2; Spottiswoode, History, ii, 304, 315; *RPC*, iii, 617; Calderwood, *History*, iii, 762, 764.

[73] *RPC*, iii, 631–2; Bowes to Walsingham, 24 Feb. 1584, *CSP Scot*, vii, no. 31; Melville, *Diary*, 142. Considering that the execution of ministers was unheard of in post-Reformation Scotland, these fears were probably exaggerated.

summoned to the Privy Council on suspicion of involvement in the attempted *coup*.[74]

The Arran regime, although in place since the previous July, was rocked by the Ruthven faction's bid to regain power. In need of an injection of confidence, it called Parliament to meet on 20 May. The legislation it passed became known as the 'Black Acts' and it is hard to portray the ecclesiastical legislation as 'no more than the reaffirmation of the system which had operated since 1560'. They declared that the king was supreme over all estates and in all matters, civil and spiritual; outlawed 'all jurisdictionis and judgementis not approvit be parliament and all assembleis and conventionis without our soverane lordis speciall licence', thus effectively banning presbyteries and preventing general assemblies which were not summoned by the crown; laid down an order for the deprivation of ministers by the state 'for worthie causis'; established an ecclesiastical commission, under Archbishop Adamson, which effectively superseded the General Assembly; and overturned the excommunication of Robert Montgomery. These acts were part of a raft of legislation designed to strengthen royal authority in all areas and entrench the power and position of the officers of state. The crown's desire for central control was further exhibited in its appointment of the provosts of most of the largest burghs.[75]

A second wave of clerical disquiet resulted. On 25 May, when the acts were publicly proclaimed in Edinburgh, Walter Balcanquhal, one of the ministers of Edinburgh, and Robert Pont, minister of St Cuthbert's just outside the capital, drew up a formal protest. James Lawson, the other minister of Edinburgh, was so vehement in his criticism of the legislation that Arran threatened to have him beheaded. Two days later, Lawson and Balcanquhal fled to England. Soon afterwards, James Melville, Andrew's nephew, crossed the border, having been warned that the Privy Council was pursuing him.[76] Initially, the crown was embarrassed by this exodus and tried, in vain, to secure their return. Around 20 ministers, students and university masters went into exile in England. While there, they attended conferences of English puritans

---

[74] Spottiswoode, *History*, ii, 309; Melville, *Diary*, 145; A.R. MacDonald, 'The Subscription Crisis and Church–State Relations, 1584–1586', *RSCHS*, 25 (1994), 225. The ministers were James Carmichael (Haddington), Patrick Galloway (Perth), John Davidson (Liberton) and Andrew Polwart (Cadder).

[75] *APS*, iii, 292–312; Donaldson, *Scottish Reformation*, 211; M. Lynch, 'The Crown and the Burghs, 1500–1625', in ed., M. Lynch, *The Early Modern Town in Scotland*, (London, 1986), 55–81, at 58.

[76] For the details of these events, see MacDonald, 'Subscription Crisis' which also demonstrates that, contrary to recent assertions, Robert Pont did not flee to England (228 n. 27).

and conducted a sustained propaganda war with Archbishop Adamson, sending letters and tracts to Scotland and the Continent. They also tried to garner support from Queen Elizabeth but with little success. Although favoured by Francis Walsingham and other prominent men, they were something of an embarrassment since they gave succour to the English puritans against whom Whitgift was campaigning. On royal instructions, two of the Scottish ministers in London were banned from preaching.[77]

As well as those who fled to England, many who remained in Scotland continued to resist the authoritarianism of Arran and Adamson. Andrew Hay, rector of the university of Glasgow and minister of Renfrew, was ordered into internal exile. David Lindsay, minister of Leith, was imprisoned for trying to gain entry to Parliament in May to protest against its legislation, as were John Howison, minister of Cambuslang, and Nicol Dalgliesh, Pont's colleague at St Cuthbert's. Continuing opposition led to the introduction of a subscription. In August, Parliament passed an oath to be subscribed by all benefice holders, schoolmasters and university regents. It consisted of a promise 'to obey with all humilitie his heines actis of the said Parliament [of May] and schaw ... obedience to our ... bischop or commissionair' on pain of loss of stipend.[78]

By the following April, only 22 ministers, or perhaps a few more, still held out against subscription but it would be distorting the truth to say that this demonstrated a widespread acceptance of the 'Black Acts'. There is little or no evidence for attempts to enforce subscription outside the archdiocese of St Andrews and, moreover, there is the thorny problem of conditional subscription.[79] The initial level of subscription was pitifully small, so the crown imposed a deadline of 16 November. If, by then, a minister had not subscribed, his stipend would be withheld. The course of events between Parliament's approval of the subscription in August and the deadline in November indicates widespread and enduring opposition to the 'Black Acts', albeit not as zealous

---

[77] MacDonald, 'Subscription Crisis', 231–2; G. Donaldson, 'Scottish Presbyterian Exiles in England', in his *Scottish Church History*, 178–190; G. Donaldson, 'The Relations between the English and Scottish Presbyterian Movements to 1604' (unpublished London PhD dissertation, 1938).

[78] *APS*, iii, 347.

[79] *Wodrow Miscellany*, i, 436. This list mentions only places within Archbishop Adamson's see. Subscription was either not enforced or not resisted elsewhere. The following interpretation differs from that offered in my 'Subscription Crisis' article, which was too hard on conditional subscribers, and with Donaldson's interpretation in *Scottish Reformation*, 214. There are similarities with the numbers who overtly resisted the Five Articles of Perth and an equally likely widespread dislike of the legislation (see Chapter 8).

as that shown by those who were gaoled or exiled. At the end of August, John Craig, one of the king's ministers who had been put into the vacant Edinburgh charges, Andrew Blackhall, minister of Musselburgh, John Brand, minister of the Canongate, John Herries, minister of Newbattle and 'sindrie others' were called before the Privy Council where they condemned the 'Black Acts' and refused to subscribe. On 16 November, they again rejected the legislation which, they argued, was contrary to God's Word. Threatened with banishment, they offered to subscribe the acts as far as they were 'agreeable to God's Word'. When, on 11 December, non-subscribers were debarred from pursuing legal cases, the balance was tipped in favour of subscription, albeit with a rider. One of the new subscribers was John Duncanson who, along with Craig, was a royal minister filling the pulpits of Edinburgh. As crown placemen, their tardy acquiescence is remarkable and is compelling evidence of the level of opposition to the 'Black Acts', if not to conditional subscription. Assessment of the apparently large-scale subscription is fraught with problems. From the point of view of the exiled James Melville, conditional subscription was a betrayal of the cause and an acceptance of the 'Black Acts', yet he was speaking from the safety of England. In the aftermath of the crisis, James Carmichael, minister of Haddington, went as far as to point out that 'men myght have subscrivit the Mess Buke or the Alcoran of Mahomet with the same condition'. On the other hand, it has been suggested that conditional subscription undermined the crown's policy completely.[80] Most ministers had dependents, so exile, imprisonment or loss of stipend were hard to face and their subscription cannot be taken to indicate that they agreed with the law.

The subscription crisis also affected the universities as many of the exiles were students or university masters. The recently founded college of Edinburgh began teaching soon after Arran came to power and within days of a purge by the crown of the burgh council, so it is no surprise that its staff did not defy the government. With Andrew Melville as principal of St Mary's college at St Andrews, however, the crown's desire to intervene there needs little explanation. In the autumn of 1584, Archbishop Adamson appointed a new principal. The universities of Aberdeen and Glasgow were reported to be out of action, the students having been ordered to return home and the masters warded for opposition to the 'Black Acts'.[81] There were even lay protests in

---

[80] Melville, *Diary*, 200–18; *Wodrow Miscellany*, i, 441; J. Kirk, 'The Development of the Melvillian Movement in Late Sixteenth Century Scotland' (unpublished Edinburgh PhD dissertation, 1972), 467.

[81] MacDonald, 'Subscription Crisis', 241–2.

Edinburgh, Ayr and St Andrews, a phenomenon which was rare in post-Reformation Scotland. It was only really repeated in the reception given to the Five Articles of Perth of 1618, so it may be taken as indicating a serious miscalculation in the crown's ecclesiastical policy.[82]

What would have happened if the Arran regime had held on to power for longer than it did? It is hard to tell, especially since the crown made no episcopal appointments during Arran's two years of power. This was a reactive, not an active government. Its overstated legislation had absolutist pretensions but its attempts to compel obedience are more reflective of paranoia than control and it is hard to imagine how it could have fulfilled its stated aims. In the summer of 1585, things were to go horribly wrong for the Arran regime. At a border conference between English and Scottish representatives, one of the Englishmen, Lord Russel, was murdered. Arran was suspected of complicity because of his preference for a French or Spanish alliance and the resultant Anglo-Scottish rift led to Elizabeth allowing the exiled nobles to return to Scotland with the ministers in tow. Once across the border, they joined up with other disaffected Scots, issuing a declaration, probably written by one of the ministers, that they would fight for religion, the king's safety, the common weal and the preservation of amity with England. This was consistent with their stance over the previous few years and it drew upon tried and tested propagandist themes. Most of the exiled lords had little enthusiasm for religion, only the earls of Angus and Mar ever being singled out as notably pious. In exile, they kept apart, remaining in the north-east of England while the ministers went to London. When the nobles followed them south in 1585 it was because Elizabeth had commanded them to do so.

Arran and Colonel Stewart were ousted and the returning exiles were given custody of the royal castles. Yet, in spite of 'all the vowes and fair promises maid to God', they did not press the religious issue. No longer of any use as propagandists or supporters, 'the good breithring war left and deserted' by the nobles.[83] A new era had dawned, however. The king's formative years were, at long last, at an end and his personal rule could begin. No longer would government be conducted by someone hiding behind the royal signature. The 19–year-old king had taken the reins of power and an atmosphere of compromise, born out of years of ecclesiastical and factional conflict, would pervade the restoration of royal government to Scotland.

---

[82] MacDonald, 'Subscription Crisis', 243–8; M. Lynch, *Edinburgh and the Reformation* (Edinburgh, 1981), ch. 8 and appendices; Sanderson, *Ayrshire and the Reformation*, 129–30.
[83] Melville, *Diary*, 225, 228.

CHAPTER TWO

Compromise and conflict, 1586–92

In August 1561 Mary, Queen of Scots, began her personal reign less than four months short of her nineteenth birthday while, in November 1585, James VI was five months past his. Unlike his mother, however, he had never left Scotland. When he started to govern his realm, he had developed a close familiarity with it. This was important for his attitudes to government, indeed it may have been the most significant distinction between himself and his mother. He probably remembered little or nothing of the civil war which was effectively over by the time he was six. Throughout the war, he was kept under close guard, well away from any fighting, largely within the confines of Stirling Castle where he was educated by George Buchanan and Peter Young. Political awareness would have begun to develop during the regency of Morton and, between 1578 and the end of 1585, political turmoil would have been more familiar than stability. Mary spent her formative years in France, returning to a country of which she knew little, a realm which had undergone dramatic religious and political upheaval. Her ecclesiastical policy was thus marked by *ad hoc* compromise, being more reactive than creative. James VI had no desire for a continuation of the sequence of short-lived regimes which had plagued the last seven years of his minority, so his initial policies promoted stability.

In Parliament at Linlithgow in December 1585, an accommodation was reached with the nobility. The next priority was the Kirk, in limbo since the fall of Arran. The ecclesiastical settlement was part of James's new policy of compromise, perhaps influenced by his secretary, John Maitland of Thirlestane. It was not a concession into which James was forced to 'mollify' the ministers' 'aristocratic allies', for they had abandoned the ministers a few months before.[1] It was agreed that a convention of ministers, Privy Councillors and the monarch would meet to agree upon an ecclesiastical settlement which could be put to a General Assembly. The conference, perhaps modelled on that held at Leith in 1572 and certainly echoing it in personnel, met at Holyrood Palace in February 1586. Much of what was discussed related to the episcopate and to the power of general assemblies. It

---

[1] R. Mason, 'George Buchanan, James VI and the Presbyterians', in ed., R. Mason, *Scots and Britons: Scottish Political Thought and the Union of 1603* (Cambridge, 1994), 131; and see above p. 29.

was resolved that an Assembly should meet in May at Edinburgh 'or where his majesty shall otherwise appoint; and to be convoked by proclamation, and letters to the bishops and commissioners, and his majesty with their advice shall set down good and solid order'.[2] The precedent being set was clearly Erastian. A new constitution for the Kirk was being formulated by a joint committee of Kirk and state, presided over by the king. Contrary to what Thomas McCrie asserted, some of the recently returned clerical exiles must have had a place at the negotiating table, if not, the works of David Calderwood and James Melville would have cried out in protest at their exclusion.[3] Scotland had an adult 'godly prince' and there was a tacit recognition that the state had the right to a role in ecclesiastical affairs. This was Erastianism only by Scottish standards; compared with Elizabeth's position as supreme governor of the Church of England, James was powerless.

A wide range of issues was discussed and the agreement reached included the retention of the episcopate and the reinstatement of presbyteries, thus overturning the spirit of one of the 'Black Acts' of 1584. Presbyteries were to be established in 'convenient places' by the General Assembly with the king's advice. Bishops were to be nominated by the crown but admitted by, and answerable to, the General Assembly. They had to have a congregation, like other ministers, but they retained rights of visitation, presentation and collation, although only with the consent of the relevant presbytery and synod. They were also to do nothing without the advice of a 'senat or presbyterie of the most learned and godly ministers' of their dioceses appointed by the General Assembly.[4] Although this idea was not entertained by a recent writer on the episcopate, this 'senat' could be seen as an attempt to create a reformed chapter.[5]

Discussion of a number of other topics, such as parliamentary representation for the Kirk, was planned but there is no record of this having taken place.[6] Another conference appears to have met in March. It agreed that the bishops should be permanent, *ex officio* moderators both of the synods in which their cathedrals lay and also of their local

---

[2] Calderwood, *History*, iv, 491–2; The Heads of the Conference, 17 and 19 Feb. 1586, *CSP Scot,* viii, no. 276.

[3] T. McCrie, *The Life of Andrew Melville* 2nd edn, 2 vols (Edinburgh, 1824), i, 278 where he wrote that only ministers 'whom he [James VI] judged more moderate' were there.

[4] Calderwood, *History*, iv, 491–4; Spottiswoode, *History*, ii, 337; The Heads of the Conference, 17 and 19 Feb. 1586, *CSP Scot*, viii, no. 276.

[5] Mullan, *Episcopacy in Scotland*, 64.

[6] The Heads of the Conference, 17 and 19 Feb. 1586, *CSP Scot*, viii, no. 276.

presbyteries.[7] The significance of this was limited by the state of the episcopate and the structure of the Kirk. At the beginning of 1586, the dioceses of Caithness and Ross were vacant; James Beaton, the Catholic Archbishop of Glasgow, was in exile in France; the General Assembly in May forbade Patrick Adamson from moderating his presbytery; the Bishop of Orkney, Adam Bothwell, was Commendator of Holyrood Abbey and was rarely if ever in his diocese; and the dioceses of the Isles and Argyll were assigned no presbyteries by the General Assembly. Out of over 40 presbyteries established by the Assembly in May, a maximum of six could thus have been moderated by bishops.

The conference in February also agreed that, before the General Assembly would be held, the provincial synods should meet on 12 April. The synod of Fife is the only one for which any record survives and there, at least, controversy continued. Questions relating to the powers, jurisdiction and constitution of synods were raised which may have affected the decisions of the General Assembly. James Melville, as moderator of the last synod in 1583, opened the proceedings with a sermon attacking episcopacy in general and Patrick Adamson in particular for his conduct over the preceding two and a half years since his suspension by that synod. Adamson was accused of dereliction of duty but he refused to recognise the synod's jurisdiction, asserting that, as archbishop, he was its superior. Failing even to appear until the third summons, he refused to answer the accusations against him, preferring instead to deny their validity on procedural points. The synod rejected his complaints, some wanted to proceed to excommunication and there ensued a dispute over the very right of the synod to censure the archbishop. When a majority voted for excommunication, the moderator refused to pronounce the sentence but his place was promptly taken by another who did. Events took a farcical turn when, on the following day, two of the archbishop's servants, acting on his authority, excommunicated Andrew and James Melville and some others for their part in the original excommunication.[8] The Kirk was in a state of flux with certain basic points, such as the constitution of the synods and the status of the episcopate, still unresolved.

On 5 April, the Privy Council proclaimed that the General Assembly was to meet on 10 May, making it clear that matters agreed at the conferences were not binding and that the Assembly itself would establish

---

[7] NLS, 'Minutes of the Synod of Fife', 12 April 1586, Wodrow Folio, 43, no. 30; A.R. MacDonald, 'The Subscription Crisis and Church–State Relations, 1584–1586' RSCHS, 25 (1994), 253.

[8] Melville, Diary, 245–6; Calderwood, History, 491–508; Spottiswoode, History, ii, 338–9; 'Minutes of the Synod of Fife'.

'a good and solide ordour for convocating of the ministerie to General Assemblies theireftir, and utheris materis concerning the Kirk of God and his trew religioun'.[9] It met in the tolbooth of Edinburgh on the morning of 10 May, the ministers in attendance presumably having been commissioned by the synods in April. 'Certayne commissioners from the Kinge declared ... that his pleasure was that they should staye ... further proceedinge, till the afternoone and then ... assemble ... at the kingis house in the chappell.'[10] They agreed and, once they had reconvened at Holyrood, the king told them that he had called the Assembly to allay allegations that he had fallen away from religion, to discuss polity and to finalise the negotiations of the conferences. He voted first for the moderator and the ministers followed his choice. The man chosen, David Lindsay, minister of Leith, was a compromise candidate, who had been for a long time close to the crown but was also imprisoned for opposition to the 'Black Acts'. The Assembly was then allowed to return to the tolbooth.[11]

Throughout the rest of its proceedings, the king was kept informed by commissioners whom he had appointed to attend and observe. It was agreed that bishops should be subject only to the General Assembly but only after James threatened to abandon the compromise between episcopacy and presbytery unless it absolved Archbishop Adamson. James was granted a role in the convocation of general assemblies and it was acknowledged that they met with his authority. The Assembly requested the right to meet annually and this was granted.[12] The atmosphere was one of compromise with a very limited royal supremacy tacitly acknowledged. The perception handed down by the presbyterian historians of the period and beyond – of a Kirk entirely free and self-governing until 1596 – is misleading and was probably formed by the rose-tinted spectacles through which some looked back after 1596.[13] For the next few years, the king would intervene with the proceedings of the courts of the Kirk if they offended him and his right to call the General Assembly was never questioned. The novelty of this situation, and thus the nature of the compromise, is striking, as is the fact that the

---

[9] RPC, iv, 60.

[10] NLS, 'The order and accidentis of the Sinod Ecclesiastical beganne at Edenboroughe the 10th Maii 1586', Advocates Manuscripts 6.1.13, fo. 33; Thomas Milles to Walsingham, 12 May 1586, CSP Scot, viii, no. 396; BUK, ii, 645. A 'tolbooth' was a burgh council building.

[11] BUK, ii, 645–7; Calderwood, History, iv, 549; 'The order and accidents of the Sinod Ecclesiastical', fo.33.

[12] BUK, ii, 649–64; Melville, Diary, 249.

[13] Melville, Diary, 412–14; Calderwood, History, v, 387; Scot, Apologetical Narration, 65.

ministry accepted the new relationship. Until 1584, when they were banned, the date and location of assemblies had always been chosen by the preceding assembly or a committee appointed for the task. Only once was this challenged when, in March 1571, the Regent Lennox asked the assembly to move from Edinburgh to Glasgow – it refused.[14] The *Second Book of Discipline* explicitly asserted that, 'the generall assembleis, aucht alwayis to be retenit in thair awin libertie and to haif thair awin place with power to the kirk to appoint tymis and places convenient thairfoir'.[15] For the first time, Scotland had a 'godly prince', an adult Protestant monarch. Was this the establishment of the very relationship that the Kirk had longed for since 1560? The implications of this for a Kirk supposedly dominated by radical, two-kingdoms 'Melvillians' in the later 1580s and early 1590s appear not to have been fully realised.[16]

The nature of the polity resulting from this General Assembly has also escaped the notice of historians. Most surprisingly, David Mullan devoted little attention to it in his study of episcopacy.[17] The compromise over the right of none but the General Assembly to censure the episcopate involved the removal of exclusive episcopal powers of visitation; the bishops could be appointed as visitors but so could any other minister. The old dioceses were abolished and replaced with new, smaller provinces for each of the commissioners of visitation (see Map 6 in the Appendix) who would be subject to the synod in which their commission operated and they could be deposed only by the General Assembly. The commissioners were to have life tenure unless deposed for misconduct.[18] There emerged the potential for a genuinely reformed episcopate, if that is taken to mean a system of oversight vested in individuals holding office for life. It was the first such scheme since the introduction of superintendents in the 1560s and attempted to iron out many of the problems of the 1570s. The commissioners and bishops were to moderate the presbyteries and synods in which they resided and would be subject to the General Assembly in this capacity. This was a remarkable

---

[14] D. Shaw, *The General Assemblies of the Church of Scotland 1560–1600* (Edinburgh, 1964), 50 and ch. 17.

[15] *Second Book of Discipline*, 233.

[16] J. Kirk, 'The Development of the Melvillian Movement in Late Sixteenth Century Scotland' (unpublished Edinburgh PhD dissertation, 1972), 479–99 where he noted recognition of the king's right to call assemblies but failed to see its implications for 'Melvillianism'.

[17] D.G. Mullan, *Episcopacy in Scotland: the History of Idea, 1560–1638* (Edinburgh, 1986), chapter 4 which is devoted entirely to Patrick Adamson instead of examining the interesting fate of episcopacy in general in the later 1580s.

[18] *BUK*, ii, 645–66; Calderwood, *History*, iv, 557–68.

settlement which could have led to a mixed polity with the General Assembly as the only court able to censure the new quasi-episcopate. It failed to flourish, however, largely as the result of the gathering strength of presbyteries, a fact which, in itself, may suggest that it had no enthusiastic clerical support.

Soon after the Assembly, the commissioners began their tasks: touring parishes, investigating the fabric of kirks, inquiring into the value of benefices and planting ministers in vacant charges. Evidence for their activities is limited but the record of one visitation survives. James Anderson, commissioner for the core of the old diocese of Dunblane and other adjacent parishes, diligently visited his province until 1589 and moderated the presbytery of Stirling until April 1588. The record of his commission begins in a very Erastian tone:

> James be [the grace] of God king of Scottis ... Forsamekle as we being dil[igent] and cairfull of the gud governement of the Kirk of God wythin oure realme ... [it then says that Anderson was nominated by the king and approved by the assembly] and thairfor we ... hes gevin, grantit and be the tenor heirof gevis, grantis and committis full powar and commissione to the said James Anderson.

It is clear where the source of power lay and, in that respect, these commissioners of visitation were remarkably similar to the superintendents. As well as having the power to conduct parochial visitations, all presentations were to be directed to Anderson and he was to examine presentees and admit them if they proved qualified.[19] No mention was made even of an advisory role for the Kirk in the capacity of the General Assembly, the relevant presbytery or even a selection of local ministers.

The commissioner for Lothian, David Lindsay, minister of Leith, was active in visitations and admissions in his presbyteries until the late spring of 1588 and was last named as commissioner in the synod of Lothian and Tweeddale in April 1589. He did not permanently moderate the presbytery of Edinburgh, although he invariably stood in whenever the elected moderator was absent.[20] One remarkable document survives from his period as commissioner for Lothian. It is a letter of admission to the benefices of the parish of Heriot in the presbytery of Dalkeith

---

[19] *Visitation of the Diocese of Dunblane and other Churches, 1586–9*, ed. J. Kirk (Scottish Texts Society, 2nd series 1984), 1; *Stirling Presb. Recs*, 220–302; Stirling Presbytery, i, *passim*; G. Donaldson, *The Scottish Reformation* (Cambridge, 1960), 137, licences for their election and the mandate for the superintendent of Lothian were all issued by the Privy Council.

[20] Haddington Presbytery, i, fos 1r, 7r and v; Edinburgh Presbytery, i, 19 April, 30 Aug., 11 Oct., 6 Sept. 1586, 14 March, 18 April 1587, 2 April 1588; *Lothian Synod*, 7.

and it dates from May 1588.[21] It was written in Lindsay's name and it opens as follows: 'Maister David Lyndesay Commissioner wisches mercie and peace to all christiens.' The tone suggests personal jurisdiction vested in David Lindsay to whom the patron of the parish directed the presentee for examination with only 'the adwyse of the presbiterie of Dalkeith'. Appended to the document was Lindsay's personal seal and the letter was dated at Leith, the 'seat' of the commissioner, not at Heriot where the benefice lay or at Dalkeith, the seat of the presbytery. Seven ministers of the presbytery of Dalkeith, whose names formed the witness list, had thus gone to Leith specially for the occasion. The episcopal nature of the whole proceeding is clear and weight is thus lent to the argument that what existed in the first two years or so of the personal reign of James VI amounted to an attempt at a reformed episcopate, in Lothian and Stirlingshire at least but perhaps more widely.

In 1587, the General Assembly demonstrated its suspicion of such responsibilities being held for life by declaring that commissioners should be appointed annually but it reappointed all the commissioners 'seeing there is no fault found with them'. In the following year, their life tenure was effectively abolished when eight of the 16 were changed and, in 1589, only one remained in office.[22] Strikingly, that survival was none other than John Erskine of Dun, superintendent of Angus and the Mearns since 1560. In spite of age and infirmity he continued in post, evidence indeed of what the Kirk of the 1580s felt about the permanence superintendents, whatever the original intention had been.[23]

In August 1590, the General Assembly resolved that there were no longer to be commissioners of visitation where presbyteries were established. In the following year, as a result of the death of Erskine of Dun, the form of discipline used in the rest of the country was to be observed in Angus and the Mearns. There was no mention, at that Assembly, of commissioners of visitation.[24] Few tears were shed either by the Kirk or the king over the demise of this system. James, admittedly, was not entirely comfortable with the presbyterian polity. At the end of 1586, one English source commented that 'Towards the discipline of the Kirk he seems not soundly affected because he has the impression that it takes away from princely authority.' Yet it is hard to sustain the claim

---

[21] SRO, 'Letters of admission by David Lindsay for a new minister of Heriot', 8 May 1588, Rattray of Craighall Rattray Muniments, GD40/14/9.

[22] BUK, ii, 702, 736–7, 745.

[23] G. Donaldson, Scotland: James V–James VII (Edinburgh, 1971), 141, where it is stated that they held office 'for life'; J. Kirk, Patterns of Reform: Continuity and Change in the Reformation Kirk (Edinburgh, 1989), 229–30, where it is stated that 'superintendents … regarded their tenure … as temporary'.

[24] BUK, ii, 775, 783.

that, from the outset of his personal reign, James was 'striving to erect' diocesan episcopacy.[25] The crown's failure to appoint any bishops between 1585 and 1600, in spite of numerous vacancies, other than the abortive attempt to make Robert Pont the Bishop of Caithness in 1587, is evidence of James's lack of enthusiasm for the restoration of full-blown episcopacy at this time. Instead, he stood back while the presbyteries came into their own as the vital agents of discipline, visitation and admission to the ministry.

The presbyteries had, of course, been re-established as part of the settlement of spring 1586. The General Assembly drew up a list of 50, stretching from Orkney to Galloway. By the end of 1593, there were 48 presbyteries in operation, if Stirling and the newly erected Auchterarder are added to the list and Dunblane removed. They covered, as with so many other aspects of government, all but the Hebrides and the western mainland north of Lennox (see Map 7 in the Appendix).[26] They were given the power to 'inquyre diligentlie of naughtie and ungodlie persons', to ensure that preaching was pure, sacraments rightly administered, discipline maintained and poor relief distributed. In 1594, they were given power to examine presentees to benefices and it was confirmed that kirk sessions were to be subject to them.[27]

Evidence for the crown's acceptance of their increasing coverage and authority can be found in the Register of Presentations to Benefices and the records of presentations in the Register of the Privy Seal. The first mention of a presbytery in these sources, covering parishes under crown patronage (about a third of the total), relates to the vicarage of Kilburnie in the presbytery of Cunningham in Ayrshire in November 1586.[28] Although only the presbytery was mentioned in this instance, for the next few years, presbyteries were normally mentioned in default of bishops or commissioners. By 1591, they were commonly mentioned, although bishops and commissioners continued to occur in many presentations. The 'Golden Act' of 1592 appears to have given a boost to

---

[25] The State of Scotland, CSP Scot, ix, no. 164; W.C. Dickinson, Scotland from the Earliest Times to 1603 3rd edn (Oxford, 1977), 374; this is echoed in K.M. Brown, Kingdom or Province? Scotland and the Regal Union, 1603–1715 (London, 1992), 90–91; Mason, 'George Buchanan, James VI and the Presbyterians', 125–6 is effectively saying the same thing by implying virtual royal authorship of the 'Black Acts' and royal approval of an anti-presbyterian tract by Patrick Adamson.

[26] BUK, ii, 648–50 and iii, 799–800; Calderwood, History, v, 245–6; M. Graham, The Uses of Reform: 'Godly Discipline' and Popular Behaviour in Scotland and Beyond, 1560–1610 (Leiden, 1996), 141 n. 65, pointing out that Dunblane presbytery no longer existed in 1593 but not noting it was split between Stirling and the newly erected Auchterarder, see Stirling Presbytery, ii, 8 May 1593.

[27] BUK, ii, 665–6, 695.

[28] SRO, Register of the Privy Seal, PS1/54, fo. 117r.

this development since it explicitly mentioned their right to receive presentations.[29] By 1593, although a few crown presentations were directed to bishops or commissioners, presbyteries were the primary recipients of royal presentations to benefices.

The development of the presbyteries can also be traced through their delegation of commissioners to general assemblies. The two presbytery registers which survive from the period before the 'Black Acts', those of Stirling and Dalkeith, show that, by their second year of existence, they were electing commissioners to general assemblies.[30] Since there were relatively few presbyteries prior to 1584, the synods must have largely maintained their role as the principal delegating bodies. With their re-establishment in 1586, more presbyteries began to take this on. The picture discernible from the six registers of presbyteries which survive from before 1596 shows some regional variations. The presbytery of Edinburgh nominated commissioners to all assemblies between 1586 and 1592; Haddington presbytery did so from at least 1588 and St Andrews and Dalkeith were doing so by 1590. The records of the presbyteries of Stirling and Glasgow suggest that, in those areas, delegation by the synod was the norm. That is not to say, however, that those presbyteries were underdeveloped, as a glance at their records would show. As early as 1589, it is clear from the records of the presbytery of Edinburgh that the General Assembly saw presbyteries as the natural bodies for delegation. In 1590 and in 1591, the presbytery used a commission from the previous Assembly to call the next one by writing to all the presbyteries of the realm.[31]

Their development as courts for hearing cases of moral discipline went along similar lines. Since most of them had emerged from a regular meeting of ministers for the exercise of doctrine, they had to be slotted into the appeals system for cases of discipline, between kirk sessions and synods. Before 1584, both Dalkeith and Stirling dealt with discipline. It is impossible to tell how quickly the role was taken on by the presbyteries created in May 1586, but only in the presbytery of Haddington is there any evidence that it came late; most of them took on disciplinary action straightaway.[32] Essentially, the presbyteries were

---

[29] APS, iii, 541 ff.

[30] Stirling Presb. Recs, 40, 107 (beginning Aug. 1581); Dalkeith Presbytery, fo. 57v (beginning at 'fo. 10', March 1582).

[31] Edinburgh Presbytery, i, 20 Jan. 1590, 8 June 1591; BUK, ii, 762–7. For a fuller discussion of the processes of election to the General Assembly see A.R. MacDonald, 'Ecclesiastical Politics in Scotland, 1568–1610' (unpublished Edinburgh PhD dissertation, 1995), 16–21.

[32] Haddington Presbytery, i, fo. 5v (March 1588); see Graham, Uses of Reform, ch. 4 for a discussion of the creation of presbyterian discipline.

firmly established by 1592 as the key courts by which the Kirk would work, even if their coverage was incomplete and their strength variable.

The 'Golden Act' of May 1592, in its legislative endorsement of the presbyterian system of kirk session, presbytery, synod and General Assembly, and in its failure to mention the episcopate, was described by the late Gordon Donaldson as 'little more than a recognition of a *fait accompli*'.[33] Yet since the act had a significant effect on the direction of presentations to benefices, the statement must be reassessed. That act of Parliament also had a wider political context which its terms, dramatic though they were, do not reveal. Although the more technical issue of the nature of ecclesiastical polity was characterised by compromise between the Kirk and the crown, deeper tensions over where authority lay simmered beneath this. The king clearly believed that he had the right to interfere with the courts of the Kirk if their activities displeased him, as was demonstrated in his threat to put the presbytery of St Andrews to the horn early in 1587 if it did not suspend a process against Patrick Adamson.[34] The prevailing opinion in the Kirk, on the other hand, was that the civil authority should support the Kirk but not interfere with it.

The principal difficulty between the Kirk and the crown in the years after 1586 related to the favour which the king showed to Catholic nobles, most notably the Earl of Huntly. Throughout the later 1580s, there were frequent calls, from general assemblies and the other courts of the Kirk, for action against Jesuits and other Catholic missionaries and equally frequent complaints against royal favour to Catholic nobles. As early as 1587, the General Assembly, fearing that the crown's resolve to take action against Catholicism went no further than unenforced legislation, called for existing acts of Parliament against Jesuits to be enforced. The Kirk felt that, in matters which concerned the state of religion in Scotland, they must exhort the civil authority to action. James VI, however, did not take kindly to such exhortations. It has been noted that the excommunication of the Earl of Huntly, among others, would technically have meant that the king would be deprived of the company of a close friend, since association with excommunicated people was expressly forbidden.[35] James was thus reluctant to enforce anti-Catholic legislation regardless of status so he responded to the Kirk's demands by demanding a role in the trial of Archbishop Adamson and insisting that two ministers who had refused to pray for Mary prior to her execution should apologise publicly. He also declared that Robert

---

[33] Donaldson, *Scottish Reformation*, 219.

[34] St Andrews Presbytery, fo. 6r.

[35] Graham, *Uses of Reform*, 156.

Montgomery, the excommunicated former Archbishop of Glasgow, should be received into the Kirk again and that the excommunication of the Catholic laird of Fintry should be annulled. The assembly responded by asserting its independence and calling for further action against Catholics.[36] This was a confrontation over differing views of the fundamental nature of sovereignty. The Kirk felt it had the right to act as the state's spiritual conscience, while the king believed that he had the right to intervene in any ecclesiastical matters which particularly concerned him.

Later in that year, Parliament passed the 'Act of Annexation' whereby the temporalities of ecclesiastical benefices (their lands) fell to the crown. The spirituality (the benefices themselves and the residences and gardens attached) were to remain with their holders. This would take property and revenue principally from prelacies – the episcopal and monastic properties. The prime motive was financial but, although it made no concessions on sovereignty, the act may also have been designed to placate the Kirk by emphasising the crown's lack of enthusiasm for episcopacy. The prospect of an increase in royal income might also have meant that the king would take less from the thirds of benefices, more of which might thus be released to the financially straitened Kirk.

In 1588, with the threat of Spanish invasion of the British Isles looming large, the wrestling match between James VI and the Kirk continued. In January, James intervened with the presbyteries of Dunblane and Stirling to prevent the excommunication of the Catholic Bishop of Dunblane, William Chisholm.[37] Chisholm had been summoned by the presbyteries to subscribe the Confession of Faith and, twice, James VI commanded that the sentence should be delayed. On the second occasion, the king himself took caution that Chisholm would leave Scotland within 40 days. He failed to do so and was finally excommunicated but the Privy Council overturned the sentence.[38] While this was going on, a convention of 'the maist wacryff [wakeful] and cearfull of the breithren' called extraordinary meetings of all synods and insisted that the king should enforce legislation against Catholics since they were seen as likely collaborators with Spain. They also demanded that he should allow the Kirk to establish a commission to root them out. Although angered by this unauthorised gathering, the political support which it enjoyed meant that he was forced to grant its requests. The commission

---

[36] *BUK*, ii, 697–701; Calderwood, *History*, iv, 627–32.

[37] Watt, *Fasti*, 78. Chisholm became suffragan for his uncle in June 1561. It is unclear who made the 'crown' nomination, but it was probably done before the 'Reformation parliament' of August 1560.

[38] Stirling Presbytery, i, 2, 9, 16 Jan. and 27 Feb. 1588; *RPC*, iv, 263–4.

reflected the fact that the pressure for action had not come from the Kirk alone, for it consisted of nobles and representatives of burghs as well as ministers.[39] In the aftermath of the failure of the Spanish Armada, the General Assembly, meeting in August, gratefully reciprocated with its own compromise in the hope that more stringent measures against Catholics would be carried out. Moderating its position of the previous year, it reserved sentence on Patrick Adamson, pending consultation with the king, and one of the ministers who had refused to pray for Mary was transferred, at the king's request, while the other was suspended.[40] In spite of this, James did not move against the Catholic threat.

Protests from the Kirk continued into 1589 as the Earl of Huntly, having made a show of conforming to Protestantism, was revealed to be in secret correspondence with King Philip of Spain, offering encouragement and support for a second Armada attempt. Although warded in Edinburgh Castle as a result of this intelligence, he was shortly released and entertained by the king at royal expense.[41] Soon, he was back in the North East, openly demonstrating both his military strength and his commitment to Catholicism. Pressure from the Kirk and from England and the rumour that Huntly intended to march south at the head of an army, persuaded James to take what appeared to be decisive action. He demanded that the earls of Huntly and Errol, another prominent Catholic, should surrender their castles to the crown on pain of treason and enter ward in Aberdeen. At the end of April, James led an armed expedition accompanied by Patrick Galloway, one of his household ministers. Huntly and his allies congregated in military array at the Brig of Dee, just south of Aberdeen but they melted away before the oncoming royal army and the king was left a clear path into his royal burgh.[42]

This gesture was enough to ensure relatively happy relations between the king and the Kirk for the rest of 1589 and into 1590. It even seems to have secured some money from Queen Elizabeth. The king had found a new enthusiasm against Catholicism which was demonstrated in May 1589 when the Privy Council passed an act against the exiled Catholic prelates, the Archbishop of Glasgow, James Beaton, and the bishops of Ross, John Leslie, and of Dunblane, William Chisholm.

---

[39] (Unknown) to Walsingham, Jan. 1588, *CSP Scot*, ix, no. 435; Spottiswoode, *History*, ii, 379; Melville, *Diary*, 267–8; MacDonald, 'Ecclesiastical Politics', 146 n. 61.

[40] *BUK*, ii, 704–23, 730, Calderwood, *History*, iv, 652–75, 685–6; Spottiswoode, *History*, ii, 380–81.

[41] Scottish Privy Council to English Ambassador, 20 Feb., Ashby to Burghley, 27 Feb., Ashby to Walsingham, 8 March, *CSP Scot*, ix nos 589, 591, 600.

[42] Donaldson, *Scotland: James V–James VII*, 189; see also *CSP Scot*, x, 25–58.

Sentences of forfeiture, conviction for barratry (simony) and excommunication were pronounced against them which were to stand unless they acknowledged obedience to the king and subscribed the 'Negative Confession' of 1581. In October, the Privy Council continued to demonstrate its godly intentions by ratifying previous acts against holding markets on Sundays and declaring that people should be appointed in every parish to ensure their enforcement.[43] In September, the synod of Lothian and Tweeddale had sent delegates to court to ask about when the next Parliament would sit, to discuss the impending royal marriage and to encourage action against Huntly and his allies the earls of Errol and Angus. Encouragement, rather than angry pressure, appears to have been all that was required, since the earls had already been called to appear before the presbytery of Edinburgh by the Privy Council.[44]

This was a happy year for relations between King James and his Kirk. A marriage with the Protestant, albeit Lutheran, Princess Anne of Denmark had been negotiated and the future for a godly Scotland looked secure. While in Scandinavia during the winter of 1589–90, the king left the country in the capable hands of the Privy Council, the Earl of Bothwell and the ministers and 'the kingdom exhibited a scene of unwonted tranquility'. Robert Bruce, one of the ministers of Edinburgh, was given a prominent role in government, although not on the Privy Council as has been mistakenly suggested, and the king maintained a personal correspondence with him on ecclesiastical affairs.[45] Before James's return, a General Assembly was held in March 1590, with the co-operation of the Earl of Bothwell. It postponed its meeting until the king's homecoming, as did the synod of Lothian and Tweeddale, meeting in April.[46]

There were hopes for great things on the king's return with his bride. Andrew Melville, like George Buchanan before him, a court poet as well as a scholar, composed celebratory Latin verses for Queen Anne's coronation and the king was so pleased with them that he ordered their publication. The coronation, however, was not without its share of religious controversy. It was unclear how a Protestant coronation should be conducted, so the synod of Lothian and Tweeddale set up a committee

---

[43] *RPC*, iv, 388, 419.

[44] *Lothian Synod*, 13, 15.

[45] McCrie, *Life of Melville*, i, 300; Melville, *Diary*, 277; *RPC*, iv, 430n; SRO, Royal letters presented by R.J. Bruce of Elmhurst Farm, GD1/240/1–4; Graham, *Uses of Reform*, 207–8, n. 17. There is no evidence that Bruce was a member of the Privy Council, as James Melville and some subsequent writers have alleged. Some of James's letters to Bruce were not written by a clerk and are entirely in James's own hand.

[46] Melville, *Diary*, 277; *BUK*, ii, 750; *Lothian Synod*, 17; Dalkeith Presbytery, fo. 117v.

in May to 'resolve ... upon the said coronatioun and ceremoneis to be ussit thairat'. They even consulted Adam Bothwell, Bishop of Orkney, because he had been involved in the rushed coronation of James VI in 1567. There is no record of what they decided but, when it came to negotiations with the king, an argument arose over anointing. The ministers argued that this was a Jewish ceremony which was removed when Christ came into the world and reintroduced only by the papacy. The king, however, pointed out that unction was universal because all kings in Old Testament times, not just Jewish kings, received it. This argument failed to persuade but a more immediate and less theoretical one proved stronger. Robert Bruce reluctantly agreed to administer unction when the king threatened to find a bishop to do it. Bruce was persuaded by none other than Andrew Melville, afraid of the consequences of episcopal involvement.[47]

The postponed synod of Lothian and Tweeddale petitioned the king about ecclesiastical representation in Parliament, action against Jesuits, the provision of stipends and the punishment of abusers of the sacraments. The English ambassador also reported that the king had agreed to consider a request for legislative recognition of presbyterianism – an idea which was filed away for later use. In relation to parliamentary representation, the synod asked that 'the Kirk be not prejudget concerning thair vote in the first conventioun and parliament'.[48] From 1578 onwards, notably in tandem with the implementation of the *Second Book of Discipline*, the General Assembly had often shown an interest in this matter. The prevailing opinion was that the current system of bishops and nominal abbots and priors sitting in Parliament for the spiritual estate was unsatisfactory since they were not accountable to the Kirk for their actions in Parliament and most of them were not even clerics. Various suggestions had been made over the years as to what sort of a system should replace this pre-Reformation constitutional remnant but no moves towards reform of the spiritual estate had yet been made. Perhaps the synod of Lothian and Tweeddale feared that the new-found closeness of the Kirk and the crown might lead to the king being willing to give the Kirk direct representation and could be taken too far by the king on his own terms. In June, a Convention of the Estates met and, unprecedentedly, it was attended by three ministers,

---

[47] *Lothian Synod*, 19; D. Stevenson, *Scotland's Last Royal Wedding: the Marriage of James VI and Anne of Denmark* (Edinburgh, 1997), 58–9; Spottiswoode, *History*, ii, 407–8; Melville, *Diary*, 279. Events like coronations highlighted the problem of a presbyterian Kirk under a monarchy which demanded a ceremonial role for the Kirk in the highly stratified world of a royal court.

[48] *Lothian Synod*, 18; Bowes to Burghley, 16 May 1590, *CSP Scot*, x, no. 403.

David Lindsay, minister of Leith, and the king's ministers, Patrick Galloway and John Duncanson.[49] Since all three were members of the synod of Lothian and Tweeddale, it may have been inside information which prompted that body to make its representation to the king. Conventions of the estates, unlike Parliament, met at relatively short notice by royal invitation and the fact that no bishops or nominal abbots attended this one would suggest that the king was making a tentative constitutional experiment. Bishops did not sit in parliaments or conventions of estates again for two years but the experiment, if that is what it was, came to nothing.

The General Assembly met at Edinburgh in August. The king addressed the Assembly, fresh from Scandinavia where the Lutheran kirks had been purged of candles and altar cloths when he worshipped. He praised the Kirk for its doctrinal purity and criticised its English counterpart for maintaining vestiges of Catholicism, its communion being 'ane evill said messe in English, wanting nothing but the liftings'. Not even the Kirk of Geneva could measure up since it 'keepeth Pasche and Yuile'. He also promised to deal with Catholics and improve the Kirk's finances. This was received with 15 minutes of spontaneous rejoicing.[50] The Assembly responded, after the excitement had died down, with a number of hard-headed requests including the legislative ratification of its polity, an organised, national anti-Catholic purge (including decisive action against Huntly and his allies) and financial provision for stipends, the fabric of kirks and for schools and universities. A number of acts in favour of the Kirk and against Catholics was passed by the Privy Council and the relationship between the Kirk and the state apparently could not have been warmer.[51]

Underlying tensions remained, however. No ratification of the presbyterian system was forthcoming in spite of a request to the Privy Council that 'the jurisdictioun of the Kirk, the generall and synodall assembleis, presbitereis and discipline presentlie in use, be allowit and authorizit be act of counsall and conventioun, gif ony sal happin to be, [and by] parliament'.[52] Proceedings against Patrick Adamson had been shelved to avoid jeopardising the king's favour towards the Kirk and James had hinted at royal supremacy in his speech to the Assembly by

---

[49] *APS*, iii, 524.

[50] *BUK*, ii, 771; Scot, *Apologetical Narration*, 57; Stevenson, *Scotland's Last Royal Wedding*, 40–41. By 1616, James had undergone a profound change of mind, see below p. 158.

[51] *BUK*, ii, 772; *RPC*, iv, 463; Bowes to Walsingham, 16 March and Bowes to Burghley, 14 Aug. 1590, *CSP Scot*, x, nos 361, 464.

[52] *RPC*, iv, 831. This Act, entitled 'Propositions Relating to the Kirk', was presented to the Privy Council, probably by the Kirk, but not passed.

asserting his right to censure the Kirk. The godly magistrate had the duty of 'conservation and purgation of religion' and it was clear that this godly prince saw more rights in that duty than the Kirk.[53] The peace between the king and the Kirk was young and delicate; the Kirk would not risk its collapse by standing on too many points of principle.

Such a honeymoon period as there was after James's return from Denmark and the General Assembly in August was short-lived. The euphoria of the Assembly soon wore off as the king's lack of enthusiasm to pursue prominent Catholics, or even to act against Catholicism in general, became clear. Most notable among them was the Jesuit, James Gordon, the Earl of Huntly's uncle. The fact that this highlighted the protection that powerful nobles could and did afford to missionaries may have been what provoked the Assembly of August 1590 to demand that something be done.[54] In October, the synod of Lothian and Tweeddale reiterated calls for action against Catholics, presumably since none had been forthcoming and, in November, the king was noted to have been acting favourably towards Jesuits whom the Kirk had been trying to pursue. Robert Bruce complained that they were being 'winked at' while friends of God were persecuted. This referred to the arrest of James Gibson, minister of Pencaitland, for allegedly having miscalled the king in a sermon. Bruce pointed out that such treatment would be better reserved for Jesuits and the king's telling response was that no Jesuit had wronged him as much as had Gibson.[55] Bruce's view, however, was that the very presence of a Jesuit in Scotland was a danger to Kirk, king and common weal. This incident, perhaps more effectively than any other, illustrates the fundamental difference in outlook which divided the instinctively tolerant king from the fervently anti-Catholic Kirk.

During 1591, tensions remained, although the situation did not come to a head. The Kirk's grievances continued to be focused on royal failure to implement existing acts of Parliament and the Privy Council against Catholicism. In May, the presbytery of Edinburgh called on the Privy Council to take 'order ... with Jesuittis and excommunicat persones' and, in July, the Assembly once more demanded that measures against Catholics be implemented. The ministers were particularly bothered by the presence, and therefore the influence, at court of the Earl of Huntly

---

[53] *Second Book of Discipline*, 40 which notes the phrase from the Concordat of Leith and 213–16 which took on this idea, giving the king the right to 'restore the trew service of the Lord' if he felt it was required.

[54] Bowes to Burghley, 21 June, Same to same, 29 June, Same to same, 23 July, *CSP Scot*, x, nos 431, 434, 454.

[55] *Lothian Synod*, 22; Calderwood, *History*, v, 112, 115–16.

and his wife, who was the king's cousin, and they demanded their expulsion.[56] There were, however, some signs of continued co-operation. Where the interests of the crown and those of the Kirk overlapped, joint action was possible. In May, the advice of the presbytery of Edinburgh was sought in relation to dealing with witches, a particular interest of the king, and in October, two ministers – Robert Bruce and John Duncanson – were appointed by the Privy Council to a commission for their detection.[57] The Earl of Bothwell had become the target of the king's wrath and found himself at the centre of Scotland's first major witch scare. In April 1591 accusations that he had consulted with witches in an attempt to thwart James's safe return from Scandinavia were levelled against him.[58] The man who had been left in command of the kingdom during the king's absence thus fell from grace and began to assert himself under arms. Therein, unexpectedly, lay the origins of the downfall of relations between James VI and the Kirk.

The king acted quickly. Bothwell was warded in Edinburgh Castle and his supporters were ordered to leave the town. He escaped in June and appeared in the field with an armed following. A proclamation was issued calling on all the other earls to be ready to resist the errant earl who was charged to render to the crown his castles of Crichton and Hailes.[59] There then followed a period of some political disorder with Bothwell in partial hiding and rumoured to be seeking support from almost any quarter. Military expeditions against him were unsuccessful and, in December, he forcibly gained entrance to Holyrood Palace in an attempt to obtain a personal pardon from the king. Although this failed, he managed to escape and, in January 1592, a further military expedition against him failed to apprehend him. By the beginning of February, Huntly had been given the leading role in the royal armed pursuit of Bothwell but, a few days later, the political nation's attention was diverted from that matter. In February, the long-standing feud between the Earls of Huntly and Moray came to a head with the murder of James, the 'Bonnie Earl', by men in the service of Huntly, at Moray's house of Donibristle in Fife.

In March, a date was set for Huntly's trial and it was declared that, if he failed to appear before the court, an army would be sent against him. He dutifully entered ward in Blackness Castle on the Firth of Forth while ministers and nobles demanded that as strong action should be

---

[56] Edinburgh Presbytery, 18 May 1591; *BUK*, ii, 784; Bowes to Burghley, 21 July 1591, *CSP Scot*, x, no. 592.

[57] Edinburgh Presbytery, 11 May 1591; *RPC*, iv, 680.

[58] Donaldson, *Scotland: James V–James VII*, 191.

[59] *RPC*, iv, 644–5.

taken against him as was attempted against Bothwell. James VI dragged his feet to such an extent, however, that his own chancellor, John Maitland of Thirlestane, sided for a time with the supporters of the murdered Earl of Moray against the king. James was still showing distinct reluctance to punish Huntly for Moray's death when the General Assembly met in May.[60] No action of any substance had been taken against the Earl of Huntly and that stood out in stark contrast to the king's persistent pursuit of the Earl of Bothwell in the previous year.

The Assembly, as was common, was held in anticipation of a Parliament. In response to some questions from the crown, the Assembly made the usual demands about pursuit of Catholics and the provision of stipends. It also called for the abolition both of the 'Black Acts' of 1584 and the 'Act of Annexation' of 1587; the restoration of the Kirk's entire pre-Reformation patrimony; the removal of prelates from Parliament and their replacement with proper representatives of the Kirk. Although Calderwood alleged that the king did promise to repeal the 'Black Acts' and allow direct representatives of the Kirk to sit in Parliament, only the former was actually carried out and then only partially.[61] The assembly's demands enraged the king, as did the behaviour of a number of ministers. Losing patience with James's lenience towards Huntly, they had praised John Knox, George Buchanan and James's late uncle, James Stewart, Earl of Moray, and regent from 1567 to 1571, implicitly criticising the king for failing to measure up to the godly government of his mother's half-brother. The combination of these factors, and royal problems with Bothwell who, seeking political support, had posed as a friend of the Kirk, appear to have provoked James, probably with the advice of his chancellor, John Maitland of Thirlestane, into dusting off the Kirk's supplication to the Privy Council of 1590 and passing the 'Golden Act'.[62] This interpretation may seem odd since the act ratified the rights of kirk sessions, presbyteries, synods and general assemblies to meet and allowed no place to an episcopate. Thomas McCrie described it as a 'triumph', and James Kirk has portrayed it as a 'victory' for the Kirk. Others have described it in terms of a concession to the Kirk with a toehold maintained by the crown, underplaying its

---

[60] The best source for the sequence of events in 1591 and the beginning of 1592 is *CSP Scot*, x, 491–677.

[61] *BUK*, ii, 786–8; SRO, 'Questions to be resolved by the assembly out of the word of God, 1592', Parliamentary Papers Supplementary, PA7/1 no. 41; Edinburgh Presbytery, i, 9 and 16 May 1592; Bowes to Burghley, 29 May and same to same, 6 June 1592, *CSP Scot*, x, nos 687 and 691; Calderwood, *History*, v, 156–8.

[62] Calderwood, *History*, v, 159; Spottiswoode, *History*, ii, 421; *RPC*, iv, 831; on the Kirk seeking noble allies see K.M. Brown, 'In Search of the Godly Magistrate in Reformation Scotland', *Journal of Ecclesiastical History*, 40 (1989), 553–81.

Erastian nature.[63] The 'Golden Act' was at once an attempt to placate an increasingly hostile Kirk and an assertion of royal power. Indeed, its inherent Erastianism was noted at the time by Robert Bowes, the English ambassador. For him, the act's most significant aspect was its declaration of the royal right to name the 'days and places for their Assemblies'.[64] He also reported that further action against Catholics had been promised by the king but that the Kirk's request for parliamentary representation had been rejected. In the summer of 1592 and for a number of years after, James Melville regarded the 'Golden Act' as having been a gift of surprising generosity for which the Kirk was to be grateful to the wise Chancellor Maitland. By 1606, however, he had realised just how potentially damaging the 'Golden Act' had been when, in a letter to the synod of Fife, he portrayed it as having been responsible for the end to 32 years of the Kirk's freedom to call General Assemblies without interference.[65]

The 'Golden Act' was Erastian for three reasons. First, by its reservation to the crown of the right to name the dates and places of general assemblies, it enshrined in law a royal right to prevent assemblies from meeting indefinitely. Although the act stated that, if the king or his commissioner at the Assembly failed to nominate a date and place, that power would fall to the Assembly, the king could exercise that power and then change his mind repeatedly without reference to the Kirk. Secondly, and perhaps more fundamentally, the very fact that this piece of legislation was carried through at all was significant. The notion that the state should ratify such things as the Kirk's form of government was, admittedly, current. Yet this idea was based upon a godly prince ratifying, without amendment, the Kirk's acts in this area. The 'Golden Act', an isolated example of civil legislative ratification of certain aspects of the ecclesiastical *status quo*, did not conform to this pattern. Thirdly, it was as significant for what it did not do as for what it did do.

---

[63] McCrie, *Life of Melville*, i, 324–5; J. Kirk, 'From Reformation to Revolution', in ed., J. Wormald, *Scotland Revisited* (London, 1991), 90–91; J. Kirk, 'The Development of the Melvillian Movement in Late Sixteenth Century Scotland' (unpublished Edinburgh Phd dissertation, 1972), 496, 501; M. Lee, *John Maitland of Thirlestane and the Foundation of the Stewart Despotism in Scotland* (Princeton, 1959), 248–9; Donaldson, *Scotland: James V–James VII*, 199; G. Donaldson, 'The Scottish Church 1567–1625' in ed., A.G.R. Smith, *The Reign of James VI and I* (Aylesbury, 1973), 50; M. Lynch, *Scotland: a New History* (London, 1991), 234; Mullan, *Episcopacy in Scotland*, 75.

[64] Bowes to Burghley, 6 June 1592, *CSP Scot*, x, no. 691; *APS*, iii, 541 ff; It is unclear when it became known as the 'Golden Act', for no contemporary source used the phrase and not even McCrie used it. See McCrie, *Life of Melville*, i, 318–25. *Dictionary of Scottish Church History and Theology*, eds N.M de S. Cameron et al. (Edinburgh, 1993), 338 gives no answer as to its origin either.

[65] Melville, *Diary*, 298, 631.

Although Parliament specifically overturned a number of the 'Black Acts' of May 1584, it did nothing to annul the first of them which legislated for royal supremacy in all matters, spiritual and temporal. The fact that it remained on the statute book, and would later be used against ecclesiastical dissidents, must be borne in mind when assessing the significance of the 'Golden Act' in its proper context. By retaining statutory royal supremacy and by specifically granting certain additional rights to the monarch, it diminished the crown's legal position *vis-à-vis* the Kirk not one whit. It could even be said to have set a precedent for the right of the civil authority to ratify, or not, matters of ecclesiastical organisation and jurisdiction. It may have been designed to placate a worried or even hostile Kirk, but its architect, Chancellor Maitland, ensured that the power of the state, far from being reduced, was enhanced. What the state could grant, the state could rescind and over the next 20 years, this would become increasingly apparent.

By the middle of 1592, the fragility of the relationship between the crown and the Kirk was once more clear. Although there had been episodes of co-operation, the period between the fall of the Arran regime and the 'Golden Act' was characterised by tension, resulting from the simple problem that the king did not see the religious and ecclesiastical world in the terms in which most of the Kirk saw it. Although he could talk in the abstract of the necessity to root out Catholicism and to promote the Protestant religion, he did not share the fervour which most of the Kirk appears to have borne against Catholicism. This factor unified the Kirk and the strong presence within it of the notion that it was the ministers' job to ensure the godly conduct of government created an atmosphere of conflict with the crown rooted in the king's disinclination, as far as the Kirk saw it, to purify the nation. There had been periods of co-operation, even of warmth, and this would recur in the future but these years did not witness 'peace' or 'harmony' between the Kirk and the king. The increasing difficulties in their relationship in subsequent years was not the breakdown of a happy relationship but the collapse of a precarious one.[66]

---

[66] Lee, *Great Britain's Solomon*, 68; Lynch, *Scotland*, 233.

CHAPTER THREE

An untidy tumble towards crisis, 1592–96

One of the most enduring commonplaces concerning the first ten years or so of the personal reign of James VI is that he began by favouring the presbyterians so that he could deal with the Catholic nobles and, once he had succeeded in doing that, he favoured the Catholic nobles so that he could deal with the presbyterians.[1] As well as encapsulating the idea that James was born with an insatiable desire for episcopacy, this view endows him with longer-term planning skills than he possessed. It assumes that, in the mid-1580s, the 19–year-old king had set his mind upon this policy and that it was achieved with perfect success. More simply, it is flawed because, before 1603, he was unable to gain the upper hand in his dealings with the Catholic nobles. They possessed enough military strength to remain unthreatened by the crown and were thus able to remain firmly undealt with, in spite of their treasonous dealings with Spain. King James acted against them occasionally, never very harshly and largely when he was forced into it by others, most notably Queen Elizabeth of England and the Kirk. He did not see them as a genuine threat and later evidence shows that the power of Huntly was not diminished. After 1594, Huntly no longer rose in arms because he did not need to and he was never seriously forced to conform to the Kirk in spite of numerous show recantations of Catholicism.

Soon after the Parliament of 1592 had risen, the Privy Council set the seal on the Erastianism of the 'Golden Act' by formally proclaiming, in accordance with the provisions of that legislation, the date and place of meeting of the next General Assembly.[2] The proclamation left both blank but the significance of the gesture was clear enough: the crown

---

[1] G. Donaldson, *Scotland: James V–James VII* (Edinburgh, 1971), 193; R. Mitchison, *A History of Scotland* (London, 1970), 152; M. Lee, *Government by Pen: Scotland under James VI and I* (Urbana, 1980), 22, although he has James dealing with all his nobility first, it is a similar view. A remnant of the idea can also be found in K.M. Brown, *Kingdom or Province? Scotland and the Regional Union, 1603–1707* (London, 1992), 86.

[2] *RPC,* iv, 758.

was demonstrating its right. It did not take some ministers long to realise the less than golden nature of the act. A convention of clergy at Edinburgh, late in 1592, sought to take advantage of the Privy Council's failure to specify the date and place by summoning an assembly of ministers and laity to meet in Edinburgh in January 1593. The failure of the 'Golden Act' to placate the Kirk other than in the short term, was demonstrated by this convention's inflammatory, not to say threatening, declaration that it was within the Kirk's power to excommunicate the king. It had met because of increasing fears over the king's failure to combat what was perceived as a rising tide of Catholicism. The convention was well attended by the laity, stirred up with a desire to use the occasion to put pressure on the king to 'tak ordour with these unnatural subjects, betrayers of thair countrey to the crewall Spainyeard'.[3] It urged the king to promise to uphold the Kirk, punish its enemies, establish a commission of nobles to execute anti-Catholic acts of Parliament, hold 'wappinschawings' for the defence of the Kirk, purge the Privy Council of any suspected of Catholic sympathies and remove Catholics from his household.[4]

The failure of these demands is illustrated in the growing tension between the king and the Kirk over the following four weeks. James Stewart, Earl of Arran, was received at court once again, having been absent since his fall in 1585, provoking public criticism by Walter Balcanquhal, one of the ministers of Edinburgh, and the summoning of Arran before the presbytery of Edinburgh. The king, at once showing extreme displeasure and implicitly endorsing Arran's government, threatened to resurrect proceedings against the ministers who had resisted his policies. Robert Bruce, another Edinburgh minister, preached that the king was surrounded by liars and John Davidson, minister of Prestonpans, offended him further by alleging that he had failed to punish Moray's murderers properly because he was still 'infected' by Esmé Stewart.[5]

Soon after this, the so-called affair of the 'Spanish blanks' came to light. A ship, about to leave the west coast, was found to be carrying one George Kerr, bound for Spain with letters and papers signed by Huntly, Errol and Angus.[6] In January 1593, the presbytery of Edinburgh, reacting to a royal intimation of intention to act, wrote to all the presbyteries in Scotland. It asked them 'to travell with the noblemen, gentlemen and baronis within thair boundis for obtening ... a voluntar contributioun to

---

[3] Melville, *Diary*, 307; *BUK*, iii, 796–813.
[4] Melville, *Diary*, 299; Calderwood, *History*, v, 179 ff. A 'wappinschaw' was a local muster for inspection of arms.
[5] Calderwood, *History*, v, 186–91; Edinburgh Presbytery, i, 5 Dec. 1592.
[6] Melville, *Diary*, 306–7.

lift a garde to his Majestie for his assistance in prosequuting this purpos intentit aganes the traffiquers with Spane'. After an armed royal expedition to the north which achieved little, the presbytery of Edinburgh sent out a similar letter in March. The presbyteries of Stirling, Glasgow, Dalkeith, Haddington and St Andrews all received a copy.[7] The tone suggests that the presbytery of Edinburgh was unhappy with the outcome of the king's expedition. It urged, once more, that money should be gathered to ensure that the king could not use lack of funds as an excuse for reneging on promises of further action.

It was thus in the atmosphere of a fortuitously averted threat to king and Kirk, combined with a strong desire for effective action against those involved, that the General Assembly met at Dundee in April. It urged the king to punish Catholics for their lawbreaking, make a public declaration against them and bar them from public office. Unwilling to be told by ministers how to do his job, the king retaliated by demanding an act of the Assembly to forbid pulpit criticism of the king or the Privy Council and urging that the ministers should preach with equal fervour against Bothwell as against the Catholic earls, because an enemy of God was an enemy of the king, and vice versa. Of five royal articles, all but one were accepted but the demand that there should be an act against criticism of the king or the Privy Council was countered with the modification, not to say loophole, that no 'rash or irreverent' speeches should be made, only just ones – not quite what the king had had in mind.

Between general assemblies, clashes between the king and the Kirk moved to the lower ecclesiastical courts, the synods and presbyteries. The frequency with which presbyteries met made them effective gatherers of money and information as well as ready sources of personnel for *ad hoc* conventions of ministers in times of crisis. It had been planned that a Convention of the Estates would try Huntly, Angus and Errol for treason in the summer of 1593 because of the revelations surrounding the 'Spanish blanks'. That Convention met at Holyrood, after a number of prorogations, but it did not proceed against the earls. In July, representatives of the presbyteries met in Edinburgh to petition Parliament, in vain, to do the same.[8] In September, the synod of Fife, increasingly wary of royal reluctance to act decisively against the rebel Catholic

---

[7] Edinburgh Presbytery, i, 23 Jan. and 20 March 1593; SRO, 'Ane letter from the presbiterie of Edinburgh to uther presbiteriis in Scotland anent payment of the kingis guard', 20 March 1593, Cunningham of Caprington Papers, GD149/265; Stirling Presbytery, i, 27 March 1593; Glasgow Presbytery, i, fo. 7v; Dalkeith Presbytery, fo. 157v; Haddington Presbytery, ii, fo. 71r; St Andrews Presbytery, fo. 49v.

[8] Calderwood, *History*, v, 225; *BUK*, iii, 814; Stirling Presbytery, ii, 3 July 1593; St Andrews Presbytery, fo. 54r; Glasgow Presbytery, i, fo. 13r; Haddington Presbytery, ii, fo. 78r.

earls, excommunicated Angus, Huntly and Errol, Lord Hume, Sir James Chisholm of Cromlix and Sir Patrick Gordon of Auchindoun.[9] It noted the king's laxity in taking action against them for their dealings with Spain and, in a collective bout of impatience, it excommunicated six people who did not even live within the bounds of its jurisdiction. The rather lame justification offered was that some of them at least had attended the University of St Andrews. To bolster this irregular act, the synod resolved to enlist the support of other synods, to which it wrote. The presbytery of Stirling recorded, on 9 October, the order of the synod of Perth and Stirling, to intimate the excommunication from all pulpits and to proceed against any of the excommunicants who might be within their bounds.[10] The latter instruction refers to Sir James Chisholm of Cromlix who was normally resident within the presbytery of Stirling.

The records of the synod of Lothian and Tweeddale reveal that it also received intimation of the excommunications. On 9 October, Andrew Lamb came as a commissioner from Fife to tell that synod 'quhat sycht god had given thame of the danger quhairin the kirk of god within this realme standis' and what the best remedy was. They were asked to call an extraordinary convention of ministers, barons and burgesses to meet in Edinburgh on 17 October and to ratify and publicise the excommunications. The synod of Lothian and Tweeddale was, however, reluctant to comply. It 'concludit that for a certane tyme sylence salbe keipit ... and that na intimatioun be maid ... to the xxviii of this instant', leaving the presbytery of Edinburgh to make the decision.[11] The presbytery of Edinburgh had already been persuaded by the Privy Council to postpone the excommunication of Lord Hume until the same date and the synod may have feared the king's reaction to such an unprocedural excommunication and felt that it would be politic not to provoke him.[12] It appears, however, although it was not recorded by the presbytery of Edinburgh, that the decision to publicise the excommunications throughout Lothian and Tweeddale had been made by 18 October, perhaps at the convention on the previous day.[13] The presbytery of Edinburgh took matters further and, on 18 October, acting as it did so often in this period as a standing commission of the

[9] Melville, *Diary*, 310; Calderwood, *History*, v, 260 ff; Spottiswoode, *History*, ii, 437–8.

[10] Stirling Presbytery, ii, 9 Oct. 1593.

[11] *Lothian Synod*, 64–5.

[12] *Lothian Synod*, 66; Stirling Presbytery, ii, 9 Oct. 1593.

[13] Bowes to Burghley, 12 Oct. and same to same, 20 Oct. 1593, *CSP Scot*, xi, nos 156 and 158.

Kirk, wrote to the moderator of every presbytery. Each was to tell those within the bounds of the presbytery who were 'well affected towards religion' to be in Perth on 24 October to lobby at the trial of the earls which was finally to take place then.[14]

The synod of Clydesdale also received a message similar to that which Andrew Lamb brought from Fife. On 11 October, ministers, nobles, barons, gentlemen and burgesses of Renfrewshire, Dunbartonshire and Lanarkshire and the presbyteries and burghs thereof, met in Glasgow. They heard that similar conventions had met in Fife 'and utheris partis of this realme' and that a general convention would meet in Edinburgh on 17 October to carry matters forward, so they elected commissioners to that convention.[15] Such conventions were designed to intimidate the government by demonstrating widespread opposition to its lenient policy towards the Catholic earls. They have even been portrayed as the Kirk asserting itself, albeit unofficially, in the capacity of a rival Parliament.[16] Royal toleration of open Catholicism among the nobility and of their dealings with Spain was an issue upon which the Kirk and a significant part of the political nation could join forces.

The king reacted angrily. He summoned Robert Bruce to ask him to stay the sentence since none of the excommunicants came from Fife.[17] Bruce told James that, as a mere parish minister, such a thing was not within his power. The convention of barons, burgesses and ministers sent James Melville and Patrick Galloway, one of the king's own ministers, as well as two barons and two burgesses to meet James at Jedburgh. In his *Diary*, Melville wrote that the king was 'crabit' and 'bitterlie inveyit against' the synod of Fife's actions.[18] He angrily agreed to hold a Convention of Estates at Linlithgow to 'tak ordour' with the matter. The response of the presbyteries to the call to organise commissioners to lobby the Convention was healthy. The Convention of Estates was again postponed but, on 5 November, the English ambassador reported that it was going ahead. The presbyteries of Dalkeith, Glasgow, Haddington, St Andrews and Stirling all recorded the delegation of ministers and laymen to lobby the Convention which met at Holyrood on 12 November.[19] It is, unfortunately, impossible to gauge the level of

---

[14] Bowes to Burghley, 18 Oct. 1593, *CSP Scot*, xi, no. 156.

[15] Glasgow Presbytery, i, fo. 15v.

[16] E.E. MacQueen, 'The General Assembly of the Kirk as a Rival of Parliament' (unpublished St Andrews PhD dissertation, 1927), esp. ch. 1.

[17] Calderwood, *History*, v, 265; Spottiswoode, *History*, ii, 437–8.

[18] Melville, *Diary*, 310–11.

[19] Dalkeith Presbytery, i, fo. 165v; Glasgow Presbytery, i, fo. 15v; Haddington Presbytery, ii, fo. 82r; St Andrews Presbytery, fo. 59r; Stirling Presbytery, ii, 28 Oct. 1593; *HKJVI*, 284.

support from a wider selection of presbyteries due to the lack of survival of records, but the king was so unnerved by the prospect of a large
number of uninvited ministers and laymen lobbying his Convention
that the Privy Council forbade all but those whom the king had called
to the Convention from entering the city.[20] In spite of the disappoint-
ment that many of the representatives of presbyteries must have felt
when the Convention passed an 'Act of Abolition', giving the earls
another chance to prove their loyalty to the crown, the act gave the
Kirk a role. The weight of feeling expressed by the Kirk's unofficial
conventions had made its mark. The king's Convention of the Estates
ordered the earls to satisfy the Kirk, in front of their respective
presbyteries or synods, before 1 February 1594 and it established a
commission, including six ministers, to examine petitions from the earls
for clemency.[21]

In the spring of the following year, as a result of the king's failure to
uphold the deadline of 1 February, the synod of Perth and Stirling
again became involved in the controversy over the open Catholicism
of Huntly, Errol and Angus, and their increasingly apparent contacts
with Spain. John Ross preached provocatively at Perth from Jeremiah
28, in which the prophet stated that God promised to break the yoke
of Nebuchadnezzar, the epitome of godless kings. Ross called the king
a 'reprobate, a traitor and rebel to God' and a son of the French
family of Guise (through his maternal grandmother), who were 'perse-
cutors of God's Church'. The synod of Perth and Stirling, in a show of
strength, merely admonished him for his excessive expressions of protest, in spite of the fact that the king had demanded his deprivation
from the ministry.[22]

In May 1594, the General Assembly met in Edinburgh and lamented
the king's continued failure to act against the Catholic earls.[23] A number
of remedies, including forfeiture and pursuit of them with a royal army,
was proposed and the Assembly demanded that, at the forthcoming
Parliament, the lords of the articles, a committee which selected and
drafted the legislation, should be vetted for godliness. The king refused
the demand to forfeit the Catholic earls but agreed that none whose
religion was suspect should be allowed on the articles. He agreed to a
number of other anti-Catholic measures but shied away from the

---

[20] *RPC*, v, 104; Bowes to Burghley, 8 Nov. 1593, *CSP Scot*, xi, no. 169.

[21] *APS*, iv, 46; Moysie, *Memoirs*, 108.

[22] Bowes to Burghley, 18 May 1594, *CSP Scot*, xi, no. 266; *HKJVI*, 317; *BUK*, iii,
844.

[23] *BUK*, iii, 821–45; Melville, *Diary*, 315–17; Calderwood, *History*, v, 307–28;
Spottiswoode, *History*, ii, 454; *HKJVI*, 315–17.

Assembly's offer of an ecclesiastically organised, local popular militia for defence against internal as well as external threats, saying that one would be established only as a last resort in time of danger. He also submitted his own set of demands to the Assembly. Because it had met without his summons, according to the act of 1592, he insisted, as he had done at the time of the previous Assembly in April 1593, that this would not prejudice his right to name the time and place of future meetings. This was acceded to and the records of the Assembly explicitly state that the date and location of the next meeting were decided upon in consultation with the king's commissioners.[24] The other royal demands clearly indicated the difficult state of relations between the king and the Kirk. He urged that the act of 1593 against criticism of the king and the Privy Council should be reissued, that ministers should be banned from associating with the Earl of Bothwell and that pulpit criticism of Bothwell should be mandatory. He demanded the excommunication of Andrew Hunter, minister of Newburn in Fife, for aiding Bothwell and the deprivation of John Ross, minister of Perth, for criticism of the king. The Assembly's reaction could be interpreted as an attempt to meet the king half-way or an assertion of their own authority. Hunter was deposed for desertion of his flock (he had left it to be with Bothwell!) but not excommunicated. The Assembly ratified the synod of Perth and Stirling's admonition of John Ross but refused to deprive him. His preaching was even approved 'except in sik heiddis as seameth to be maist offensive', and he was ordered to speak reverently of the king in future.[25] James's view of the Assembly's response to his demands was clear. He banished John Ross.

This was indeed a testing time for relations between Kirk and crown. The anonymous writer of *The Historie and Life of King James the Sext* wrote that, by the time of this Assembly, James was 'in suspicion with them all [the ministers] in general and with dyvers of thayme in particular'.[26] In an account by James Melville of an encounter with the king at this time, the tension is amply illustrated. James VI expressed regret that the Kirk seemed hostile to him. Melville replied that the problem was one of mutual suspicion and that it could be resolved if they were open about their grievances with each other. The king, therefore, complained about the Assembly having met without royal permission and about its excommunication of Lord Hume for Catholicism. Melville replied that all conventions of ministers were lawful, with or without the king's permission, and that Hume had been excommunicated because

---

[24] *BUK*, iii, 805, 813, 836, 842, 845; Calderwood, *History*, v, 323.
[25] *BUK*, iii, 844; *HKJVI*, 317.
[26] *HKJVI*, 315.

he was a professed Catholic who might be absolved as soon as he had recanted and satisfied the Kirk of his soundness of religion.[27] The tone of Melville's account of the meeting makes it hard to imagine how this could have 'cleared the air' and led to increased understanding.[28] Mutual suspicion remained, resulting from the king's unhappiness with the independent tendency in the Kirk which itself was caused by the Kirk's unhappiness with James's failure to act against the Catholic earls.

During the summer of 1594, letters came to the presbytery of Edinburgh from the synods of Aberdeen and of Angus and the Mearns asking them to urge the king to move against the earls.[29] Pressure from numerous quarters, including England, appears to have forced his hand. The Catholic earls had ignored ultimatum after ultimatum and further royal procrastination would undermine the king's credibility as the one who actually ruled Scotland. The General Assembly of May had decided that two commissioners from every presbytery should wait in Edinburgh to lobby Parliament in June. It duly met, with the king, according to Spottiswoode, having received agreement from the Kirk for a renewal of the ban on irreverent speeches as a *quid pro quo* for forfeiture of the Catholic earls.[30] Perhaps because of James's desire for ecclesiastical support, with the baptism of Prince Henry imminent, it was enacted that all presbyteries were to summon suspected Catholics to press them to satisfy the Kirk regarding their religion. If they failed to do so, the presbyteries should report this to the Privy Council which would summon them under pain of rebellion and escheat of lands and goods.[31] Parliament forfeited Huntly, Angus and Errol and preparations for a military expedition against them were set in motion.[32] James, however, continually postponed the baptism, thus delaying the armed campaign. By September, Bothwell had thrown in his lot with the Catholic earls and, at a stroke, a fundamental problem between the king and the Kirk was obviated. Bothwell had previously attempted to pose as the champion of the Kirk, a position left vacant since the death of the Protestant Earl of Angus in 1589. This had led the ministers, eager to have a noble ally, to be more forgiving of his reckless acts than they were of the Catholic nobles. Royal favour to the Catholics had been combined with a deep-seated dislike of Bothwell ever since the witchcraft scandal. The arch-enemy of the king had now joined the

---

[27] Melville, *Diary*, 316.

[28] M. Lee, *John Maitland of Thirlestane and the Foundation of the Stewart Despotism in Scotland* (Princeton, 1959), 276.

[29] Bowes to Burghley, 21 July 1594, *CSP Scot*, xi, no. 294.

[30] Spottiswoode, *History*, ii, 454; Calderwood, *History*, v, 328.

[31] Stirling Presbytery, ii, 17 and 24 April, 10, 17 and 24 July 1594.

[32] *APS*, iv, 56–61.

arch-enemies of the Kirk. Thrown together in desperation, these nobles left themselves open to a united attack from Kirk and crown. The king could declare that 'a Bothwell and a Papist shall now be all one'.[33]

At the end of September, the Earl of Argyll took an army north, under the king's lieutenancy. It ended indecisively in the Battle of Glenlivet with Huntly losing more men, including Gordon of Auchindoun, but holding the field after Argyll withdrew. Huntly had presented armed resistance to a royal army, so the king was forced to act. In October, David Lindsay, minister of Leith, presented a royal letter to the synod of Lothian and Tweeddale requesting fasting and prayer for the success of the royal expedition and asking that the ministers would inform those whom James had left in charge of government of any practices against state or religion. Not surprisingly, the synod agreed.[34] The synod of Perth and Stirling, meeting on 2 October, received a similar request and ordained a fast in defence of the king, the 'true religion' and Christians in general and against defenders of 'idolatry'.[35] Every synod probably received a similar letter. The king took a force to the North East in pursuit of the Catholic earls and with him went a number of churchmen: James Melville, Andrew Melville, Patrick Galloway and James Nicolson. If the previous year and a half had demonstrated the efficiency of the Kirk in applying pressure on the state, it soon became apparent how quickly differences could be buried for united action against what the Kirk had insisted was a common enemy, even if it had taken some time to persuade the king of this.

When the royal force reached Aberdeen, it was found that the rebel army had withdrawn. The king remained in the North East for the rest of October, arranging for Huntly's castle of Strathbogie and Errol's castle of Slains to be slighted. At the beginning of November, he returned south, leaving a small force behind under the command of Ludovic Stewart, Duke of Lennox, with the task of searching out and apprehending the rebel earls and their associates. Co-operation with the Kirk continued, with one of the ministers who had accompanied the expedition north, James Nicolson, along with Peter Blackburn, minister of Aberdeen, and David Lindsay, being appointed to advise Lennox in his lieutenancy.[36]

The rebel earls continued to maintain their troops and stand in readiness for further fighting.[37] Widespread fear of political disruption

---

[33] Bowes to Burghley, 24 Sept., *CSP Scot*, xi, no. 373.

[34] *Lothian Synod*, 77.

[35] Stirling Presbytery, ii, 9 Oct. 1594.

[36] *RPC*, v, 187–8; News from Aberdeen, 8 Nov., *CSP Scot*, xi, no. 401.

[37] News from Scotland 26 Nov., News from Scotland 12 Dec., *CSP Scot*, xi, nos 408 and 427.

continued and, by the end of the year, rumours of plans by the earls to rerun 1567 by deposing the king and setting Prince Henry in his place were circulating. The following year began with a new intensity of ecclesiastical activity centred on the presbytery of Edinburgh.[38] During February and March, ministers from other parts of Scotland met, as the 'commissioners of the general assembly', with the presbytery, keeping in touch with the progress of events in the North East. In February, Huntly and Errol undertook, under caution of £40 000, to leave Scotland by the middle of March and not to return without royal permission. In March, the excommunication of Bothwell was proclaimed in Edinburgh and a Convention of the Estates at Holyrood confirmed a royal command banishing Huntly and Errol.[39] By the end of the month, Huntly, Errol and Bothwell had all left the country, Bothwell never to return. The General Assembly, meeting at Montrose in June demonstrated the Kirk's contentedness by passing off without controversy. The mood was relaxed, the only bone of contention being the Assembly's refusal to ban summary excommunication, something which the king had wanted, presumably hoping that his recent action against the Catholic earls would have endeared him to the Kirk more than it did.[40] The two rounds of synods during 1595, meeting in April and October, also showed no hostility towards the crown, with the figureheads of Scottish Catholicism now banished.

Co-operation was the theme of 1595, with ministers being invited to help in the examination of arrested Catholics and in discussions over various matters of state. In December, perhaps following the example suggested by the Kirk two years previously, and as a consequence of a request from some ministers, the Privy Council resolved to use the presbyteries to aid national defence. Fear of Spanish invasion had reached a height unknown since the days of the Armada in 1588 and the council ordered each sheriff to liaise with the barons and ministers in each presbytery to devise ways of defending the realm. Any suggestions were to be reported to the Privy Council and each presbytery was given permission 'to convene the people in armour at [the Privy Council's] first call to resist incursions of the Spaniard or of any other papist'.[41] This, it must be emphasised, did not give the presbyteries an independent power of military muster. Whatever they did in this sphere, they were to be an arm of the state's defence policy

---

[38] A.R. MacDonald, 'Ecclesiastical Politics in Scotland, 1586–1610' (unpublished Edinburgh PhD dissertation, 1995), ch. 3.

[39] Nicolson to Bowes, 19 Feb. 1595, *CSP Scot*, xi, no. 472; RPC, v, 212.

[40] *BUK*, iii, 852.

[41] *RPC*, v, 233; McCartney to Bowes, 5 Dec. 1595, *CSP Scot*, xii no. 80.

and it is in such a context that they may indeed be seen as the first effective link between the centre and the localities in Scotland, in the temporal as well as the spiritual kingdom.[42] By January 1596, Roger Aston, an English agent, was able to say that 'the ministers and the King were never so great'.[43]

It was in 1596 that presbyteries were coming into their own as responsive bodies which could carry out tasks set by central institutions. Perhaps this was why, with hindsight, 1596 was looked upon as an *annus mirabilis* in a number of narrative histories. It was claimed that the purity of the Kirk had reached a zenith by the beginning of this year, a claim which might relate, at least partially, to the presbyteries' coming of age.[44] Although clear evidence is lacking, with the absence of Huntly and Errol and the renewed threat of Spanish invasion, many of the courts of the Kirk may have found themselves able to act against Catholics with little interference, even with some state support, and were thus more effective than ever. Portrayal of 1596 as a year of triumphant hope had its origins in an atmosphere clouded by the events of the second half of that year and by subsequent erosion of the independent authority of the courts of the Kirk.

Much of the activity of the Kirk after the first few months of 1596 suggest that is was riven with anxiety, as if aware of impending crisis. The Catholic threat was enough to prompt a level of lay participation in the General Assembly not seen for years. The presbytery of Stirling alone sent five lairds along with the earls of Mar and Argyll, the latter probably still smarting from his defeat at Huntly's hands.[45] At the Assembly at Edinburgh in March, renewed tensions with the king became evident. He attended for the first time since 1590, bringing five nobles with him and, in his address, he implied that he had called it to meet. As if preparing for a confrontation, the Assembly asked to see a copy of the 'Golden Act' of 1592. It wanted to see exactly where it stood in civil law.[46] The moderator, Robert Rollock, principal of the college of Edinburgh, thanked God for the royal presence by which, he claimed, the king did 'declare to the comfort of all the good men … present' that he professed their religion and wished to see it advanced.

---

[42] J. Wormald, *Court, Kirk and Community: Scotland 1470–1625* (Edinburgh, 1981), 165.

[43] Nicolson to Bowes, 23/24 Jan. 1595; Aston to Bowes, 28 Nov. 1585; Aston to Bowes 18 Jan. 1596: *CSP Scot*, xi, no. 451 and xii, nos 70 and 110.

[44] Scot, *Apologetical Narration*, 65; Calderwood, *History*, v, 387; Melville, *Diary*, 506; 'Ryseing and Usurpation', 7: M. Graham, *The Uses of Reform: 'Godly Discipline' and Popular Behaviour in Scotland and Beyond, 1560–1610* (Leiden, 1996), 156.

[45] Stirling Presbytery, ii, 3 March 1596.

[46] Bowes to Burghley, 26 March 1596, *CSP Scot*, xii, no. 146; *BUK*, iii, 859.

He went further, comparing James to the Roman Emperor Constantine and the biblical David, perhaps in the hope that he would live up to the comparison. The king replied that he had never regarded it as a dishonour to be with the Assembly 'counting it more honour to be a Christian than a King'. He declared that he had come to show his good disposition towards 'God, His religion and ministry', and his resolve against those who would subvert them. He also asked for their advice on resisting the common enemy, reminding them that his door was always open if they felt that he or any of his household required admonition.

Some aspects of this Assembly suggest a desire for reconciliation and continued co-operation, others suggest otherwise. The king promised the augmentation of stipends and the plantation of 400 vacant kirks with ministers, a carrot he was to dangle in front of the Assembly frequently in years to come. He also admitted personal shortcomings. On the other hand, the Assembly made it clear that it suspected royal backsliding and complained about the king's continued favour to suspected Catholics. Many ministers suspected Catholicism among the Octavians, a commission established at the beginning of 1596 in an attempt to rescue the crown's disastrous financial situation. James Melville thought half of them were Catholic and the commission included, most significantly, Alexander Seton, the future Earl of Dunfermline, whose Catholicism was well known.[47] The king had also allowed the property of the forfeited earls to fall to their wives rather than distributing their lands to others, which would have made their restoration difficult. The Duke of Lennox, whom the king had made lieutenant in the North East after his expedition in 1594, was the Countess of Huntly's brother. This was more than enough to raise the Kirk's suspicion that the estates were kept intact so that the lands could easily be restored to their former holders whenever they returned or so that the lands could be passed to the heirs. The Assembly urged complete forfeiture and military preparedness against invasion, indicating dissatisfaction with the crown's initiative in this area. Yet here, also, was an Assembly prepared to ratify the act against public criticism of the king and extend its scope to readers.[48] The state of play is difficult to discern but attempts to please combined with assertions of power on both sides reflect renewed unease.

This Assembly's most significant act was to undertake the 'renewal of the covenant with God'. In an atmosphere of deep self-reproach, the

---

[47] Melville, *Diary*, 330; Donaldson, *Scotland: James V–James VII*, 217 n.14 lists who they were.

[48] Calderwood, *History*, v, 408–20; *BUK*, iii, 862.

Kirk bound itself together, promising diligence and moral rigour.[49] It lamented backsliding in religious observance in the royal household, entertainment of suspected Catholics at court, corruption of all estates, a negligence of justice and corruption in the ministry.[50] All those who attended renewed the covenant with confession and purgation on 30 March and the idea was passed on to the synods and the presbyteries to ensure that the exercise would be as national as possible. Why, if the Kirk had reached such a state of perfection, did it consider it necessary for all ministers, the length and breadth of the realm, to examine their hearts and their conduct, purge themselves and make a fresh start? The covenant was renewed at the synod of Perth and Stirling on 5 May and at the synod of Fife on 12 May.[51] If it was taken up by all the synods, and due to the frustrating paucity of record material it is impossible to say, its impact on the self-consciousness of the Kirk would have been immense.

Combined with this spiritual renewal came the prospect of a major opportunity for a share of political power. The strength and prominence of the presbyteries were made evident in the scheme for a 'constant platt', or perpetual system, for the provision of stipends which emerged in the spring of 1596.[52] Devised by the king's secretary, and one of the Octavians, John Lindsay of Balcarres, a crucial aspect of the plan was that the revenues from dissolved prelacies, both episcopal and monastic, would be used to augment stipends. As a consequence, what had passed for the clerical estate in Parliament would cease to exist. As each bishop or 'abbot' died, he would be replaced with a representative of a presbytery until 51 such ecclesiastical parliamentarians were in place. The internal stability which might have resulted from this link between the organisational structure of the Kirk and the state could have been a great benefit to both. James Melville felt that 'the breithring of best judgement' would have accepted this scheme, and it is hard to believe that the majority of ministers would not have found it very attractive.[53]

---

[49] *BUK*, iii, 869–70; J.B. Torrance, 'The Covenant Concept in Scottish Theology and Politics – Its Legacy', *Scottish Journal of Theology*, 34 (1981); S.A. Burrel, 'The Covenant Idea as a Revolutionary Symbol: Scotland 1596–1637', *Church History*, 27 (1958), 338–50, at 340–42.

[50] Calderwood, *History*, v, 406–9.

[51] Stirling Presbytery, ii, 12 May 1596; Melville, *Diary*, 353. The records of the synod of Lothian and Tweeddale end in April 1596. Burrel, 'The Covenant Idea as a Revolutionary Symbol' 341; T. McCrie, *The Life of Andrew Melville*, 2nd edn, 2 vols (Edinburgh, 1824) 384–5 where a spontaneous spread of the idea 'from presbytery to presbytery' is suggested.

[52] Melville, *Diary*, 331–46; Calderwood, *History*, v, 421–33.

[53] Melville, *Diary*, 343–5.

As the result of events later in the year, however, the scheme never left the paper upon which it was written. It is worth remembering this judgement of James Melville, especially when it is set against his later assertions that the Kirk had never wanted a place in Parliament. It is also interesting that Thomas McCrie, presumably to make certain ministers' views appear to have been consistent, omitted to mention parliamentary representation in his description of this scheme.[54]

It is not difficult to imagine how these two factors, spiritual renewal and the prospect of a major stake in secular politics, combined to raise the expectations of the Kirk. The higher they were raised, the further and the more easily they would fall. In late June or early July, Huntly secretly returned to Scotland. The king would not reveal whether he had given his permission for this and it was certainly the case that the Kirk, whom Huntly had still to satisfy in relation to his religion, had had no say in the matter. In spite of calls for royal action from many quarters, nothing, save promises which, to the Kirk, had an all too familiar ring, resulted. The synods, easier to convene at short notice than a General Assembly but possessing influence which the presbyteries lacked, quickly assumed their role as a means of bringing pressure to bear on the state. Fife was the first to move. Early in August, an extraordinary synod met at Kirkcaldy 'and all the principal barons and gentlemen were there',[55] illustrating again the fact that, when it came to combating the combined dangers of Catholicism and foreign threats, many of the laity were with the Kirk. The support of the presbytery of Edinburgh was sought and it wrote to the synod of Aberdeen in September asking it to excommunicate the countesses of Huntly and Errol.[56] Four commissioners were sent from Fife to the king demanding that he should not accept any offers from Huntly until he had left Scotland again and showed signs of renouncing Catholicism.[57] Nothing resulted and, on 5 October, the presbytery of Edinburgh received another letter from Fife asking it to set a date for a meeting of the 'commissioners of the general assembly' to discuss the imminent dangers of the Kirk.[58]

According to James Melville, the presbytery of Edinburgh met commissioners of 'divers synodalls' between 20 October and 17 December but there is evidence that they had already begun to tackle the matter of

---

[54] McCrie, *Melville*, i, 382; and see below pp. 83–5, 177–8 for a discussion of James Melville's later views on parliamentary representation.

[55] Advices from Scotland, *CSP Scot*, xii, no. 244.

[56] Edinburgh Presbytery, ii, 31 Aug. 1596; Bowes to Burghley, 23 Sept. 1596, *CSP Scot*, xii, no. 269.

[57] Bowes to Burghley, 17 Sept. 1596, *CSP Scot*, xii, no. 262.

[58] Edinburgh Presbytery, ii, 5 Oct. 1596.

Huntly's return as early as September.[59] This appears to have been in the form of the commissioners of the General Assembly. There are numerous references to such a body in the years immediately preceding 1596, but not until then does its nature and composition become clear. Its remit was certainly wide, the assembly of 1596 having appointed it to report on 'universal repentance, and earnest turning to God: And of order taking for resisting the enemies and maintenance of the liberty of the religion and country'.[60] It would appear that it was some sort of standing commission of the General Assembly and that a similar group had been appointed in 1595 because, in 1596, reference was made to the reading of its commission from the previous year. Frustratingly, however, there is no record either of its remit or its personnel. During 1594 and 1595, however, a number of ministers from Fife, Lothian, Angus, Lanarkshire and the Borders had met with the presbytery of Edinburgh and, although there is no record of their appointment, they appear to have been the commissioners of the General Assembly.

In the last few months of 1596, the commission emerged into the full light of day amidst a political crisis for the Kirk. The commission, 'apointed be the Generall Assemblie to sie to the dangers of the Kirk at all occasiones', met at Cupar in September to resolve upon a course of action. Delegates demanding that measures should be taken against the Catholic earls, for Errol had also returned, were sent to the king at Falkland Palace. They were, significantly, the same men as had accompanied James on his 'raid' in the autumn of 1594: Patrick Galloway, James Nicolson, and James and Andrew Melville. The king reacted angrily, complaining that they had met without royal permission. Andrew Melville took this opportunity to point out, in words now famous, that James VI was but 'God's sillie [i.e. weak] vassall'. He took the king's sleeve and told him that, in Scotland, 'thair is twa Kings and twa Kingdomes ... Thair is Chryst Jesus the King, and his Kingdome the Kirk, whase subject King James the Saxt is, and of whase kingdome nocht a king, nor a lord, nor a heid, bot a member'. These were not statements likely to lead to reconciliation.[61] This is the cliché which passes for Andrew Melville and it has been ripped out of context and portrayed as a 'Melvillian' maxim, the encounter supposedly epitomising relations between Kirk and state in Scotland in the late sixteenth century. The significance of his statements, however, lies in the fact that they were the sort of sentiments which had rarely been expressed since

---

[59] Melville, *Diary*, 372.

[60] *BUK*, iii, 857–9; MacDonald, 'Ecclesiastical Politics' ch. 3 discusses the commission's development.

[61] Melville, *Diary*, 369–71.

the fall of Arran. This was the language of crisis and confrontation, signifying the collapse of an uneasy coexistence between a deeply anti-Catholic Kirk and a king with little zeal for the persecution of those who did not follow the Reformed faith.[62]

In spite of royal assurances that he had been ignorant of the return of the Catholic earls until after the event and a promise that they would receive no favour until they had left again and even then, would 'gett na grace … till they satisfeid the Kirk', no action resulted.[63] Perhaps the ministers were impatient, perhaps they were tired of waiting in vain for promises to be fulfilled. At the behest of the synod of Fife, the commissioners reconvened at Edinburgh in October with much to consider.[64] They began by writing to every presbytery to inform them of the danger which had resulted from the return of Huntly and Errol and, with the advice of the presbytery of Edinburgh, they announced that a General Assembly would meet in January to choose the best means for the preservation of the religion and the common peace.[65]

The commissioners of the Assembly sat in Edinburgh throughout November and into December acting in many different spheres.[66] At the beginning of November, a rotating standing commission of 12 was established: six from the presbytery of Edinburgh, one from the North, one from central Scotland, two from the West and two from the South. They sent delegations to the king and the Privy Council, demanding action against Huntly, Errol, their wives and Lady Livingstone, Errol's daughter and an openly practising Catholic. Alexander Seton, president of the Court of Session and one of the Octavians, was referred to the commissioners by the synod of Lothian and Tweeddale for dealings with the Catholic earls. They even found time to deal with a dispute over a benefice in the presbytery of Glasgow. The commissioners were acting, and were seen by the rest of the Kirk, as a privy council for the Kirk, wielding the power of the General Assembly between its meetings.

---

[62] Lynch, 'Preaching to the Converted? Perspectives on the Scottish Reformation', in eds, A.A. MacDonald et al., *The Renaissance in Scotland: Studies in Literature, Religion, History and Culture Offered to John Durkan* (Leiden, 1994), 301–43, at 336 notes the situation-specific nature of this incident.

[63] Melville, *Diary*, 371.

[64] Melville, *Diary*, 372; Calderwood, *History*, v, 443; Bowes to Burghley, 20 Oct. 1596, *CSP Scot*, xii, no. 283; NLS, 'Copie of the minute buik of the actis maid be the commissioineris of the generall assembly', Wodrow Quarto, xx, no. 18.

[65] Melville, *Diary*, 372; Bowes to Burghley, 12 Nov. 1596, *CSP Scot*, xii, no. 291; 'Copie of the minute buik', 20 Oct. 1596.

[66] For accounts of the last three months of 1596, see: 'Copie of the minute buik'; Calderwood, *History*, v, 443ff; Melville, *Diary*, 371–2 and 508 ff; Spottiswoode, *History*, iii, 9 ff.

Most crucially of all, they were closely involved in the trial of David Black, minister of St Andrews, for allegedly delivering a seditious sermon in October. It had been deeply critical of the king, his progenitors and Queen Elizabeth of England. He had asserted that the Catholic earls had returned with the knowledge and consent of the king and that this revealed 'the treacherie of the Kingis harte'. He claimed that 'all Kingis wer the devillis childrene', that the devil guided the court and 'he callit the Quene of England ane atheist'. Praying after his sermon, he had said that, as for Queen Anne, 'we have no caus to pray for hir, scho will nevir do us gude'.[67] On 12 November, Black was summoned to the Privy Council and the commissioners of the General Assembly resolved that he should reject its right to judge him and set to examining the Bible to justify this. On 17 November, they resolved to compose a declinature, a written justification for Black's rejection of the Privy Council's authority. As Arthur Williamson has observed, 'the moment ... cooperation [between king and Kirk] failed, basic questions about the nature of authority ... would surface'.[68] The commissioners of the General Assembly were insisting on the separation of the two kingdoms in spite of conciliatory overtures from the king, who had promised action against the Catholic earls as long as Black agreed to stand trial.[69] Thomas McCrie, writing in the early nineteenth century, took on the views of Calderwood and James Melville, portraying Black's trial as having been set up as a test case by the crown and the commissioners themselves looked upon it as an attempt by the king to set a precedent by which freedom of speech could be restricted, so they resisted staunchly any royal pressure to compromise. Their view of the situation is encapsulated in their allegation that 'the ministeris of God his word ... [were] ... chairgit and trublit upon calumneis and trifling dilationis quhairas in the mean tyme the inemeis of the treuth was favorit and overlukit'.[70]

Black duly came before the Council and rejected its authority to judge him in matters of doctrine, which encompassed all that was said in sermons or extempore prayers. He demanded that, in the first instance, the charges should have been brought before the presbytery of St Andrews which would then have been able to judge whether his sermon was seditious or heretical. If it was found to be the former, the case should then, and only then, be remitted to the civil authority. The Privy Council cited the first of the 'Black Acts' of 1584, which had granted

---

[67] *RPC*, v, 334–5.

[68] A. Williamson, *Scottish National Consciousness in the Age of James VI: the Apocalypse, the Union and the Making of Scotland's Public Culture* (Edinburgh, 1979), 50.

[69] 'Copie of the minute buik', 16 Nov.

[70] 'Copie of the minute buik', 12 Nov.; McCrie, *Melville*, i, 395.

the crown jurisdiction over all estates in all matters and Black retaliated by citing the 'Golden Act's' recognition of the authority of the courts of the Kirk. He also cited Paul's First Letter to Timothy, which gave no role to civil authority in its basic instructions for church organisation, to justify the Kirk's right to its separate jurisdiction. The case was continued until the end of the month.[71] As November wore on, tension rose. More than just the standing committee appointed at the beginning of the month were in the capital. The commission fanned the flames by questioning Queen Anne's religious orthodoxy and criticising her for surrounding herself with Catholics – the Countess of Huntly and Lady Livingstone were two of her closest companions. Events took a new turn every few days. The commissioners of the General Assembly pressed for the removal of the Countess of Huntly from court and of Princess Elizabeth from the custody of Lady Livingstone. The king pressed for a resolution to the question of where the bounds between the civil and ecclesiastical jurisdictions lay and this became the focal point of the controversy.

Although the commissioners had appointed an Assembly to meet in January, they needed swift responses which could be as representative as possible of the Kirk as a whole. On 20 November, they resolved to send a copy of Black's declinature to every presbytery for endorsement. This was the clearest demonstration of the political effectiveness of the presbyteries. They met every week or fortnight, included all ministers and covered a small enough area to be quickly responsive to local problems while being relatively easy to co-ordinate nationally. The voice of the presbyteries was the voice of the Kirk. They were already being kept abreast of events in Edinburgh, having been warned by the commissioners of the dangers to the Kirk as a result of the return of Huntly and Errol and, on 11 November, the commissioners had appointed ministers to inform them of all acts of Parliament and Privy Council in favour of the Kirk. Just how widespread subscription of Black's declinature was it is impossible to tell. Of the five presbytery records which survive from the time, three record an endorsement of it – those of Peebles, Edinburgh and Stirling.[72] The register of the presbytery of St Andrews does not contain such an endorsement but, by the end of November, virtually all its ministers were in Edinburgh, so they probably subscribed it there. The only presbytery which definitely did not

[71] RPC, v, 326.

[72] Peebles Presbytery, i, fo. 3r; Edinburgh Presbytery, ii, 23 Nov. 1596; Stirling Presbytery, ii, 24 Nov. 1596; see also St Andrews Presbytery, fo. 77. There is a gap in the register of Haddington presbytery from 18 Nov. to 8 Dec. when the declinature would have been subscribed.

subscribe the declinature was Glasgow.[73] As in so many other instances, the lack of record material means one is left guessing. An assertion was later made that about 400 ministers subscribed it and, although written years later, its author was 28 at the time. If it was a realistic figure, it constituted over two-thirds of the ministry.[74] However many subscribed, the king was furious. He saw that presbyteries, although potentially effective tools of the state, posed a threat because they increasingly tended to act in defiance of the crown. Fundamental questions relating to the authority of the presbyterian system began to emerge from the court for the first time.

On 24 November, perhaps fearing that presbyteries would wilfully misinterpret the act of the Privy Council relating to military musters, they were forbidden to 'mak convocatioun of divers baronis and utheris his Hienes liegis'.[75] On the same day, the council denied any favour was given to Catholics and the king summoned James Nicolson, moderator of the commissioners of the General Assembly. King James demanded to be given copies both of Black's declinature and of the commissioners' letter of commission from the last Assembly. Both were sent and the letter was judged by the king to be 'seditious and treasonable'.[76] He then banned all gatherings of ministers without royal permission and ordered the commissioners of the Assembly to leave Edinburgh. They decided to stay, declaring that their duty was to the welfare of the Kirk and to the law of God above the laws of man. They urged the king to drop the case against Black until the common enemy was dealt with and until a General Assembly was held to resolve all disputes.

The commissioners continued to advise David Black during his trial and to send delegations to the Privy Council. On 9 December, Black was found guilty of sedition and warded north of the Moray Firth. Two days earlier, it had been proclaimed that the order banning convocations by ministers did not include the normal meetings of the courts of the Kirk.[77] Now, and arguably in contradiction of that clarification, the

---

[73] Glasgow Presbytery, i.

[74] Scot, *Apologetical Narration*, xi–xii, 72. According to his supposed date of birth (1558), Scot was 24 on matriculation at St Andrews (1582) and therefore 38 in 1596; 1568 is a more likely date of birth with 14 as his age on matriculation. Lynch, 'Preaching to the Converted?', 313; W.R. Foster, *The Church before the Covenants* (Edinburgh, 1975), 153. The national figure of 539 ministers excludes Argyll and the Isles but they were poorly planted, hence their frequent exclusion from commissions of visitation, the absence of presbyteries there and their exclusion from the Register of Assignation and Modification of Stipends in 1596–97.

[75] *RPC*, v, 333; Spottiswoode, *History*, iii, 19.

[76] 'Copie of the minute buik', 24 Nov.

[77] *RPC*, v, 344.

General Assembly, which had been called by the commissioners to meet in January, was cancelled by the crown and replaced with a convention of ministers called by the king to meet on 5 February. The proclamation intimating this specifically stated that the new meeting would resolve, once and for all, the polity of the Kirk and the bounds of ecclesiastical and temporal jurisdiction. The commissioners of the General Assembly were again ordered to leave Edinburgh.[78] On this occasion they obeyed, with the provocative proviso that it was permissible, although not expedient, to remain. Responsibility for carrying on the fight was passed to the ministers of Edinburgh who, on 16 December, were summoned before the Privy Council but refused to appear unless the commissioners of the Assembly were recalled.[79] There is some evidence that this was actually entertained but events overtook such a plan. Twenty-four burgesses who were guarding the manses of the ministers of Edinburgh, a move which was seen to lay 'a heavy imputation upon his majesty', were ordered to leave the town. One, Edward Cathkin, informed the ministers and told them that Huntly, who had been at court, had prompted the action. On the following morning, Walter Balcanquhal, in his sermon, publicised this, criticised those about the king and exhorted the nobles and lairds who were present to stand to the maintenance of the Kirk and to meet with the ministers of Edinburgh after the service.[80]

A large number gathered and a delegation, consisting of Lords Lindsay and Forbes, the lairds of Bargany and Blairquhan and the ministers Robert Bruce and William Watson, went to the king who was in the nearby tolbooth with the Lords of Session. The delegation complained that the ministers and the godly were persecuted while Catholic nobles were shown royal favour. King James refused to answer them and locked himself in another room. The delegation returned to the nobles and lairds who raised a clamour of complaint which spread to a crowd gathered outside. Wild rumours of danger from armed Catholics resulted in calls to arms among the crowd which was pressing upon the tolbooth. A very ugly incident may have resulted had not Alexander Hume, provost of Edinburgh, calmed the mob. The king immediately sent a delegation to the ministers who were quick to distance themselves from what had happened, rashly blaming the disturbance on the king's rejection of their petition. On invitation by this delegation, another was sent to James by the ministers and things seemed to have calmed down, the king asking them to come before the Privy Council

[78] Melville, *Diary*, 513; Calderwood, *History*, v, 501; Bowes to Cecil, 17 Dec. 1596, *CSP Scot*, xii, no. 315; Spottiswoode, *History*, iii, 26.

[79] Calderwood, *History*, v, 509–10.

[80] Calderwood, *History*, v, 511–13; Spottiswoode, *History*, iii, 27.

that afternoon with their petitions. The royal mood changed in the interim, however, and their petitions were refused. The next morning, James left for Linlithgow, taking the Privy Council with him and leaving a proclamation condemning the 'treasonable uproar' which had put the king and Council at risk of their lives. Edinburgh was declared an 'unfit place for the ministration of justice' and the central courts were removed.

Matters were not improved when Lord Hamilton turned up at Linlithgow with a letter subscribed by Bruce and Balcanquhal inviting him to Edinburgh to support them. Some sources allege that it had been tampered with but others say that Hamilton produced the authentic copy which implied that they would place the crown on his head if he would support their cause. That was the final straw. The council of Edinburgh, desperate not to lose the status and revenue which being the centre of law and government provided, made a grovelling apology to the king for having allowed the 'riot' to occur. This was accepted along with a substantial sum of money and they were ordered to imprison the ministers who escaped such a fate by flight, Bruce and Balcanquhal to England, Watson and Balfour to Fife. By the end of December, the king and the courts were back in Edinburgh.

The truth surrounding the 'riot' is hard to extract from the conflicting narrative sources. The sequence of events is not particularly mysterious but difficulties of interpretation lie in the cause of the standoff between the crown and the ministers. Some suggest that Black's trial was taken up by the king to assert his claim to supreme authority and to divert attention from the controversies over Huntly by targeting the ministry, yet one source alleges that certain ministers deliberately portrayed it in that light to provoke a decisive confrontation.[81] One root of the problem which does seem to be generally agreed upon is that certain gentlemen of the king's bedchamber, unhappy at the power and influence of the Octavians, sought to discredit them. This was apparently done by passing to the ministers allegations about some of the Octavians' Catholicism, notably the Lord President, Alexander Seton, the Lord Advocate, Thomas Hamilton and the Comptroller, James Elphinstone.[82]

Whether it was fate or design which was the central factor in the events which included the 'riot' of 17 December, it had far-reaching effects on the Kirk and its relationship with the state. The most striking consequence which became visible after the dust had settled was a major realignment of clerical opinion. What is most interesting about the last few months of 1596 is the personnel involved in the commission

---

[81] Calderwood, *History*, v, 505–7; Spottiswoode, *History*, iii, 13.
[82] Spottiswoode, *History*, iii, 39; Calderwood, *History*, v, 510–11.

of the General Assembly. Archbishop Spottiswoode, writing his *History* decades later, claimed that a minority of ministers among the commissioners, those he termed 'the wiser sort', had wanted to obey the first command to leave Edinburgh.[83] He intended the reader to understand that he was one of that number, or at least minded to agree with them for, although he was not named among the commissioners of the assembly, he was certainly in Edinburgh at the time and, according to William Scot, he both subscribed Black's declinature and was active in encouraging others to do the same.[84] The allegation that Spottiswoode was an *agent provocateur* smells strongly of a hindsight-ridden desire to portray him as having always been on the wrong side. That this was not the case is supported by the tone of Spottiswoode's account of the last three months of 1596 which is strangely reluctant to condemn the actions of the commissioners in the fulsome terms which one would expect from an archbishop.[85]

The close involvement in opposition to the king of many who were later to become noted loyalists to the crown is striking. Indeed, some were later to become bishops: David Lindsay became Bishop of Ross and Peter Blackburn became Bishop of Aberdeen in 1600; Andrew Knox became Bishop of the Isles in 1605 and, of course, Spottiswoode himself became Archbishop of Glasgow in 1603. James Nicolson, moderator of the commissioners of the General Assembly, became a minister to the royal household in 1602, was the bishops' choice as moderator of the hand-picked Linlithgow Assembly of 1606 and became Bishop of Dunkeld in 1607, while Patrick Galloway was also one of the king's own ministers. The most plausible explanation for this seems to be that the commission of the General Assembly was genuinely representative of the sentiments of the Kirk as a whole and that it was swept along by deep indignation at the king's lack of action against Huntly and Errol. The apparent support for the commissioners from some nobles, lairds and burgesses of Edinburgh served only to make them feel that their actions were justified and widely approved. The clerical mainstream was united around opposition to the king's attitude to these powerful Catholic nobles. In the heated atmosphere of the last months of 1596, this grievance became entangled with the issue of where ultimate authority lay. As a result of the king's refusal to take decisive measures against Huntly and Errol, he was subject to severe criticism from the

---

[83] Spottiswoode, *History*, iii, 17–19.

[84] Edinburgh Presbytery, ii, inserted between the meetings on 26 Oct. and 9 Nov. is a list of those on the exercise which includes Spottiswoode; Scot, *Apologetical Narration*, 72; Lee, *Government by Pen*, 32 accepts this view of Spottiswoode.

[85] Spottiswoode, *History*, iii, 10–28.

ministers. Seeing themselves as the guardians of the realm's godliness, they believed that they had the right to instruct him in such matters. He took a very different view. There was nothing he appears to have liked less than being given orders. David Black's intemperate outbursts from the pulpit gave James the perfect opportunity to show who really was in charge. The stakes had been raised and, with professional and religious zeal, the whole commission of the General Assembly stood solidly behind the right of the ministers to judge their peers. As Thomas McCrie wrote, 'that there was anything like an opposition among the ministers to the course which was taken, I have seen no good reason to believe. The fact is that there never was more unanimity in the church than was displayed in this course'.[86]

David Calderwood and William Scot portrayed the whole episode as a royal plot to destroy the independence of the Kirk. The fact that the proclamation intimating that a convention of ministers would meet in February 1597 was issued prior to the 'riot' of 17 December led them to conclude that plans for changes in the Kirk's polity had been drawn up long before.[87] This was intended to reduce the significance of the 'riot' and explain subsequent events by portraying them as part of a premeditated royal plan rather than as a reaction to a series of events culminating in an unsavoury incident in which the ministers of Edinburgh played a significant part. That the king had intended to clarify the bounds of the two jurisdictions and entrench what he saw as his right to supremacy before 17 December 1596 is unquestionable. That was made clear in the proclamation calling the meeting of ministers to Perth which was issued before the 'riot'. The conduct of the commissioners of the General Assembly had been enough to convince James that such a course of action was necessary. Indeed, in 1609, Alexander Hume, minister of Logie, in his 'Ane afold admonitioun to the ministerie of Scotland', blamed the downfall of the pure presbyterian polity and independence of the Kirk on the ministers of Edinburgh 'who raschlie behaved them selfis in that tumult at Edinburgh, the 17 day of December 1596'.[88] Lord Hamilton's revelations put the 'riot' in a new light and it may have been them which caused James to believe that the threat which the Kirk posed was greater than he had previously thought. It thus strengthened his resolve to establish more clearly the bounds of the jurisdictions and perhaps to do so in a way which gave the crown even greater authority

---

[86] McCrie, *Life of Melville*, i, 397.

[87] Calderwood, *History*, viii, 44–5; Scot, *Apologetical Narration*, 79; Lee, *Government by Pen*, 21 shows one modern historian accepts this interpretation.

[88] A. Hume 'Ane afold admonitioun to the ministerie of Scotland', in *Wodrow Miscellany*, i, 569–90, at 585.

than he had originally planned. The 'riot' did not cause James to call the convention at Perth but it may well have persuaded him to conduct it as he did.

CHAPTER FOUR

The road to consensus, 1597–1602

Convinced that the ministers had sought too much freedom to interfere with affairs of state, James VI began decisively to take matters ecclesiastical into his own hands for the first time. The importance of this cannot be overemphasised, for only now, 11 years into his personal reign, did he begin actively to subvert the Kirk's administrative autonomy. On 6 January he began as he intended to continue by banning ecclesiastical courts, other than the kirk session, from meeting in Edinburgh. The presbytery was to meet in Leith and the synod in Musselburgh.[1] Keeping them out of the capital would, he hoped, prevent trouble on the royal doorstep. Twelve days later, the presbytery of Edinburgh, in consultation with Haddington and Dalkeith, called a synod for 1 February to reply to a royal demand to fill the town's pulpits, vacant after the flight of the four ministers.[2] Three royal commissioners attended and announced that the king was concerned that preaching should be maintained in Edinburgh. The commissioners commanded the synod to appoint interim ministers and to give their names to the Privy Council, saying that failure to carry this out would 'show the great slander and inconvenience which will arise thereupon as a thing done by faction with the advice and favour of the late ministers now fugitives from our laws'.[3]

The king's commissioners commanded the restoration of David Ogill, suspended by the presbytery of Haddington for preaching in Edinburgh. They ordered the synod to censure that presbytery and to summon the ministers of Edinburgh before the General Assembly on pain of excommunication. Finally, the synod was told to investigate the presbytery of Edinburgh's reaction to the flight of the ministers to 'eschew ... trial ... for the crime of the late treasonable uproar'.[4] The synod was cautious. It agreed to compile a rota for the empty pulpits of Edinburgh; it alleged that Ogill was suspected of offences other than

---

[1] *RPC*, v, 357; *APS*, iv, 107; Advices from Edinburgh, 11 Jan. 1597, *CSP Scot*, xii, no. 333; Calderwood, *History*, v, 537.

[2] Edinburgh Presbytery, ii, 18 Jan. 1597; Haddington Presbytery, ii, fo. 4v.

[3] Haddington Presbytery, ii, fo. 4v-r.

[4] Bowes to Burghley and The King's Commissioners and the Synod of Lothian, both 1 Feb. 1597, *CSP Scot*, xii, nos 359 and 360; The three commissioners were John Preston of Fentonbarns (a Senator of the College of Justice), Edward Bruce (commendator of Kinloss) and William Oliphant.

preaching in Edinburgh (he himself admitted fault and asked the royal commissioners not to press the matter); and it let the presbytery of Edinburgh answer for itself. Dismay was expressed at the king's desire to summon the ministers of Edinburgh and, in an echo of David Black's stance in November, it requested that they be accused before their presbytery which was the proper place for their trial.[5] Three days later, the synod petitioned the king, warning him against missing the real enemy, Catholics, while he targeted ministers. It insisted that the weal of the Kirk and of the king were inseparable, calling on him to support the Kirk, regretting that some ministers were being 'ill used' and requesting that he would proclaim his good intention towards them. It specifically asked that the ministers who had refused to preach in Edinburgh would be relaxed from the horn, that the General Assembly be continued until its previously agreed date and place, that he would not publish an account of the 'riot' in case it gave a bad impression abroad, and that he would allow the fugitive ministers of Edinburgh to return. All these requests were refused. James asserted that they had nothing to fear from the meeting at Perth, that the publication of an account of the 'riot' was necessary to prevent misreporting of his actions and that the ministers of Edinburgh would be allowed liberty only if they submitted to his will.[6]

To prepare the ground for Perth, the king sent Sir Patrick Murray, a gentleman of the royal bedchamber, to the North East. He was to emphasise that James was supreme in all matters and to urge disapproval of the 'riot', to order them to receive Huntly's submissions to the Kirk and to ignore the presbytery of Edinburgh in this matter. It had been common for other presbyteries and synods to contact it for guidance but, with the presbytery of Edinburgh having been closely involved in the events of the last few months, the king was anxious to ensure that it would have no such role in the future. Murray was also to deliver to the presbyteries of the North East 55 questions on polity devised by the king. He was to say that other presbyteries had accepted them, that a commission had been established for the augmentation of stipends and that they were to send 'ane part of the most discreit' of their members to Perth.[7]

---

[5] The King's Commissioners and the Synod of Lothian, 1 Feb. 1597, CSP Scot, xii, no. 360; Haddington Presbytery, ii, fos 3r–4r, show that Ogill was reprimanded for having preached in Edinburgh without the presbytery's permission, rather than for having preached per se and that he appealed to the synod against that reprimand.

[6] Bowes to Burghley, 20 Feb. 1597, CSP Scot, xii, no. 374; NLS, 'Humble petitions proponit to his majestie be the Synodal of Lowthiane on Fryday the fourt of Februar 1596 [i.e. 1597]', Wodrow Folio, 43, no. 47.

[7] Instructions to Sir Patrick Murray, Feb. 1597, CSP Scot, xii, no. 385.

To avoid being accused of contacting the presbytery of Edinburgh, the presbytery of Aberdeen wrote to 'the ministers of Lothian' on 30 January, saying that it had been charged to confer with Huntly and to lift his excommunication if he satisfied them. They had been ordered to subscribe a declaration that they condemned the ministers of Edinburgh, accepted the dissolution of the commission of the General Assembly and would absolve Huntly as quickly as he had been excommunicated. In addition, they were commanded to hold a synod on 8 February to respond to these instructions. They therefore sought the advice of the synods of Lothian and Tweeddale, Angus and the Mearns, and Moray, with representatives of the last two being invited to their meeting.[8] The synod of Aberdeen acknowledged the king's authority over them as subjects but refused to recognise that this extended to ecclesiastical matters. It remitted to the General Assembly a reply about the right to judge the content of sermons since that was one of the 55 questions. It also denied that it saw the presbytery of Edinburgh as holding any authority and refused to pass judgement on the 'riot', professing ignorance of its circumstances.[9] The king's task was not proving easy.

The synod of Fife decided that two from each presbytery should meet at St Andrews on 21 February to draw up a response to the 55 questions. It sent seven ministers to the king to request that the Assembly might meet, as originally planned, at St Andrews in April, fearing that its freedom might be compromised by the coincidence of the meeting at Perth with a Convention of the Estates. This was echoed by the synods of Lothian and Tweeddale, and Angus and the Mearns.[10] Fife demanded the release of the ministers of Edinburgh and David Black and insisted that nothing should be published by the crown in prejudice of the 55 questions. Fife's delegates, and those from Lothian and Tweeddale, were sent to Perth out of obedience to a royal command, not to acknowledge it as a General Assembly. They were to deal only with the 55 questions, they were warned against private reasoning by which it was feared that the court might win over individuals and they were to request that all matters should be remitted to the General Assembly in April.[11] The presbytery of Stirling expressed its misgivings by instructing

---

[8] Presbytery of Aberdeen to the ministers of Lothian, 30 Jan. 1597, *Letters and State Papers*, no. xviii; Untitled paper, *CSP Scot*, xii, no. 403; Calderwood, *History*, v, 538.

[9] James VI to Sir Patrick Murray, 3 Feb. 1597, *The Warrender Papers*, ed. A.I. Cameron, 2 vols, (Scottish History Society, 1931–32), ii, no. ci.

[10] Calderwood, *History*, v, 578–90; Melville, *Diary*, 386–9; Bowes to Burghley, 1 Feb. and same to same, 26 Feb. 1597, *CSP Scot*, xii, no. 359 and 380.

[11] *BUK*, iii, 908–9; Melville, *Diary*, 387; Calderwood, *History*, v, 578; 'Humble petitions proponit to his majestie be the Synodal of Lowthiane'.

its commissioner to report back diligently so that it could discuss what answers should be given in a future assembly.[12]

That the battle-lines remained drawn, albeit less overtly, was clear. One contemporary alleged that James had packed the meeting and chosen Perth because Huntly and Errol were in arms nearby, a factor which might intimidate dissidents.[13] Although the latter may have been the case, there is no evidence that the assembly was packed. There was, indeed, 'moe out of the North than wer wont to be seen at any Generall Assembly', yet that need not have been very many, judging by the pitiful attendance from that region in previous years. The northern ministers were outnumbered by more than two to one by their southern brethren.[14]

Once the ministers had gathered at Perth, the king asked them to declare the meeting an extraordinary General Assembly. They complied, although only after a threat that no further assemblies would be permitted if they did not. James was not willing, at this stage, to be conciliatory and was prepared to use threats to stamp his authority on the Kirk. It should be noted that, in calling this meeting, the Assembly scheduled for April in St Andrews had not been brought forward, nor had James thus 'made good his powers of summons' for assemblies.[15] These things were achieved only after the meeting had convened. David Lindsay, minister of Leith, was appointed moderator by the king. He had been prominent in the events of the previous months and was thus one of the first to repent of what he had done and fall in with the king. In May 1586, James had nominated Lindsay and the ministers had voted him in. Now they were not even given the opportunity to approve the royal choice.[16]

By this time, the 55 questions, designed to wrongfoot the Kirk, had been reduced to a more manageable 13 articles. The first suggested that anyone had the right to question the polity of the Kirk, while the rest

---

[12] Edinburgh Presbytery, ii, 8 Feb. 1597; Peebles Presbytery, i, fo. 6r; Stirling Presbytery, iii, 23 Feb. 1597; see also Bowes to Burghley, 26 Feb. 1597, *CSP Scot*, xii, no. 380 where Bowes suggested that delegates went to Perth only out of obedience to the king. The fact that he was based in Edinburgh may, however, have affected his opinion.

[13] Bowes to Burghley, 1 Feb. 1596, *CSP Scot*, xii, no. 359.

[14] Spottiswoode, *History*, iii, 45; Scot, *Apologetical Narration*, 88; Melville, *Diary*, 403; MacDonald, 'Ecclesiastical Politics', Appendix 1(b), esp. 326–7.

[15] M. Lee, 'James VI and the Revival of Episcopacy in Scotland: 1596–1600', *Church History*, 43 (1974), 55; W.R. Foster, *The Church before the Covenants* (Edinburgh, 1975), 121; R. Mason, 'George Buchanan, James VI and the Presbyterians', in ed., R. Mason, *Scots and Britons: Scottish Political Thought and the Union of 1603* (Cambridge, 1994) 134.

[16] *BUK*, iii, 889–90; Scot, *Apologetical Narration*, 88–9; Calderwood, *History*, v, 606–24; Bowes to Burghley, 9 March, and Advices from Scotland, March 1597, *CSP Scot*, xii, no. 309 and 402.

implied the need for restrictions on its jurisdiction and its right to criticise secular authority. Only four were accepted.[17] The assembly was then summoned before the Convention of Estates, a new set of conditional answers was drawn up and all but one were agreed to, the other being remitted to the next assembly.[18] Narrative historians alleged that the activities of Sir Patrick Murray, threats, private persuasion and promises to release David Black and the ministers of Edinburgh had been used to draw many to favour the king's course. Whatever was the case, by turning a convention of ministers which met to discuss certain royal articles into a General Assembly, King James had established a precedent for his right to set the agenda of future assemblies. That this had not been without difficulty, showed that opposition to the drift of his ecclesiastical policy remained.

Robert Pont, as moderator of the Assembly of March 1596, went to St Andrews on 27 April to keep the diet appointed at that meeting. Few others came, so he took formal legal instruments of protest and left.[19] James Melville was to look back upon this as the death of free general assemblies, lamenting that, after March 1597, 'the court began ... to govern all' because the king called assemblies which had once been called by Christ (i.e. the Kirk), debate was controlled, the Word of God was ignored, fear of God had been replaced with fear of the king and the freedom of the Kirk had been subordinated to the 'polytic esteat of a frie monarchie'.[20] The king was asserting his authority, but he would not be able to do so without the support of general assemblies and subsequent years would show that obedience to the king often proved an overriding factor with many ministers. The fact that most synods and presbyteries regarded the St Andrews assembly as having been superseded by those at Perth in February and at Dundee in May suggests that there was little concern over such royal intervention, even if there was enduring opposition to acts which the king wanted those assemblies to pass.

That resistance to royal assertions of authority continued after 17 December 1596 is undeniable, but the first half of 1597 saw the resolve of those who would stand up to the king melting away. In March, the presbytery of Edinburgh demanded the return of the capital's ministers but that was the last time in 1597 that it crossed the king. By July, the

---

[17] *BUK*, iii, 889–90. They forbade the Kirk's courts from acting against anyone living outwith their bounds, banned summons without charge, banned ministers from ministering to any but their own flock and commanded presbyteries to enforce these regulations.

[18] *BUK*, iii, 894–6.

[19] *BUK*, iii, 912; Melville, *Diary*, 412; Calderwood, *History*, v, 626.

[20] Melville, *Diary*, 412–14.

presbytery of Peebles was supplying ministers to fill the Edinburgh charges.[21] The presbytery of Stirling presents a striking example of the effect of James's decisive action. In February, it excommunicated Lady Livingstone, Errol's daughter, for persistent refusal to renounce Catholicism and over two years of evasion of the presbyteries of Glasgow and Stirling. It then wrote to the king's ministers asking them to admonish James for continuing to receive her at court and for allowing her to retain custody of Princess Elizabeth but no more was heard on the matter.[22] With the chance of royal support for the victimisation of Lady Livingstone gone, her husband took his revenge. On 27 April, he evicted Adam Bellenden, minister of Falkirk, where he was patron, refused him his stipend and forbade anyone from giving him shelter. In spite of requests from the presbytery for moderation, Lord Livingstone did not relent. In a last gesture of defiance, the homeless minister was elected moderator of the presbytery in August *in absentia* even though he managed to attend only three out of a possible 19 meetings of the presbytery in the rest of 1597.[23]

The first General Assembly after 1596 to be convened as such met at Dundee in May 1597 with the king in attendance. In April, fears were expressed that it might be packed but such crude means were not required.[24] As at Perth, a Convention of the Estates met in the town at the same time and, by this juxtaposition, James asserted his right to wield both the civil and ecclesiastical swords. He may even have been toying with the idea of reducing the Assembly to a status similar to Convocation in England. The English ambassador, Robert Bowes, claimed that James had invited particular laymen to the Assembly and that some presbyteries had 'employed especial commissioners' to achieve greater unity against the crown than at Perth. In spite of this, Bowes felt that 'the most part of the commissioners from the North (with many others)' would fall in behind the court and that, if the king did not win the day, he would adjourn the Assembly. The last three words of what Bowes wrote are crucial. The 'especial commissioners' were the unprecedentedly large delegations sent by presbyteries who remained opposed to the crown but 'many others', even outside the North, would stand with the king. Bowes knew that most northern ministers would

---

[21] Edinburgh Presbytery, ii, 15 Mar. 1597, *et passim*; Peebles Presbytery, i, fo. 13r.

[22] See Stirling Presbytery, ii and iii and Glasgow Presbytery, i, throughout 1595 and 1596; for the specific incidents mentioned here see Stirling Presbytery iii, 9 and 16 March 1597 *et passim*.

[23] Stirling Presbytery, iii, 27 Apr., 4 May, 10 Aug., yet Bellenden later became Bishop of Dunblane.

[24] Bowes to Burghley, 3 April 1597, *CSP Scot*, xii, no. 405.

take the royal view but he also knew that many from the South would do likewise. The ministers of Edinburgh and David Black had been relaxed from the horn to make the Assembly amenable to the absolution of the Catholic earls and the approval of the Perth Assembly.[25]

King James opened proceedings by promising augmentation of stipends and provision of vacant parishes. Robert Rollock, principal of the college of Edinburgh, was, according to James Melville, elected moderator by 'manie and grait persuasiones ... usit with the breithring bathe in publict and privat'.[26] This is the first record of what could be described as a 'whip' system. Sir Patrick Murray had even tried to woo James Melville and his uncle Andrew. The former later stated, apparently forgetting his earlier comment, that here the Assembly lost its freedom 'by purchessit voitis'.[27] The crown's system of persuasion, combined with a growing reluctance to defy it, succeeded. The Catholic earls were absolved, the Perth Assembly was approved, summary excommunication was suspended and the commission of the General Assembly was re-established.[28] This commission was ostensibly akin to that which had been discharged at the end of 1596 but it proved to be a quite different creature. The king:

> declarit that ... ther were sundrie matters of weght and importance ... quhilk could not be commodiouslie intreatit and concludit in this present Assemblie ... therfor his Majestie desyrit the brether to considder wither ... ane generall commissioun sould be grantit to certaine of the most wyse and discreit of the brethren, to conveine with his Majestie for effectuating of the premisses.[29]

A commission of 14 was appointed with a quorum of seven. Half of them had been among the 16 named as commissioners in the previous November and a further three had represented the presbytery of Edinburgh on the rotating committee at that time. The other three from Edinburgh presbytery, Bruce, Balfour and Balcanquhal, had been directly involved in the 'riot', so were excluded from consideration.[30] The significance of this continuity cannot be exaggerated, for it was not the

---

[25] Bowes to Burghley, 11 May 1597, *CSP Scot*, xii, no. 439; Melville, *Diary*, 416; Calderwood, *History*, v, 623; Stirling Presbytery, iii, 3 March 1596, 4 May, 1597; St Andrews Presbytery, fos 70v, 80r. In 1596, both Stirling and St Andrews sent three ministers; in 1597, Stirling sent six and the whole of St Andrews presbytery was commissioned.

[26] *BUK*, iii, 927; Melville, *Diary*, 415–16.

[27] Melville, *Diary*, 527.

[28] Spottiswoode, *History*, iii, 58–60; Melville, *Diary*, 529.

[29] *BUK*, iii, 927–8.

[30] *BUK*, iii, 928; Calderwood, *History*, v, 447; NLS, 'Copie of the minute buik', Wodrow Quarto, xx, no. 18, 5 Nov. 1596.

replacement of one group with another. Ten out of 14 new commissioners had been involved in the old one. The king was taking control of the Kirk and the General Assembly had acknowledged his supremacy by agreeing to appoint this commission. No longer stoutly challenging the king, as it had almost unfailingly done throughout the later 1580s and early 1590s, it, and thus many who had previously defied him, willingly became another element of his absolutist pretensions. James Melville, a member of the new commission, was later to describe its re-establishment as (yet another) 'deid-stroke' to the Kirk's freedom, 'the very neidle to draw in the Episcopall threid', and a 'fatall Trojan horse'. In similar vein, David Calderwood called it 'the King's led horse'.[31] Its remit was wide, the Assembly granting it power:

> to take sole ordour anent the provisioun of Ministers to the townes of Edenburgh, Dundie, and Sanct Androes, his Majesties and the Princes houses; to give thair advyce and opinioun to his Majestie, anent the planting of every ... kirk within this realme; to make such overture as they can best devyse twiching the constant platt; and generally to give thair advyce to his Majestie in all affaires concerning the weill of the Kirk, and entertainment of peace and obedience to his Majestie within this realme; with expresse power and command ... to propone to his Majestie the petitiounes and grieves, asweill of the Kirk in generall, as of every member thereof in particular.[32]

Thus, according to James Melville, was 'transferrit the haill power of the ... Assemblie in[to] the hands of the king and his Ecclesiastic Counsall, these Commissionars'.[33] By establishing this formal mechanism of contact between Kirk and king, the previously accessible James VI, perhaps because of the danger he had felt on 17 December 1596, distanced himself from individual ministers and presbyteries. He was beginning to retreat from the Stewart tradition of intimate monarchy before he took the high road to England in 1603.

The commission quickly began to act as a judicial committee of the Kirk headed by the king. After the Assembly, it appointed four new ministers to Edinburgh. In June, it overturned a decision by the presbytery of St Andrews to depose a minister for criticism of David Black and it suspended Robert Wallace, Black's erstwhile colleague, who was involved in a dispute with the king's secretary, Lindsay of Balcarres. In

---

[31] Melville, *Diary*, 417, 529; Calderwood, *History*, viii, 47–8; M. Lynch, 'Preaching to the Converted? Perspectives on the Scottish Reformation', in eds, A.A. MacDonald et al., *The Renaissance in Scotland: Studies in Literature, Religion, History and Culture Offered to John Durkan* (Leiden, 1994), 336.

[32] *BUK*, iii, 928.

[33] Melville, *Diary*, 417.

July, in a visitation of the University of St Andrews, it removed Andrew Melville from the rectorship and barred theology students and masters from attending presbytery meetings.[34] These rules applied only to St Andrews and, since most regents who normally attended general assemblies held parochial charges, only those at St Andrews who did not (Andrew Melville and John Johnston) would have been excluded. The measure was put into force on 15 July, when the provost of St Andrews came to the presbytery with a royal command 'nocht to permit or suffer anie to sitt in the presbyterie as judges in discipline of maneris that war nocht actuall ministeris'.[35] Later in the year, the new reluctance to defy the crown was revealed by the same presbytery. John Rutherford, reinstated by the commission after deposition for criticism of Black, asked what punishment should be given to those opposing his ministry – two Sundays in sackcloth on the stool of repentance was the presbytery's reply.[36]

There is a significant difference between reluctance to defy the king and agreement with his policies. What happened from December 1596 until midway through the following year was a concentrated demonstration of royal anger at the events surrounding the trial of David Black and of James's determination that such a thing would not happen again. A majority of the ministry, faced with the choice between obedience to the powers that be, as enjoined by Paul in his letter to the Romans, and defiance of them in the name of ecclesiastical independence, opted for the former. A defiant rearguard action was fought by a few, but the failure of that action soon became apparent. By the summer of 1597, James had obtained a Kirk no longer defying him as a matter of course. What he had yet to achieve was a Kirk with which he could work without the fear of unrest or the need for coercion.

During the following years, a degree of peace and stability returned to the Kirk. The major issue which occupied the last years of the sixteenth century was parliamentary representation. The Assembly at Dundee in May 1597 had, in response to the king's expressed desire to see ministers appointed to vacant prelacies sitting in Parliament, recommended this to the presbyteries.[37] It saw the possibility of financial gain for the Kirk through the acquisition of the revenues of these prelacies

---

[34] Bowes to Burghley, 31 May 1597, *CSP Scot*, xii, no. 454; St Andrews Presbytery, fos 73–5 and 80–81; Melville, *Diary*, 417–18; Calderwood, *History*, v, 647–51; NLS, Advocates Manuscripts 29.2.8, fos 55–116, esp. 'Sclanderis Committit be the ministerie of St Andros to be reformet be his majestie and Commissioneris of the general assemblie, 22 Junii 1597', at fos 111–16; Moysie, *Memoirs*, 134.

[35] St Andrews Presbytery, fo. 81r.

[36] St Andrews Presbytery, fo. 88r.

[37] *BUK*, iii, 930–32.

and, since numerous assemblies had sought some form of ecclesiastical representation in Parliament since the later 1570s, such a scheme would be the completion of unfinished business, the fulfilment of the settled will of the Kirk.

A sudden change in the attitude of those ministers who continued to defy the king – loosely called the 'Melvillians' but never properly identified by generations of historians – is thus not surprising. James Melville and others began to deny that the Kirk had ever wanted parliamentary representatives. It has recently been claimed that James and Andrew Melville 'sharply disagreed' on the issue but this is probably due to the fact that the two expressions of opinion date from either side of the 1596/97 watershed.[38] Andrew and James Melville, and some others, realised that any form of parliamentary representation which would now result would reflect the new atmosphere of royal authority. Their basic opinions had not changed but their political marginalisation led them to reject the very idea of ecclesiastical representation in Parliament.

In December 1597, the commissioners of the General Assembly petitioned parliament for the Kirk's restoration as one of the estates. The evidence suggests that the revival of this issue was the king's idea, so it could be inferred that, by this time, he had decided to reintroduce episcopacy, in some form at least. The petition was successful, Parliament passing an act allowing ministers presented to prelacies to sit and vote for the Kirk. The commissioners wrote to all the presbyteries informing them that the next Assembly had been brought forward from May to March to discuss this very important issue, the resolution of which should not be delayed. They emphasised that this deal had been hard-won from the nobility with royal support and was the best that they could hope for. It was to be included in a package for a 'constant platt', a scheme for perpetual provision of stipends which would end the complicated annual process of a minister obtaining a top-up from the thirds of benefices, held by the crown and distributed by the Lords Modifiers. The commissioners urged the presbyteries to appoint representatives to the Assembly who would approve the proposal, warning that acts unfavourable to the Kirk might be passed otherwise.[39] In January 1598, the king reminded them that the assembly had been

---

[38] Lynch, 'Preaching to the Converted?', 303–4. The assertion is, unfortunately, not referenced.

[39] APS, iv, 130; BUK, iii, 931–2; that James intended only to appoint to the bishoprics, not the abbacies, is suggested in a letter he wrote to Lord Hamilton, reassuring him that his possession of Arbroath Abbey would not be threatened, SRO, Hamilton Manuscripts, GD406/1/60.

brought forward and told them to send their 'maist learned wys and experimented' to it.[40] The synods were summoned to meet on 21 February to prepare for the assembly and Sir Patrick Murray was sent to Fife as the king's commissioner. James Melville warned against creeping hierarchy if they agreed to parliamentary representation, while David Ferguson, minister of Dunfermline, described it as a Trojan horse for episcopacy. In spite of these dire warnings, the synod approved parliamentary representation, 'the quhilk seiming guid'. The English ambassador, George Nicolson, reported that the synod of Lothian and Tweeddale discussed the matter and remitted the decision to the Assembly.[41]

The prominent role of the commission of the General Assembly was demonstrated when they met with the king prior to the Assembly at Dundee in March.[42] The English ambassador suggested that James's presence was necessary writing that, 'If the king had not gone, the ministers would surely have prevailed, but now it will go doubtful what will be the end of these things'.[43] It is impossible to be certain exactly who 'the ministers' were, but it is likely that Nicolson meant the ministers of the Edinburgh area with whom he was familiar and where opposition to parliamentary representation appears to have been strong. The king was taking no chances. He nominated the moderator's privy conference, the group which met to discuss the business of the Assembly, and he ordered Andrew Melville and John Johnston to leave Dundee. They had been commissioned by the presbytery, not the university, in breach of the rules established at the visitation of the University of St Andrews in the previous summer. The whip system operated again, the king calling individual ministers to him to persuade them to vote for parliamentary representation.[44]

The synod of Lothian and Tweeddale submitted grievances against the commissioners of the General Assembly, so the accusers, the delegates from that synod, were removed and the rest of the Assembly approved the commissioners' proceedings, the complaints being 'buried and obliterat'.[45] In a conciliatory gesture, the king forgave the ministers of Edinburgh for their part in the 'riot' of December 1596 and expressed his desire to restore the Kirk's patrimony and to see discipline firmly established, promising to put pressure on those who held tacks of

---

[40] Edinburgh Presbytery, ii, 3 Jan. 1598; Peebles Presbytery, i, fo. 19v; Stirling Presbytery, iii, 18 Jan. 1598.

[41] Melville, *Diary*, 436; Nicolson to Cecil, 25 Feb. 1598, *CSP Scot*, xiii, pt i, no. 126.

[42] Melville, *Diary*, 439.

[43] Nicolson to Burghley, 5 March 1598, *CSP Scot*, xiii, pt i, no. 128.

[44] Calderwood, *History*, v, 683; Melville, *Diary*, 440, 530–35; Scot, *Apologetical Narration*, 100.

[45] *BUK*, iii, 935–6, 941; Scot, *Apologetical Narration*, 100.

teinds to pay what they owed. For this, he said, parliamentary representatives were required, but he denied that there would be a 'Papisticall or Anglican' episcopate. Only the wisest ministers would be his bishops. The Assembly approved the idea of votes for the Kirk in Parliament, much to the chagrin of James Melville. For him, responsibility lay with Gilbert Body, 'that drunken Orkney ass', northern ministers and others voting for worldly reasons. There is no evidence that only 'a small majority' voted in favour.[46] Indeed, judging by the prevailing opinion at the synod of Fife, it is unlikely that any but a small minority opposed the principle of parliamentary representation. James Melville's tendency to rewrite history is demonstrated in two different accounts of the Assembly's vote on this question in his *Diary* and *A True Narratioune of the Declyneing Aige of the Kirk of Scotland*. In the former, written closer to the events, he claimed that it was the votes of lay commissioners which won the day but, in the latter, written in 1610, he claimed that it was the votes of laymen 'that had no commissioune'.[47] The vote as originally described was legal and Melville later changed his description to make it appear otherwise.

This Assembly demonstrated that the theory of two kingdoms and strict questions of polity, were not of paramount importance to the majority of the clergy, to whom serving their parishes and surviving on meagre stipends in a time of high inflation were likely to have been higher priorities: 'For them, the interaction between the two kingdoms was more important than their separation.'[48] If giving prelacies to ministers released money to aid the Kirk at the parochial level, they were happy to support it. It was decided that there should be 51 representatives of the Kirk, as there had been before the Reformation, and that their election should be shared between Kirk and king; much more Erastian than the scheme proposed in 1596. The matter was remitted to the presbyteries which were to report to the synods. Each synod would then appoint three representatives for discussions with the king and some ministers chosen by him.[49] The king gathering a representative group of ministers to discuss important issues was to become a common means of trying to achieve consensus and it was an idea which he was to carry into his English reign, most notably in the Hampton Court Conference of 1604.

There were allegations that the Assembly of March 1598 was packed and intimidated, summed up in the rhetorical plea written many years

---

[46] J.H.S. Burleigh, *A Church History of Scotland* (Edinburgh, 1983), 206.
[47] Melville, *Diary*, 440, 534.
[48] Lynch, 'Preaching to the Converted?', 304.
[49] *BUK*, iii, 946.

later: 'What availeth reasoning where force swayeth the matter?', but there is no evidence for packing in the crown's favour.[50] On the contrary, as in 1597, there were attempts by those who opposed the crown's policies to fill the Assembly with their ranks and it was this which led to another significant act. Although the king had achieved a good deal in the assemblies of 1597, they had proved troublesome, partly because presbyteries could send unlimited delegations. In 1598, in a last-ditch effort to have their views prevail in a Kirk which no longer agreed with them, 'the hail presbitrie' of St Andrews was commissioned and 'the maist part' of the presbytery of Edinburgh, now free to elect those warded for their activities in December 1596, was also sent.[51] This had not been normal before 1597 when those presbyteries had been in the mainstream of clerical opinion. Only now, when the rest of the Kirk was slipping away from them, did they take drastic measures. Their efforts were to no avail because too many ministers disagreed with them. They had already failed to prevent the Kirk's recognition of royal power over assemblies in the previous year. In spite of what Calderwood and James Melville would have posterity believe, the encouragement of the 'Northland' ministers is overstated. Of the 59 identifiable probable attenders in 1598, only ten came from north of Dundee.[52] This assembly took the decisive step of restricting the representation of the ministry at future assemblies to no more than three per presbytery. For the general assemblies of 1600, 1601 and 1602, the pattern of delegation was thus altered and a more representative gathering of ministers than had been seen in 1597 and 1598 was guaranteed. As a result, much less royal effort was required to achieve agreement at these meetings.

At the end of this Assembly, John Davidson, minister of Prestonpans, submitted a written protest alleging that this, and the two preceding assemblies, had been illegal. He deplored the confusion and corruption which he claimed had reigned since the discharge of the commission of the General Assembly in December 1596 and formally dissented from the decisions of the Assembly. According to the official record, none was prepared to support him. Sources more favourable to him were to claim that more than 30 or even as many as 80 signed his protest but they allegedly withdrew their names before its submission, bringing their very existence into question, as does the document itself which has

---

[50] Melville, *Diary*, 530–31; Calderwood, *History*, v, 688, 694; 'Ryseing and Usurpation', 10.

[51] St Andrews Presbytery, fo. 89r; Edinburgh Presbytery, ii, 7 March 1598; Calderwood, *History*, v, 629; Melville, *Diary*, 414–15; Spottiswoode, *History*, iii, 71.

[52] A.R. MacDonald, 'Ecclesiastical Politics in Scotland, 1586–1610' (unpublished Edinburgh PhD dissertation, 1995), Appendix 1(b).

only Davidson's signature and plenty of space for others.[53] In accordance with the proper form, the king then pursued Davidson before his presbytery.[54]

In the aftermath of the Assembly, the king's attempt to restore to his revenues James Beaton, the exiled Catholic Archbishop of Glasgow now living in France, resulted in an outcry from Patrick Simson, minister of Stirling. The English ambassador, George Nicolson, commented that this was 'more like to make the King more resolute anent the establishing of bishops ... and the infringing of the ministers' ampleness'.[55] It was already felt by some that James intended to restore the episcopate and, soon after this, Nicolson wrote that 'the King will have it that the bishops must be' and that 'sundry good and wise men suspect the King to have some mystery in establishing of bishops as also some high platt by restoring the Bishop of Glasgow and putting thus at the ministers'.[56] These 'wise men' were probably those, such as Robert Bruce and James Melville with whom English ambassadors were close. They too suspected that there was more to the planned placing of ministers in Parliament than met the eye. They feared that the king was seeking to restore a powerful episcopate through which he could control the Kirk and they suspected that parliamentary representation was the first step in that direction.

They were not far wrong, as is witnessed in James VI's *Basilikon Doron*, written in the summer of 1598 and its prototype, *The Trew Lawe of Frie Monarchies*. It should be acknowledged that 'Not only were these works cut from the same intellectual cloth at about the same time, but they must also be seen as peculiarly the products of the context which was Scotland in the 1590s', or even the later 1590s.[57]

---

[53] *BUK*, iii, 947, (0); NLS, 'Mr John Davidson's protestation in the general assembly, March 1598', Wodrow Folio, 42, no. 43; Calderwood, *History*, v, 697–9, (30–60); Melville, *Diary*, 535; Scot, *Apologetical Narration*, 104, (40–60); Row, *History*, 191, (0); 'Ryseing and Usurpation', 10, (60–80). Figures in brackets denote the number of ministers alleged to have subscribed the protest. That most must have voted for parliamentary representation and the restriction of presbytery delegations undermines the credibility of these figures.

[54] Haddington Presbytery, ii, fos 28, 29v; SRO, 'Instructionis for Mr Williame Melvile ... and Mr David MacGill ... for accusation of Mr John Davidson', Earl of Stair Papers, GD135/2711/6.

[55] *APS*, iv, 169; Nicolson to Cecil, 15 July 1598, *CSP Scot*, xiii, pt i, no. 177.

[56] Nicolson to Cecil, 25 July and same to same, July 1598, *CSP Scot*, xiii, pt i, nos 179 and 182.

[57] A. Williamson, *Scottish National Consciousness in the Age of James VI: the Apocalypse, the Union and the Shaping of Scotland's Public Culture* (Edinburgh, 1979), 45; R. Mason, 'George Buchanan, James VI and the Presbyterians', in ed., R. Mason, *Scots and Britons: Scottish Political Thought and the Union of 1603* (Cambridge, 1994), 135.

The former, written in 1597, deals with royal power in very basic, theoretical terms, stating simply that parliamentary statute constituted only advice to the king who held absolute authority within his realm. It said nothing specifically about the Kirk.[58] *Basilikon Doron*, on the other hand, was a detailed manual for government, written by James for his son and heir Henry. It shows that James had developed a very jaundiced view of the more staunch ministers. Had he written the work three or four years earlier, the tone would undoubtedly have been less harsh and it would be wrong to suggest, as many historians are inclined to do, that the opinions expressed in this work had been held by James since the middle of the 1580s.[59]

James went so far as to express regret about the very nature of the Scottish Reformation since it was 'maid be populaire tumulte and rebellion and not proceeding from the princes ordare as it did in Englande'.[60] His loss of regard for the ministers who continued to stand out against royal intervention in the Kirk was demonstrated by an extreme view of their intentions. He wrote that:

> finding the guste of government sueit they begouth to fantasie to thame selfis a democratike forme of gouvernement ... [and] they fedd thame selfis with that hoape to become tribuni plebis, and sa in a populaire gouvernement be leading the people be the nose to beare the suey of all the reule.[61]

It is easy to detect here James's reaction to the 'riot' of December 1596. He saw it as having been, potentially, a revolt of the commons led by the 'fyrie ministers' and if this was what would result without sufficient royal control of the Kirk then such control was clearly necessary.

As far as participation of the clergy in government was concerned, James recommended that Henry should favour modest and learned ministers, rewarding them with bishoprics and other prelacies, 'annulling that vyle act of annexation' of 1587. He recommended that Henry should 'banish thaire [the ministers'] parity, quhilke can not agree with a monarchie [an early form of 'no bishop, no king'] but ... also ... reestablishe the aulde institution of three estates in parliament quhilke can na otherwayes be done'. Finally, he promised 'to make ... a faire

---

[58] J. Craigie, ed., *Minor Prose Works of James VI* (Scottish Texts Society, 4th series, 1982), 57–82.

[59] For example M. Lee, *Government by Pen: Scotland under James VI and I* (Urbana, 1990), 21.

[60] *The Basilikon Doron of King James VI*, ed. J Craigie, 2 vols (Scottish Texts Society, 3rd series 1944 and 1950), i, 74.

[61] *Basilikon Doron*, i, 74–5. In the sixteenth century, 'democracy' was used in the sense in which 'anarchy' would be used today.

entree' in the process for Henry.[62] This demonstrates just how far James had come since his attempts to work with the Kirk during the later 1580s and earlier 1590s had fallen on stony ground. He was now convinced that the best means of being at peace with the Kirk was by controlling it through bishops. He made it clear that he had tried to reason with the ministers who opposed the crown but that it had been in vain.[63]

He closed the passage concerning the Kirk with the advice that Henry should suffer neither 'vaine puritane ... nor proude papall bishoppis', echoing what he had said to the General Assembly and evidence, if it were required, that James's priority was not so much episcopacy *per se* as control and the contentment which that could bring.[64] To James, neither overmighty bishops nor overmighty ministers were desirable. He wanted pliable men who relied upon him for their status, men upon whom he could depend to carry out his government, for he was becoming increasingly aware that he might not be ruling his ancient kingdom directly for much longer.

The principal task which occupied the king and the Kirk over the next few years was establishing a system of ecclesiastical representation in Parliament. Of the surviving presbytery records, there is evidence for discussion of the question only in the books of the presbytery of Edinburgh. It approved of the principle as long as the Kirk's representatives, which it wanted to call 'commissioners', did not hold office for life and were appointed by the king from leets drawn up by the Kirk. The presbytery of St Andrews planned a discussion but none was recorded.[65] There are no other indications of presbyteries having been active in a debate which was mainly carried on in the synods which were to meet on the first Tuesday of June 1598. This was later alleged to have been a royal ploy to make it impossible for them to know of each other's deliberations but it had been common for them to meet at the same time before 1597.[66] There is evidence for opposition to the proposals for parliamentary representation only in Fife. Perhaps anticipating problems, the king sent two commissioners to that synod and, although there was little opposition to the principle of representation in Parliament, members from three of its four presbyteries opposed certain aspects of the proposals for selection, tenure and payment of the envisaged parliamentarians. Cupar, like Edinburgh, was happy for the king to choose from leets supplied by the Kirk,

---

[62] *Basilikon Doron*, i, 79–80.

[63] *Basilikon Doron*, i, 80.

[64] *Basilikon Doron*, i, 81.

[65] Edinburgh Presbytery, ii, 30 May 1598; St Andrews Presbytery, fo. 91v.

[66] 'Ryseing and Usurpation', 11.

for the representatives to have life tenure and for them to be called bishops. The other three wanted exclusive nomination by the Kirk, annual election by the General Assembly and the title of 'Commissioner of the Kirk'.[67] According to James Melville, the royal commissioners secured three pliable delegates from the synod who were then given power only to report the synod's conclusions to the conference. In a later account, it was alleged that delegates from all the synods had been appointed by royal commissioners. There is no evidence for this and it is hard to see how any synod which opposed the sentiments of its delegates would have stood by while they went off to discuss such an important issue. The very fact that James Melville himself was a delegate to just such a meeting in 1600 suggests that these conferences genuinely reflected a wide range of opinion.[68]

The scheme, devised in August 1598 at a conference with the king at his palace at Falkland in Fife, bears out the consensual nature of proceedings on this issue. There were to be 51 'commissioners', chosen by the king from leets of six supplied by the Kirk for each place. Certain 'caveats' were agreed upon to limit their powers. They were to receive the revenues from their prelacies only once all the kirks, schools and colleges financed therefrom were paid for; they should not vote in Parliament without the Kirk's warrant; they should be annually accountable to the General Assembly for their conduct; they should not alienate the revenues of their prelacies; they would be compelled to serve a congregation and they would be subject, as all ministers were, to their presbytery, synod and the General Assembly. If deposed from the ministry, they would lose the right to sit in Parliament.[69]

Archbishop Spottiswoode later suggested that the king had accepted these 'caveats' because he knew he would be able to erode them in the future and because he wanted a swift end to negotiations, wishing to concentrate on gaining European support for the English succession. He was, unwittingly, depriving James of due credit for it is likely that he realised that, with the Kirk showing increasing favour to royal policy, he might face little difficulty in securing approval for this scheme. It did take some lengthy negotiations but this was a period in which James, seeking a policy which would ensure his supremacy but carry the approval of the majority of the ministry, was just finding his feet. He was even eager to include those who staunchly opposed his plans. If he did indeed intend to go much further with the restoration of an episcopate, he saw his way to success led through the route of compromise.

[67] Spottiswoode, *History*, iii, 70, 73; Melville, *Diary*, 441–2.

[68] Melville, *Diary*, 442, 489; 'Ryseing and Usurpation', 11.

[69] Spottiswoode, *History*, iii, 72–6.

The conclusions of the conference were to be discussed by the General Assembly but none met in 1599 because further conferences, held in an attempt to obtain unanimous agreement over parliamentary representation, failed to reach a resolution. Conferences in July and August 1599, involving the commissioners of the General Assembly and delegates from the synods, met 'to lay the ground ... for erecting bishops at the next General Assembly'.[70] On 19 November, during a further conference, the king lost patience with those who had not come round to his point of view. He remitted the matter to the next Assembly, threatening that, if they did not accept his scheme, the Kirk would remain in financial straits and he would appoint his own ecclesiastical estate in Parliament.[71] Early in the following year, there were renewed allegations of royal intimidation of opposition ministers. Robert Bruce was allegedly threatened with the loss of his stipend if he did not vote for parliamentary representation at the forthcoming Assembly.[72] This, and the king's threats of the previous November, suggest that he was trying to achieve as much unity as possible by intimidating the rump of uncooperative ministers, of whom Bruce was certainly one. He would surely not have wasted his time on such likely intransigents if coercion of more moderate ministers had been necessary.

When the Assembly did meet, in March 1600 at Montrose, James was again present. The numerical weakness of the ministers opposed to the king's policies, in the first Assembly to meet under the new rules for delegation, is suggested by the accounts of James Melville and David Calderwood. They alleged that, by a number of ministers whom they favoured being on the leet for moderator, the votes of the 'best breithring' were split and Robert Wilkie, minister of St Andrews, principal of St Leonard's College and favourable to the king's course was chosen.[73] Rather than revealing 'faultlines within Melvillian ranks', this demonstrated that the ministers opposing royal policy were outnumbered.[74] Had the 'best breithring' been thwarted at this turn merely by splitting their votes for moderator, the king's policy would have fallen at the first vote on a substantive issue. An allegedly royalist moderator could not have been enough to sway the Assembly.

Although the vast majority of ministers broadly favoured the scheme, James did underestimate the level of opposition to some of its aspects.

---

[70] Nicolson to Cecil, 8 May, 1599, *CSP Scot*, xiii, pt i, no. 372; Calderwood, *History*, v, 738.

[71] Calderwood, *History*, v, 746–62; Melville, *Diary*, 446–62.

[72] Nicolson to Cecil, 26 Jan. 1600, *CSP Scot*, xiii, pt ii, no. 493.

[73] Melville, *Diary*, 469; Calderwood, *History*, vi, 2.

[74] Lynch, 'Preaching to the Converted?', 316.

Seeking the unanimity pursued in the conferences, the moderator's privy conference tried to resolve the issue with a set-piece debate between four ministers opposed to parliamentary representation and four in favour. The king and Privy Council were the audience and, not surprisingly, no agreement was reached. The whip system was used, once more, to ensure approval of the royal scheme and Andrew Melville was again excluded, having been commissioned by his presbytery.[75] A place in Parliament *per se* was not in controversy, indeed the only issue sufficiently in dispute to require a vote was whether the Kirk's representatives should be annually elected or appointed indefinitely, barring serious misconduct. The vote was close: 51 voted in favour of annual election and 48 voted against. The king, certainly not 'rebuffed decisively', wanted life tenure. Realising he was close to success, he offered what had been agreed the previous August, that they should have life tenure but would have to give an annual account of their conduct to the General Assembly. This stratagem, by no means indicating a royal defeat, worked and Melville and Calderwood gave no figures for the second vote, perhaps because it revealed the opposition to have been embarrassingly small.[76] Minor modifications of the 'caveats', rather than coercion of the ministry, had been enough to win the day for the king.

In the Kirk at large, things were generally quiet, although there were a few lingering murmurs of dissent as well as renewed zeal against Catholicism. The General Assembly of 1598 had given the lead in this by ordering the countesses of Huntly, Sutherland and Caithness to subscribe the Confession of Faith and, in 1600, various acts were passed against Catholicism and the harbouring of Jesuits.[77] In June 1599, the presbytery of Linlithgow told its counterpart in Stirling that its excommunication of Lady Livingstone had been intimated in the kirks of Lothian. The king's failure to remove his daughters from her custody was lamented and he had been petitioned on the matter. The presbytery of Stirling endorsed those actions and passed the information to those of Glasgow and Auchterarder. In December, the presbytery of Edinburgh pressed the king for action against Catholics by a delegation, the sort of thing which had not been seen for three years.[78] In the

---

[75] Melville, *Diary*, 469; Scot, *Apologetical Narration*, 113; Calderwood, *History*, vi, 16.

[76] 'Ryseing and Usurpation', 14; Nicolson to Cecil, 25 March 1600, *CSP Scot*, xiii, pt ii, no. 503; Lee, 'James VI and the Revival of Episcopacy', 63; G. Donaldson, *Scotland: James V–James VII* (Edinburgh, 1971), 202 gives a false impression of the annual election *versus* annual account incident.

[77] *BUK*, iii, 948, 952.

[78] Stirling Presbytery, iii, 13 June 1599; Edinburgh Presbytery; ii, 11 Dec. 1599.

North East too, the presbyteries were acting with unwonted freedom against recusants, including Errol, his wife and their household. This freedom of action was to continue until the regal union and beyond.[79] That this was once more possible without royal interference, suggests that the severe tensions of 1596–97, which led the King to view ecclesiastical action against Catholics as a personal criticism and clerical criticism as virtually treason, had dissipated.

In the summer of 1600, a test of loyalty which few ministers failed was made available to James. The young Earl of Gowrie, rehabilitated son of the leader of the Ruthven regime of 1582–83, returned to Scotland in the summer of 1600. His younger brother, a gentleman of the king's bedchamber, came to the king while he was hunting near Perth on 5 August, inviting him to Gowrie's house in the town where the young earl would reveal details of a foreign Catholic plot against Scotland. James accompanied him to Perth and, inside the house, an incident occurred the true details of which will never be known. The king, fearing for his life, cried for help from the window. When it arrived, he accused the brothers of attempted murder and they were killed on the spot. That the king's life was threatened is unlikely. Had they wanted, two men could have at least caused him serious injury before help arrived. Whatever the true circumstances of the so-called 'Gowrie Conspiracy', everyone except five ministers of Edinburgh was prepared to accept that James had escaped assassination by the grace of God alone. Willingness to give thanks for his deliverance did not, therefore, denote conservative loyalty.[80]

The king immediately commanded the ministers of the capital to proclaim that he had been miraculously delivered from mortal danger. Somewhat perversely, Robert Bruce, Walter Balcanquhal, James Balfour, John Hall and William Watson, 'refusit', because they had nothing other than (official) hearsay to go on. In spite of his description of it as a 'maist hid and horroble conspiracie, intendit ... to have cut af the King', James Melville felt that it was used by the king to 'undo' those ministers but, judging by the reaction of the rest of the Kirk, the ministers of Edinburgh brought their fate upon themselves.[81] One week after the 'conspiracy', the king provided £1 000 from the revenues of Scone Abbey near Perth to be given to the poor in thanksgiving. On the

---

[79] Ellon Presbytery, i, 1599–1602, *passim*, see esp. fos 29v, 30r, 33v, 67–8, 80r, 85r; Aberdeen Presbytery, 1600–1602, *passim*.

[80] Balfour, *Works*, i, 407; M. Graham, *The Uses of Reform: 'Godly Discipline' and Popular Behavior in Scotland and Beyond, 1560–1610* (Leiden, 1996), 240 portrays thanksgiving in this way.

[81] Melville, *Diary*, 485–6; Calderwood, *History*, vi, 28–45; Spottiswoode, *History*, iii, 84–9.

same day, the five ministers were called before the king and Privy Council to explain themselves. They insisted that they had given thanks for his delivery from danger but that they could not say what that danger was because no trial had taken place. They refused to give thanks in the terms which the crown demanded so they were discharged from public speaking and banished outwith ten miles of the capital.[82] The synods were ordered to meet on the third Tuesday of September to devise a standard form of thanksgiving for the king's escape from his alleged would-be assassins.[83] The crown was using the synods, just as they had operated prior to 1597, to secure a quick response from as much of the realm as possible. The fact that no one objected is testament to a general acceptance of the royal version of events. Even the synod of Fife was happy to obey. James Melville, having been elected moderator, went to the king himself to show him the form of thanksgiving which it had established.[84] Only the presbytery of Edinburgh, having lost five of its members, was upset with the king. In December 1600, it challenged the right of the commissioners of the General Assembly to choose their replacements and, throughout 1601, it demanded their reinstatement. That it was out of line with the majority of ministers is demonstrated by the General Assembly's vote by a two to one majority, in 1601, in favour of the transportation of three of the former ministers of Edinburgh for their reaction to the 'Gowrie Conspiracy'.[85]

The king's drive to restore episcopacy took a decisive step in October 1600. Another conference of delegates from synods met at Holyrood and the first three parliamentary bishops were appointed. Discussions were conducted over the fate of the ministers of Edinburgh and the three ministers who resolutely opposed the restoration of episcopacy (the delegates from Fife), William Scot, minister of Kennoway, John Carmichael, minister of Newburn, and James Melville, were sent to confer with the former ministers of Edinburgh. While they were absent 'the king with his commissionars, and the breithring' nominated David Lindsay, minister of Leith, as Bishop of Ross, Peter Blackburn, minister of Aberdeen, as bishop there, and George Gledstanes, minister of St Andrews, as Bishop of Caithness.[86] The king and the other delegates

---

[82] *RPC*, vi, 147–9

[83] *RPC*, vi, 157.

[84] Melville, *Diary*, 488.

[85] Edinburgh Presbytery, iii, 24 Dec. 1600 and 1601 *passim*; Calderwood, *History*, vi, 120.

[86] Melville, *Diary*, 488–9; Calderwood, *History*, 95–6. A chance discovery in the SRO revealed that, as far back as 1576, David Lindsay had connections with Ross. SRO, Receipt, David Lindsay to Alexander Ross of Balnagown, 1 April 1576, Balnagown Castle Manuscripts, GD129/1/box44/bundle 180 (uncatalogued).

had disregarded both the spirit and letter of the 'caveats' agreed in 1599 and ratified by the Assembly in 1600. A precedent was thus set, giving him the right to make episcopal appointments without using leets drawn up by the Kirk and thus to choose who would sit in Parliament for the Kirk.

The next Assembly, originally planned for St Andrews in July, met in May at Burntisland on the south coast of Fife with the king again present. Again, allegations were later made that the leet for the election of the moderator was almost filled with ministers of what James Melville called the 'better sort' so that John Hall, whom William Scot called a 'dissembler', was elected ahead of Patrick Simson, minister of Stirling.[87] The fact that Hall was one of the ministers of Edinburgh banished in 1596 and had initially refused to accept the official version of the 'Gowrie Conspiracy' hardly makes him a prime candidate for a royal stooge. As in 1600, if those who opposed the king's policy were actually in the majority, as Melville, Scot and Calderwood implied by suggesting that they were thwarted by underhand tactics, then they would have outvoted the others during the Assembly. The fact that they did not tells its own story.

King James warned that disagreements would benefit only the Catholics. He admitted his own shortcomings, professing his zeal for religion and pledging to 'live and die in the trew relligioun' and intimated his desire to see the pulpits of Edinburgh refilled. Even James Melville admitted that this was 'to the grait confort of all the Kirk'.[88] The tone of the king's speech was remarkably reminiscent of his address to the Assembly of August 1590, which rejoiced at his zeal. This was a king more at peace with his Kirk than he had been for many years. The Assembly passed off without controversy, except for the contribution of one minister who did not attend. John Davidson, who had got into trouble in 1598 for alleging the illegality of the Assembly, wrote to this one and his letter was read out by the moderator. He accused the Assembly of meeting in the name of the king rather than in the name of God, while Catholicism flourished and went unpunished, and he called on them to beware of episcopacy creeping into the Kirk.[89] The letter was denounced as seditious and its author warded in Edinburgh Castle, then within his own house and, after protesting his faithfulness to the king, he was allowed freedom to travel within his parish.

---

[87] Scot, *Apologetical Narration*, 117; Calderwood, *History*, vi, 105.

[88] Melville, *Diary*, 494, 544; *BUK*, iii, 969; Calderwood, *History*, vi, 125.

[89] Calderwood, *History*, vi, 110–12, 125–7; *RPC*, vi, 243; NLS, 'Original Chargis King James to Mr John Davidson to enter ward in his own house May 20, 1601', Wodrow Folio, 42, no. 45.

The Assembly voted to restore James Balfour, William Watson and Walter Balcanquhal to the ministry but to transport them to charges outwith the capital and Robert Bruce, the only remaining suspended Edinburgh minister, in exile in England, was invited to return by the king and Patrick Simson, minister of Stirling, successfully helped to persuade him.[90] This new found harmony provided an opportunity for another attempt to regularise the payment of ministers' stipends. Endemic economic instability meant that the finalisation of a 'constant platt' remained one of the king's unfulfilled promises to the Kirk and, in 1601, moves were made to rectify that. The commissioners for the constant platt, appointed by the General Assembly in that year, sought royal co-operation in organising a survey of all benefices. During the following year, the presbyteries of Aberdeen, Edinburgh, Ellon and Peebles all recorded royal letters requesting details of the value of the benefices within their bounds. The presbyteries of Glasgow, St Andrews and Stirling neither recorded such a letter nor show any evidence of having compiled a list of benefices. As a result of the uneven response, the commissioners for the constant platt were forced to report to the Assembly at Holyrood in 1602 that they were unable to proceed due to the lack of co-operation from a number of presbyteries.[91]

The General Assembly of 1602, again originally planned to meet in St Andrews in July, was prorogued until November. The delay was supposedly necessary to give time for the last Assembly's acts against Catholics to be put into effect and to allow for the finalisation of the platt. The move to the king's palace of Holyrood was significant because Andrew Melville was, by this time, warded in St Andrews 'for having rallit [railed] against the king', and Robert Bruce was warded outwith a six-mile radius of Edinburgh.[92] Both could have gained access to an Assembly at St Andrews and caused trouble, neither could go to one at Holyrood. In a petition to the Assembly, the synod of Fife, alone in its opposition, submitted a list of complaints about the king's role in ecclesiastical affairs and his failure to take decisive action against Catholics.[93] These were put to a committee of 12 members of the Assembly which came up with answers which were generally dismissive of their urgency, arguing that

---

[90] Calderwood, *History*, vi, 120–21; 130–38.

[91] Aberdeen Presbytery, fo. 71r; Edinburgh Presbytery, iii, 27 Jan. 1602; Ellon Presbytery, i, fo. 89; Peebles Presbytery, i, fos 85–8; T.M. Devine and S.G.E. Lythe, 'The Economy of Scotland Under James VI a Revision Article' *SHR*, 50 (1971), 91–106; K.M. Brown, *Bloodfeud in Scotland, 1573–1625* (Edinburgh, 1986), 266.

[92] *BUK*, iii, 973; Melville, *Diary*, 545; Calderwood, *History*, vi, 157–8; *RPC*, vi, 397–8; Thomas Douglas to Cecil, 21 July 1602, *CSP Scot*, xiii, pt ii, no. 835, see also PRO State Papers Scottish, SP52/68/86. The Calendar has 'called' but the MS clearly reads 'rallit'.

[93] *BUK*, iii, 989 ff; Calderwood, *History*, vi, 173 ff; Melville, *Diary*, 549–53.

most of the topics about which they complained were in hand. In accepting the king's right to deal with ministers for matters raised in their sermons and failing even to answer questions about the Edinburgh ministers and the absolved earls' failure to adhere to their conditions of absolution, the Assembly was at odds with the synod of Fife. The synod of Fife was, in fact, at odds with the majority of the Kirk. Spottiswoode was later to argue that these grievances were inspired by 'private discontents of such as grieved to see the affairs of the church carried by others than themselves'.[94] That is how he saw the rump of dissident ministers.

One of Fife's complaints was that the commissioners of the General Assembly were running the Kirk in a manner prejudicial to the synods and presbyteries. The commission had been augmented in 1598 and 1601 to 27 and its powers increased with the consent of the Assembly. Its response was that the commissioners could conduct themselves only according to the acts of general assemblies and, because it formally approved their proceedings, this was deemed to have been the case. The commission was reduced to 25 and all three new bishops were included.[95] It was not planned at the time, but this commission continued unchecked and unchanged for six years.

At this Assembly the king made further promises relating to stipends, suppression of Catholicism and the plantation of ministers in vacant parishes, all three being closely related in the minds of many. In return, the Assembly ordained an annual thanksgiving on 5 August for the king's deliverance from the, 'Gowrie Conspiracy' and asked Robert Bruce to declare his satisfaction with the king's version of events. Without remark or protest, it granted that the Bishops of Ross and Caithness, David Lindsay and George Gledstanes, should have powers of visitation in their own dioceses.[96] This Assembly was so amenable to the king that, when he chose the last Tuesday of July 1604 for the next meeting, no dissenting voice was raised. This was the first time since the Reformation that the Kirk had willingly planned a year without an Assembly. One view attributed the loss of annual assemblies to the ambitions of the bishops but since there were only three and they had no real power, it seems that James, anticipating Elizabeth's death and wishing to leave 1603 free of inconveniences, was largely responsible for the suggestion which the Assembly accepted.[97]

---

[94] Spottiswoode, *History*, iii, 105.

[95] *BUK*, iii, 989, 994, 996; Melville, *Diary*, 549–52; Calderwood, *History*, vi, 165, 174–7; MacDonald, 'Ecclesiastical Politics', Appendix 6(b) listing the commissions from 1597 onwards.

[96] Calderwood, *History*, vi, 168, 180, 184; Scot, *Apologetical Narration*, 120.

[97] *BUK*, iii, 1008; Melville, *Diary*, 554; 'Ryseing and Usurpation', 17; Spottiswoode, *History*, iii, 107.

Calderwood claimed that, at this Assembly, 'the King and his man, Mr Patrick Galloway, ruled as they pleased'.[98] This was because, by that time, what pleased them pleased the Kirk. Over the years since 1596, with an initial struggle during 1597, opposition to the crown's intervention in the affairs of the Kirk had dwindled and those who remained opposed to the king were sidelined, bereft of support. With increasingly representative assemblies after 1598, it became even more clear that the majority within the Kirk was amenable to royal policy. This was not, as many have tried to suggest without really providing any evidence, due to the exclusion of what had been a dominant 'party' prior to 1597. It was also not the result of significant alterations in the geographical origins of those attending assemblies after 1596. The composition of assemblies before 1597 compared to those which met after 1596, cannot be said to reveal an unrepresentative platform on which sustained tension with the crown could have rested. Contrary to one recent assertion, the proportion of ministers attending general assemblies may have been closer to one in five or even one in four than one in 12.[99] The view that, before 1597, '[Andrew] Melville appears to have converted to his views the majority of ministers, or at any rate the majority ... who regularly attended the General Assembly' must be reconsidered, for it is largely without foundation.[100] Many ministers from the supposed 'Melvillian heartland' of Fife, Lothian and the South East continued to attend assemblies after 1596 and those parts of Scotland continued to dominate assemblies. After 1596, James did not depend 'chiefly upon the votes of the northern ministers for carrying his measures'. The difference between the assemblies of 1590 and 1602, the only ones for which full sederunts survive, is striking in its insignificance. At the former, 42 per cent of ministers came from Fife, Lothian and the South East, while at the latter the figure was 39 per cent.[101] As for the 'Northland ministers', there were seven from the west Highlands, the North East and parts further north in 1590; in 1602 that number had risen to ten, hardly a massive influx. The notion that, by

---

[98] Calderwood, *History*, vi, 186.

[99] Lynch, 'Preaching to the Converted?', 313, 317. The figure of one in 12 assumes that every parish was filled. The truer figure should be based on *c.* 600 or fewer since, in 1596, there were 539 ministers outside Argyll and the Isles (both sparsely populated and poorly provided); 99 ministers attended the 1590 assembly alone (*BUK*, ii, 762–7).

[100] G. Donaldson, 'The Scottish Church 1567–1625', in ed., A.G.R. Smith, *The Reign of James VI and I* (Aylesbury, 1973), 45.

[101] See *BUK*, ii, 762–7 and iii, 974–9 for sederunts; see also MacDonald, 'Ecclesiastical Politics', Appendix 1(a) and (b) for chronological and alphabetical attendance lists of ministers; T. McCrie, *The Life of Andrew Melville*, 2nd edn, 2 vols (Edinburgh, 1824), ii, 18.

moving the Assembly to northern locations after 1596, James was able to manipulate their composition is thus also a red herring: the assemblies of 1593 and 1595 had met in Dundee and Montrose respectively and there is no evidence that the Assembly of 1601, at Burntisland in Fife, was more opposed to royal policy than those which met elsewhere.[102]

John Spottiswoode, David Lindsay, Peter Blackburn and James Law, who received some of James VI's first episcopal appointments, were not only frequent attenders at assemblies before 1597 but also they were very much involved in ecclesiastical politics at the highest level. Nearly two-thirds of ministers who attended assemblies before the end of 1596 continued to do so thereafter. Not only did the geographical distribution of ministers at the General Assembly remain very much the same, so did the personnel. This continuity of personnel and change of sentiment may be explained by the fact that, on the crucial issue of the king's inaction against Catholics in the later 1580s and early 1590s, the ministry united in dissent. As a consequence of the events of the last few months of 1596, such opposition became viewed by the king as almost treasonous and its perpetrators dangerous revolutionaries. Many thus shied away from such extremism and left a rump of ministers still holding opinions no longer fashionable.

General assemblies characterised by tension between Kirk and king became a thing of the past and the conciliatory atmosphere after 1598 is testament to that. A *via media* had been found, between the extremes of ecclesiastical independence and Erastian absolutism, which was acceptable to the bulk of Scottish churchmen. Certainly, the Kirk would not have independently suggested the restoration of episcopacy. As Jenny Wormald put it, 'No bishop, no king' can be reversed, for it is 'unlikely that anyone other than the king would have brought about the restoration of bishops as such'.[103] Yet most ministers did not take such a dogmatic view of polity that they would implacably oppose them. A similar view has recently been emphasised in England, where concentration

---

[102] Many historians have accepted unquestioningly these notions. See: D.G. Mullan, *Episcopacy in Scotland: the History of an Idea, 1560–1638* (Edinburgh, 1986), 82; Donaldson, *Scotland: James V–James VII*, 200–201 and 'Scotland's Conservative North in the Sixteenth and Seventeenth Centuries', in his *Scottish Church History* (Edinburgh, 1985), 191–203, esp. 196; M. Lynch, *Scotland: a New History* (London, 1991), 231; Burleigh, *Church History of Scotland*, 205; for the assemblies of 1593 and 1595 see *BUK*, ii, 795, 846.

[103] J. Wormald, 'No Bishop, no King: the Scottish Jacobean Episcopate, 1600–1625', in ed., B. Vogler, *Bibliotheque de la Revue d'Histoire Ecclesiastique: Miscellanea Historiae Ecclesiasticae*, viii (Louvain, 1987), 259–67, at 263. I am grateful to Dr Wormald for this reference.

on Puritans and Arminians in the early seventeenth-century Anglican church has been questioned since it ignores the bulk of the clergy.[104] In Scotland, the compromise, involving an episcopate with severely limited powers representing the Kirk in Parliament as well as recognition of a limited royal supremacy, was, however, stifled before it could flourish.

---

[104] P. White, 'The *via media* in the Early Stuart Church', in ed., K. Fincham, *The Early Stuart Church, 1603–1642*, (London, 1993), 211–30. Although White's thesis has been challenged by N. Tyacke in 'Anglican Attitudes: Some Recent Writings on English Religious History, from the Reformation to the Civil War', *Journal of British Studies*, 35 (1996), 139–67, it is no less applicable to Scotland. I am grateful to Julian Goodare for this reference.

CHAPTER FIVE

The regal union and the collapse of consensus, 1603–1606

On 26 March 1603, Sir Robert Carey arrived in Edinburgh to inform an undoubtedly delighted James VI, King of Scots, that he had also become James I, King of England. Preparations for a triumphant journey south immediately got under way while the marches erupted into a last-chance frenzy of cross-border raiding. The king went to St Giles' on 3 April where John Hall congratulated him, gave thanks and exhorted him to gratitude and the maintenance of the truth. After the sermon, James made a farewell address, thanking God that he had 'sattled boith Kirk and kingdome … and left it in that estate quhilk he meinit nocht to hurt or alter ony way'. He then made another promise which he was not to keep, that he would return to Scotland every three years.[1]

On the following day, his magnanimity was shown to be boundless when he received Robert Bruce, the one minister who remained obstinate about the 'Gowrie Conspiracy'. Bruce was reported to have been impressed with how friendly the king was and James felt that they were reconciled.[2] On 5 April, James VI left for London. Passing Haddington, the ministers of the synod of Lothian and Tweeddale rushed out to bid him farewell and to seek reassurance that Catholicism would be repressed, that stipends would be augmented and that, with James entering a country with an improperly reformed Kirk, there would be no further ecclesiastical innovations. He was happy to reassure them on all three matters. All the signs were good. The polity of the Kirk as it stood was acceptable to the majority of the ministry and, reassured that this state of affairs was to continue, they could be content that, even with their king absent, the Kirk would remain at peace with itself and with the crown. Even the presbytery of Edinburgh made a special effort to congratulate James on his English coronation.[3] Things would change profoundly in 1604.

Perhaps surprisingly, the first signs of the problems of dual monarchy emerged in the North East, an area held in contempt by Calderwood

---

[1] Spottiswoode, *History*, iii, 137–8; Melville, *Diary*, 554.

[2] Calderwood, *History*, vi, 217–19.

[3] Edinburgh Presbytery, iii, final folio. The King's reply is the last entry.

and James Melville for its acquiescence to the king. The presbyteries there, which had recently enjoyed a free rein to call Catholics to account for recusancy, found that the crown was commanding them to call off their dogs. In 1603, the commissioners of the General Assembly ordered the presbytery of Aberdeen to suspend action against Lord Glamis, later Earl of Kinghorn, and in 1604, they became involved with the presbytery of Deer. In February, that presbytery was beginning to lose patience with the Earl of Huntly who had been given chance after chance and had led them a merry dance but was no closer to satisfying them as to his religion. He was, after all, a Catholic, but he had been absolved from excommunication in 1597, after which he had shown no signs of abandoning his old faith. The presbytery, found him to be 'remayning as yit no less obdured and hardenit in his superstition and idolatrous opinions of papistrie than he was in the beginning' and decided that further continuations of the case against him would only endanger the Kirk. The process of excommunication began. Two weeks later, the presbytery received a letter from the commissioners of the General Assembly and Sir Alexander Straiton of Lauriston, the king's commissioner in ecclesiastical affairs, addressed to all the presbyteries of the synods of Aberdeen and Moray. It was accompanied by a letter from the Privy Council to the presbytery of Aberdeen and another from Peter Blackburn, Bishop of Aberdeen. This bundle of correspondence ordered the suspension of proceedings against Huntly until the king's further will was known. The presbytery had no option but to obey.[4] Huntly was the most powerful Catholic noble in Scotland and a good friend of Spain with whom James, as King of England, was seeking peace. To upset Huntly could upset that delicate process. The interests of English foreign policy were overriding the interests of the Kirk, just as, in the 1590s, James's desire not to offend potential continental supporters of his succession to the English throne had caused him to be lenient towards his powerful Catholic nobles, uniting the ministry against the crown. It was again an important element in a process which would, once more, turn the Kirk against the king.

The spring of 1604 witnessed a dramatic reversal in the king's popularity within the Kirk. The year had started badly for any who had anticipated that the succession of James VI to the English throne could have led to further Reformation there. It is not clear to what extent the Hampton Court Conference in January contributed to Scottish ecclesiastical opposition but the Scots certainly knew of its proceedings. The king's resounding condemnation of presbytery and his insistence on

---

[4] Aberdeen Presbytery, fo. 106r; Deer Presbytery, i, fos 12–13r.

conformity to an episcopalian polity, a preference already shown in his *Basilikon Doron*, must have made many ministers fear a royal push towards conformity on the English model.[5] In March, the presbytery of St Andrews, whose opposition to the new episcopacy was well known already, began to act against it. Some ministers protested that George Gledstanes, minister of St Andrews and Bishop of Caithness since 1600, had been 'adwancit to honour to sit in counsaill Parliament and chekker'. On 12 April, the presbytery introduced a new system of fines for absence from its meetings. The fine was to be double for those whose residence was in St Andrews itself, a thinly veiled attempt to get at their minister-bishop who was often absent on crown business.[6]

Added to the unease which news from Hampton Court must have caused, came the prospect of an incorporating union with England. Parliament was to discuss the matter and the synods, meeting in the spring, sent delegates to the commissioners of the General Assembly requesting an Assembly before Parliament. This concerted appeal may reflect a widespread fear of conformity with England for, with the exception of the synod of Fife, this was the first sign for many years of misgivings from synods about the ecclesiastical policy of the crown.[7] The commissioners of the General Assembly refused their call, while David Lindsay, Bishop of Ross, and Patrick Galloway, one of the king's ministers, came from the king to reassure them that an Assembly was unnecessary since Parliament would only choose commissioners to negotiate union. They were also assured that the Kirk would remain unaffected by whatever form of union resulted.[8] Yet a matter of principle was at stake; the synods' delegates wanted an Assembly so that it could advise the Kirk's parliamentary representatives as to how they should vote, according to the 'caveats' drawn up in 1599 and approved in 1600. The first 'caveat' stipulated that the parliamentary representatives 'should not propone to council, convention, or parliament, in name of the Church, any thing without express warrant from the Church ... under pain of deposition'.[9] This was unambiguous and the fact that the Parliament would not discuss matters directly affecting the Kirk made no difference to the fact that the new bishops, who sat in Parliament 'in name of the Church' should not have been able to do anything

---

[5] K. Fincham and P. Lake, 'The Ecclesiastical Policies of James I and Charles I', in K. Fincham, ed., *The Early Stuart Church, 1603–1642* (London, 1993), 23–51; F. Shriver, 'Hampton Court Revisited: James I and the Puritans', *Journal of Ecclesiastical History*, 33 (1982), 48–71.

[6] St Andrews Presbytery, fos 123–4.

[7] Calderwood, *History*, vi, 257–61; Melville, *Diary*, 555.

[8] Melville, *Diary*, 555–7.

[9] Spottiswoode, *History*, iii, 74.

in Parliament without the explicit warrant of the Assembly. This, indeed, is not an impossible proposition. General assemblies had commonly met before and during parliaments and the royal burghs' convention normally met simultaneously with parliaments and drew up a 'party line' for its representatives.[10]

That this lobbying of the commissioners of the General Assembly resulted from fear of the consequences of union is reflected in the fact that the commissioners of synods drew up instructions for the Kirk's parliamentary representatives. They approved the general idea of union as good for religion and the common weal but insisted that all acts of Parliament and General Assembly which favoured the Kirk should be safeguarded and that no ecclesiastical innovations should result. A tract, written later in the year by a layman, approved the union and reflected this anxiety. Its author was clear that he felt that there was 'na reformit kirk in Europe [which] injoyis the puritie of the evangell in greater sinceritie than Scotland'. Obviously fearing a greater risk to the Kirk in Scotland, he nevertheless balanced his conclusion by warning that if the 'religioun of ather of the saidis natiounis sal be imparit' then those opposed to union 'wil be furnist with ane michtie and forceable argument'. The ministers also insisted that the bishops' 'caveats' should be observed.[11] Denied a General Assembly before Parliament met, the Kirk, in the form of representatives of the synods, was demonstrating a profound lack of faith, both in the commissioners of the General Assembly and in the king's reassurances. They were also striving to ensure that agreed constitutional arrangements were maintained, in the face of pressure from the crown for change.

The General Assembly was to meet in July but, because of delays to the holding of Parliament which eventually convened in that month, it was prorogued by Parliament, on royal instructions, until union was concluded, or at least until July 1605.[12] It is easy to imagine the panic this may have caused in a Kirk already concerned about union with a country whose church many saw as too close to Catholicism for comfort. They were to have no say in union negotiations involving those who supposedly represented them in Parliament and their national assembly had been indefinitely postponed. The episcopal 'caveats' had

---

[10] *The Records of the Convention of the Royal Burghs of Scotland*, ed. J.D. Marwick, 7 vols (Edinburgh, 1866–1918), e.g. vol. 1597–1614, 21–2.

[11] J. Russel, 'A Treatise of the happie and blissed unioun', in B. Galloway and B.P. Levack, eds, *The Jacobean Union: Six Tracts of 1604* (Scottish History Society, 1985), 75–142, at 89; Melville, *Diary*, 557; see also, B.P. Levack, *The Formation of the British State: England, Scotland and the Union, 1603–1707* (Oxford, 1987), ch. 4, esp. 105, 109, 117–18.

[12] Calderwood, *History*, vi, 268; Melville, *Diary*, 560–61; Forbes, *Records*, 376–7.

been breached, so what faith could they have in royal reassurances on other matters?

In July, the presbytery of St Andrews chose to keep the original date set in November 1602, in spite of the prorogation.[13] Perhaps surprisingly, given the events of the spring, St Andrews was the only presbytery to do this, yet their action led to an upsurge in opposition to the crown. The three commissioners from St Andrews went to Aberdeen and formally constituted themselves as a General Assembly, asserting the liberties of the Kirk and taking legal instruments to record that they had done so.[14] The first meeting of the presbytery after their return took place on 9 August when their protest was registered in the presbytery book.[15] As a consequence of this gesture, the 'guid breithreine of the north', shamed into action by the arrival of the ministers from St Andrews, called on the synod of Aberdeen to write to all synods, asking them to send delegates to meet with the synod of Fife in September to discuss further action. An organised national campaign of resistance had begun in the North East.[16]

At its next meeting, the synod of Lothian and Tweeddale accused the two bishops whose parishes lay in its bounds, John Spottiswoode, Archbishop of Glasgow, and James Law, Bishop of Orkney, of attempting to overthrow the Kirk, presumably because they were involved with the government and its plans for union and because they had ignored the 'caveats'.[17] In this atmosphere of heightening tension, the synod of Fife met in September, along with delegates from other provinces. The laird of Lauriston arrived with letters of discharge, fearing they would declare their meeting a General Assembly but they did not, so he approved it. The ministers gathered there agreed that it was acceptable to hold a General Assembly without royal consent, arguing that, just as barons, nobles and burghs could hold their own courts without royal permission, so could the Kirk. Lauriston, desperate to avoid further confrontation, acknowledged the logic of this but urged them to await the king's licence to hold an Assembly because, if they failed to do so, James would discharge an unofficial one. He suggested that they should adjourn and meet again with the commissioners of the General Assembly at Perth in October.[18]

---

[13] St Andrews Presbytery, fo. 126v.

[14] *BUK*, iii, 1009; Melville, *Diary*, 561–3; Calderwood, *History*, vi, 265.

[15] St Andrews Presbytery, fo. 127r; Melville, *Diary*, 564.

[16] Melville, *Diary*, 565; Calderwood, *History*, vi, 268; this and subsequent defiant actions by ministers from the North East are not mentioned in Donaldson's 'Scotland's Conservative North', presumably because they seriously undermine its thesis.

[17] Calderwood, *History*, vi, 268; 'Ryseing and Usurpation', 16.

[18] Melville, *Diary*, 565–6; Calderwood, *History*, vi, 270.

In response to this explosion of dissent, the king formally declared his religious sincerity, emphasised that he had done nothing without the consent of a General Assembly and expressed anger at 'certane turbulent and unquiet spreitis amangis the ministerie' who met without royal permission on any pretext which suited them.[19] He also ordered that James and Andrew Melville and a number of others involved in the meeting should be warded. The Privy Council, perhaps under the moderating influence of the Earl of Dunfermline and probably aware of the true extent of the opposition, refused to carry out the order.[20] All decisions had been remitted to the convention at Perth and the Council may have felt that to act before it had deliberated could be counterproductive. It was clear that opposition was growing and it was equally clear that James was increasingly out of touch with the sentiments of the ministry. For this protest movement to have been instigated by ministers from the North East, hardly an area notorious for subversion, and for it to have involved delegates from all the synods, more than just a few 'turbulent and unquiet spreitis' must have been unhappy.[21]

In October, the principal demand of the ministers was that a General Assembly should be allowed to meet. They also complained that freedom of speech was being restricted, that the government of the Kirk was now in the hands of the commissioners of the General Assembly who had taken on the power of the Assembly and that the bishops voted in Parliament without direction from the Kirk. The commissioners replied that they held office from one General Assembly until the next, at which they would give an account of their proceedings. Posing as victims of circumstance, they claimed that the situation was not of their making 'for thai wer wearie of the office … [but] the king would acknowledge no uther to deall with him bot them, and that we would find iff we attemptit any thing without them'. The commissioners claimed to be as harsh censurers of the bishops as any of the delegates from synods, while the bishops (all incidentally commissioners) bizarrely affirmed their enthusiasm for the 'caveats', in spite of having broken them already. One bishop even declared 'I wold he were hanged above all theives that presseth not to the uttermost to see the Cautions keept'.[22]

---

[19] *RPC*, vii, 13.

[20] Calderwood, *History*, vi 271; M. Lee, 'King James's Popish Chancellor', in eds, I.B. Cowan and D. Shaw, *The Renaissance and Reformation in Scotland* (Edinburgh, 1983), 170–82; M. Lee, *Government by Pen: Scotland under James VI and I* (Urbana, 1980), 33.

[21] Lee, *Government by Pen*, 32–3 where the author failed to realise that it was not just the unspecified 'Melvilleans' who opposed the drift of royal policy.

[22] Calderwood, *History*, vi, 271–2; Melville, *Diary*, 566–8; Scot, *Apologetical Narration*, 130.

The problem was that the complaints arose because it was nearly two years since the last Assembly had met and another was not planned for a further year. The system which had been established to review the conduct of the bishops and the commissioners required annual assemblies and was thus failing to function.

Eventually, the commissioners agreed to pass four requests to the king. Firstly, the ministers asked that an assembly might be allowed without offending James. They reiterated the old request for financial help for the Kirk and they asked that order would be taken with Catholics since, far from receiving secular support in its fight against Catholicism, the government continually thwarted its efforts in this respect. Their final request was injudicious since it amounted to meddling in the affairs of James's other kingdom. The deadline for the English clergy to subscribe to the articles agreed to at Hampton Court in January was approaching, so it was requested that 'the godlie and ffaithfull britherine' in England who were 'vexit with the bischoppis' might get latitude from James and that those already deprived might be restored.[23] The threat to English Puritans was increased because Richard Bancroft, whose views on presbyterianism in general and on the Kirk in particular were made clear in 1589, had just been made Archbishop of Canterbury. This would have done nothing to calm the nerves of those ministers who feared a royal desire to see presbyteries wither and bishops reign supreme. No royal reaction is apparent but it could not have been favourable. In December, John Spottiswoode, Archbishop of Glasgow, carried a petition to the king from the synod of Lothian, again requesting permission for an Assembly to meet. Their request was refused.[24]

In spite of royal pressure, pursuit of Huntly by the presbyteries of the North East continued into 1605. In September 1604, the king had ordered the Privy Council to forbid the presbytery of Aberdeen from further proceedings against him and, at the end of that year, Huntly wrote to the king, thanking him for this. As well as providing the dubious information that, if a General Assembly met, it would provide a forum for opposition to James's beloved union, he provocatively wrote: 'I finde the ministrie heir the mair malicious aganis me, the mair

---

[23] Melville, *Diary*, 568–9; Collinson, *Elizabethan Puritan Movement*, pt 8, ch. 5; Fincham and Lake, 'The Ecclesiastical Policies of James I and Charles I', 26.

[24] Calderwood, *History*, viii, 55. In 1589, Bancroft delivered a sermon which was highly critical of presbyterianism and of James VI's toleration of it. See W.D. Cargill Thomson, 'A Reconsideration of Richard Bancroft's Paul's Cross Sermon', *Journal of Ecclesiastical History*, 20 (1969), 233–66; G. Donaldson, 'The Attitude of Whitgift and Bancroft to the Scottish Church', *Transactions of the Royal Historical Society*, 4th series, 24 (1942), 95–115.

your most michtie majestie wreittis in my favours, for they have presentlie summonit me to Aberdein to the second day of Januar.'[25] The resolve of the ministers of the North East was illustrated on 11 January, when the presbytery of Aberdeen sent Bishop Blackburn, along with representatives of other presbyteries, to the Privy Council to counter Huntly's requests to the king for immunity from the censures of the Kirk. At the same meeting, it was reported that commissioners from the synod of Aberdeen, on visiting Huntly to request his subscription of the Confession of Faith, received only a charge from the Privy Council suspending all censures of the Kirk against him. The outrage of the presbytery is striking. It declared that:

> thair wes nevir sic ane chairge direct be his hienes auctoritie against the Kirk sen the first reformatioun of religioune within this realme ... inrespect that the said chairge wes not only uncouthe but appointit to be a begyning off ane ... triell quhairwith God is to temp his Kirk for probation off the faith off his elect and chosyn chyldrene that they quha persevaris unto the end may be saif.[26]

The presbytery was divided as to how to proceed but its anger at its treatment by the civil authority is clear and the council continued to prevent it from acting against Huntly.[27]

By the time the presbytery of Deer was again discharged from further action against Huntly, it had reached the final stage in the process of excommunication. The case was passed to the synod of Aberdeen for, in May, both the presbyteries of Deer and Ellon recorded an order that each was to provide £6 to pay the expenses of commissioners from the synod 'direct to the coonsall'.[28] Although on the verge of losing patience with Huntly, the events of the previous 12 months had been enough to turn the presbyteries of the North East against the king.[29] The frustration, resulting from being thwarted by the crown, may have been a major factor in the involvement of so many ministers from that region in the illegal General Assembly held at Aberdeen in July.

The events surrounding the Assembly of 1605 are difficult to clarify. During the spring, those in control of government in Scotland, began to have misgivings about the wisdom of allowing it to meet. In March, immediately after Robert Bruce had finally been deposed from the ministry and banished to Inverness by the commissioners of the General

---

[25] Huntly to James VI, 20 Nov. x 10 Dec. 1604, *Letters and State Papers*, no. xxxi.

[26] Aberdeen Presbytery, fos 155v, 157r.

[27] *RPC*, vii, 19, 468; Privy Council to James VI, 1 Feb. 1605, *Letters and State Papers*, no. xxxiii.

[28] Deer Presbytery, i, fos 47v, 55r; Ellon Presbytery, i, fo. 127v.

[29] *RPC*, vii, 37, 468.

Assembly, Archbishop Spottiswoode wrote to the king. He lamented that there were daily invectives against the bishops from the pulpits of Edinburgh and urged the king to command the commissioners of the General Assembly to nip the trouble in the bud before it got out of hand.[30] By May, the unrest which had been noted in March had not abated and Lauriston wrote to James. The tone of panic is clear. He reported that the synod of Fife, which he had warned against holding it, planned to ensure that the General Assembly at Aberdeen in July went ahead, 'for preventing of quhilk attempt, the commissioners and I haif declarit your Majesties plesour heirin, and haif requyrit, yea commandit, tham and al other sinods in North Britane to forbeir ony sik meiting'. In spite of this, he feared that a meeting would go ahead. Spottiswoode recorded that the Assembly was to be cancelled because 'they intended to call in question all the conclusions taken in former assemblies for the episcopal government'.[31]

Meanwhile, 'the ministrie of the North, finding themselffes depryved of their expected comfort of the Generall Assemblie, and greatlie impedit ... in ther own lawfull proceidings ... against the Marques of Huntly', sent John Forbes, minister of Alford, to the king to complain of these things which they were sure could not have been devised by him. In response to the ban on the presbytery of Aberdeen proceeding against Huntly, the synods of Moray and Aberdeen demanded the right to act. Opposition was mounting and central control was increasing. All synods and presbyteries were forbidden to excommunicate any noble without the permission of the commissioners of the General Assembly who had, by this time, obtained the status of an ecclesiastical privy council, which was further enhanced with the declaration that there was to be no appeal from them to the General Assembly. James could normally govern with his council, calling Parliament only if absolutely necessary for taxation or the enactment of some particularly important legislation; his government of the Kirk was beginning to conform to that pattern.[32]

---

[30] PRO, 'Proceedings of the commissioners of the general assembly, 1 March 1605', State Papers Domestic James I, SP14/13 no. 1. This is a much fuller version than that in *Calendar of State Papers Domestic Series, James I, 1603–1610*, ed. M.A.E. Green (London, 1857), 200; Lauriston to James VI, 4 March 1605 and Archbishop of Glasgow to James VI, 22 March 1605, *Ecclesiastical Letters*, i, nos viii and ix.

[31] Lauriston to James VI, 2 May 1605, *Ecclesiastical Letters*, i, no. x; Spottiswoode, *History*, iii, 157; Forbes, *Records*, 380–81.

[32] Synods of Aberdeen and Moray to James VI, 20 Feb. 1605, *Miscellany of the Spalding Club*, 5 vols (Spalding Club, 1844–52), ii, 'Extracts from the Manuscript Collections of the Rev. Robert Wodrow, 1605–1697', no. i; *RPC*, vii, 19; Melville, *Diary*, 627; Calderwood, *History*, vi, 391–2.

John Forbes, to the relief of many, returned with good news. The king pledged to make no innovations in the Kirk and to support all actions against disobedient nobles, and Forbes undertook that all things would be done 'in quyetnes and peace'. Thus 'the Kirk assuredly hoped to have found no impediment to their nixt Assemblie, the 2d of Julii, at Aberdein'.[33] It was not to be. In June, letters were sent to the presbyteries intimating the prorogation of the Assembly, although it was alleged that some letters gave 2 July as the date which was discharged while others banned a meeting on 5 July.[34] There is evidence for the receipt of this letter only in the records of the presbytery of Haddington. It was subscribed by the laird of Lauriston and Patrick Galloway, moderator of the last Assembly in November 1602 and was registered on 19 June. Ignoring the letter and in defiance of the crown, the presbytery appointed a commissioner to attend the assembly.[35] The presbytery of Deer sent commissioners and has no record of the letter of discharge, while the other five presbyteries whose records are extant for this period recorded neither the appointment of commissioners nor the receipt of the king's letter.[36] At the time of the letters of discharge being sent out, Forbes was in Edinburgh. He immediately went to the Lord Chancellor, Alexander Seton, Earl of Dunfermline, from whom he received a promise that, as long as those who gathered for the Assembly confined themselves to constituting the Assembly, appointing a new date and dissolving, he would stay the discharge.[37] Those who met may well have thought that they did so legally.

Twenty-seven ministers from 14 presbyteries as far apart as Kirkcudbright and Ross arrived in Aberdeen to keep the Assembly, turning up either on 2 July or two or three days later.[38] The majority appeared on the former date, set in 1604, to find that the laird of Lauriston was there too. In his apparently acquiescent presence, the

---

[33] Forbes, *Records*, 381–3.

[34] *BUK*, iii, 1013; Scot, *Apologetical Narration*, 132; Forbes, *Records*, 377n, 385; Melville, *Diary*, 570–71, 574.

[35] Haddington Presbytery, ii, fo. 122. The presbytery of Haddington dated the letter 7 July, in error or to mislead posterity by making it look as if they received the letter after the assembly had met.

[36] Deer Presbytery, i, fo. 55(a)r; see Ellon Presbytery, Aberdeen Presbytery, Glasgow Presbytery, Paisley Presbytery, Stirling Presbytery.

[37] Forbes, *Records*, 385–6. Alexander Seton, Earl of Dunfermline, had been one of the Octavians. As a Catholic, he realised the vulnerability of his position, so he tried to be as even-handed as possible with the Kirk.

[38] A.R. MacDonald, 'Ecclesiastical Politics in Scotland, 1586–1610' (unpublished Edinburgh PhD dissertation, 1995), Appendix 1(b), 332; Lee, *Government by Pen*, 49 states that 'a very small number' attended without realising the number of presbyteries which sent them.

ministers heard a sermon and elected a moderator. Then Lauriston read out a letter from the Privy Council discharging the Assembly and ordering them not to appoint a new date without royal permission. The Assembly was duly dissolved but, in defiance of the charge, a new date in September was chosen, the ministers not wishing to see the Assembly prorogued *sine die*. Only then did Lauriston 'suddenly wake up to what he had done'.[39] Realising his mistake at having allowed them to meet at all, he declared that their proceedings had been unlawful and had been done without his approval. According to Forbes, Lauriston then ordered a messenger to proclaim a royal command that the ministers might not meet and that the provost and bailies of Aberdeen should do all in their power to prevent any meeting from proceeding. In an attempt to cover his tracks, Lauriston subsequently claimed that he had made this proclamation at the mercat cross of Aberdeen the day before the Assembly met.[40]

John Welsh, minister of Ayr, was the first to reach Edinburgh, ahead of Lauriston. He informed Chancellor Dunfermline of the events at Aberdeen, who approved what the ministers had done. It was Lauriston's version of events, however, which was the first to reach the king.[41] Although James would have been angered by what really happened, he was led to believe that the ministers had defied a public discharge. The severity of the resulting persecution may thus have been the result of Lauriston's successful attempt to make it appear as if he had not sanctioned the meeting in the first place. Maurice Lee's assertion that 'it was not possible to mislead him [James] for very long' is certainly not accurate in this case. It was perfectly possible to mislead him if he was inclined to believe an inaccurate account of events.[42] Contrary to recent opinions on the episode, Dunfermline did appreciate the broader ecclesiastical situation and kept an eye on the sentiments in the Kirk. Far from having a 'lack of confidence in dealing with presbyterian dissent', he was the only major figure in government to notice the growing tide of opposition within the Kirk. Had he been allowed to pursue the

---

[39] Lee, *Government by Pen*, 49.

[40] Forbes, *Records*, 387–94; Melville, *Diary*, 573; Calderwood, *History*, vi, 284; Spottiswoode, *History*, iii, 158–9; *BUK*, iii, 1014–15; *RPC*, vii, 471.

[41] Forbes, *Records*, 401–2; *BUK*, iii, 1018; *RPC*, vii, 189–202 (published under the snappy title *A Declaration of the Just Causes of his Majesties proceiding against those ministers who are now lying in prison attainted of high treason*, (Edinburgh, 1605) [in SRO, P33/33/14]. This episode bears out Lee's thesis on 'government by pen' where he suggests that it was as much controlled by what those in power told the king as it was by James himself: M. Lee, 'James VI's Government of Scotland after 1603', *SHR*, 55 (1976), 41–54, esp. 53 and *Government by Pen*.

[42] M. Lee, 'James VI's Government of Scotland after 1603', 44.

moderate policy which he wanted, the difficulties which the crown was later to face might never have arisen.[43] Dunfermline maintained a Scottish perspective on how the crown should treat the Kirk, whereas his sovereign took an increasingly British view in which the internal politics of Scotland could not take priority. The king's desire for the advancement of episcopacy, the advancement of Anglo-Scottish ecclesiastical conformity, meant that the situation in which James left the Kirk in 1603 could not be maintained and that any attempts to preserve it would have to be resisted.

The government acted swiftly. On 9 July, the Privy Council denounced the ministers who had held the Assembly and, ten days later, the king wrote to Secretary Balmerino. He declared that the meeting at Aberdeen savoured of 'nothing els bot … seditioun and plane contempt of us and our authoritie'. He called it an 'oppin breache and violatioun of the lawis and statutis of this realme' and demanded that those involved should be tried because 'thay committed ane manifest contempt and disobeydyance' by acting with the full power of an Assembly. The Privy Council promised to oblige.[44] The commission of the General Assembly, not to be outdone, declared the unofficial Assembly in Aberdeen to have been illegal and, anticipating a wave of support for those who had met there, ordered all kirk sessions, presbyteries and synods to refrain from justifying it.[45] It is tempting to infer from the commissioners' enthusiasm for the indefinite prorogation of general assemblies that they were keen to remain in office, accountable to none but the king. The increasing clerical opposition to the crown's ecclesiastical policy after the Assembly at Aberdeen would have made them no more inclined to change their minds. Indeed, certain ministers asserted that general assemblies were not being held precisely because the bishops did not want to be judged according to the 'caveats' and because the commissioners feared censure.[46]

In the aftermath of the Aberdeen Assembly, the synod of Fife took the lead in asserting the freedom of the Kirk. At an extraordinary meeting in August, it declared that the holding of general assemblies was necessary to ensure the Kirk's liberty because it was the only way of dealing with Catholicism and differences of opinion which, it admitted, existed among the ministry. It asserted the legality of the Assembly and,

---

[43] Lee, 'King James's Popish Chancellor', 170–83; K.M. Brown, *Kingdom or Province? Scotland and the Regal Union, 1603–1707* (London, 1992), 90.

[44] *RPC*, vii, 101, 474.

[45] *BUK*, iii, 1018–19.

[46] Melville, *Diary*, 590–91, which is part of a contemporary declaration by 'The Britherin'.

consequently the prorogation of it to the last Thursday of September. It agreed, however, not to keep that meeting in deference to the king's command and a further prorogation of the Assembly until May 1606 was proposed for which the king would be petitioned. This was to be circulated to the other synods for their approval and a national fast was declared for 15 and 22 September.[47] At the beginning of September, all the presbyteries in the synod of Aberdeen agreed to the new prorogation, the presbytery of Ellon doing so 'provyding the brethren presentlie in ward in Blaknes consent'. A number of those who had attended the Assembly were already imprisoned in Blackness Castle on the Firth of Forth. It was also decided to send a supplication to the king to seek consent for the new date, so the presbytery offered to pay the expenses of the bearers along with the other presbyteries of the synod. The presbyteries of Deer and Aberdeen suspended all meetings while some of their number were summoned before the Privy Council.[48] The government, in thwarting their action against Catholics and in reacting so harshly to the Assembly, had ill-judged its actions and created stout resistance in an area which was normally acquiescent. The Earl of Dunfermline, far from lacking confidence with presbyterian dissent or having overestimated the potential clerical backlash, was the only man in government aware of the extent of opposition. His desire to compromise was not what the king wanted and his loss of influence in government to the Earl of Dunbar, sent north at this time to sort things out, can be attributed to this episode.[49]

In November, the presbytery of Aberdeen wrote to the presbytery of Ellon, 'Schawing that thai haid spokin with sum brethren of everie presbiterie within the diocie of Abirdene, And haid thocht it meit that everie presbyterie … suld collect xl merkis [£26 13s. 4d.] for releiff off the brethren in waird.'[50] Expressions of solidarity with the warded ministers came from other areas. The presbytery of Haddington, having admonished its commissioner for failing to go to Aberdeen, received a messenger from Dalkeith who intimated to them all that had been done at Aberdeen by those who had made the effort. At the beginning of September, the presbyteries of Dunbar, Haddington and Dalkeith agreed

[47] Melville, *Diary*, 582–4.

[48] Ellon Presbytery, i, fos 134r, 136v; Deer Presbytery, i, fo. 62r; Aberdeen Presbytery, fo. 167v.

[49] Lee, 'King James's Popish Chancellor', 177–8; Lee, *Government by Pen*, 56; Brown, *Kingdom or Province?*, 90. Dunbar, formerly Sir George Home of Spott, led the opposition to the Octavians (one of whom was Alexander Seton, later Earl of Dunfermline). He became Lord Treasurer in 1601, went south with James in 1603 becoming Chancellor of the Exchequer in England until 1606. He was made earl in 1605.

[50] Ellon Presbytery, i, fo. 136v.

to the national fast. Haddington also endorsed Fife's prorogation of the Assembly and offered to help to pay for a supplication to the king for his approval, adding:

> that seeing we understand his majestie hes bein abusit in respect no sut hath bene delyverit (as ane letter direct from his Majestie bearis) craving ane generall assembly, quhairas the Sinod of Lawthiane and Tweddell convenit at Tranent direct ane letter to his Majestie craving maist humblie ane generall assemblie and send to his Majestie be Mr John Spottiswood.[51]

This presbytery was well aware of the difficulties involved in communicating with a distant monarch through unreliable channels – Spottiswoode was Archbishop of Glasgow and had no desire to carry the unwelcome requests of Scottish ministers to their king.

The records of the presbytery of St Andrews have a significant gap covering the summer of 1605. The presence of one corner of a page suggests that it has been torn out and thus the record of any letter of discharge of the assembly and of the appointment of commissioners are missing. When, why and by whom this was done cannot be known. In September, the text used for the exercise was temporarily changed from the Book of Revelation to the Letters of Timothy 'for learning the groundes of discipline' or polity. Soon after, a letter arrived from the Privy Council assuring them of the king's love for the Kirk and asking them not to be offended by the treatment of those in ward. It, somewhat disingenuously, blamed the persistence of Catholicism in Scotland on the Kirk because it had stirred up trouble, thus preventing decisive action from being taken. How its prevention of the north-eastern presbyteries' actions against Catholics could be squared with this was not explained. The presbytery's reply was intemperate to say the least, insisting that the warding of Protestant ministers gave succour to Catholics and that it would break the law rather than its principles. It also criticised the harsh treatment received by the warded ministers, pointing out that they had acted on commission by their presbyteries and not as individuals. This was to become a common argument employed in their defence and it was never addressed by the crown. In November, the presbytery of St Andrews commissioned three ministers to present a supplication to the Privy Council for the release of the warded ministers with whom they had been in frequent contact via David Rait, one of their number.[52] Not surprisingly, it was ignored.

West central Scotland conspicuously failed to support either the Assembly of 1605 or those prosecuted for attending it. The records of the

---

[51] Haddington Presbytery, ii, fos 124–7.
[52] St Andrews Presbytery, fos 135–7; Calderwood *History*, vi, 333–8.

presbyteries of Glasgow and Paisley do not even mention the Assembly. In spite of this, the presbytery of Paisley was a particular victim of the close attentions of the Privy Council in other matters. During 1605, there were three separate instances of processes by the presbytery of Paisley being suspended or discharged by the council. This compares with a total of three for all other presbyteries during that year.[53] The supremacy of the civil jurisdiction was exercised, it would appear, without regard for the sympathies of the presbytery concerned.

In spite of the synod of Fife's prorogation of the Assembly until May 1606, the Privy Council had tried to stave off a repeat of the events of July by proclaiming, on 12 September, that the Assembly should not be held according to the prorogation made at Aberdeen, to the last Tuesday in September. Crassly, none other than the Earl of Huntly was ordered to ensure that no such meeting would take place, a move which could not have been designed to pour oil on troubled waters. Two weeks later, in reaction to the wave of opposition from the presbyteries, the king appointed an Assembly to meet in July (without specifying the year), declared his religious sincerity and criticised those who disrupted the Kirk for making things easier for Catholics. He also declared that the final decision over the date and place of general assemblies lay with Parliament after a legal Assembly had provided suggestions.[54] There was no legal basis for this, it was not the position according to the 'Golden Act' of 1592, so it can only be seen as an exercise of the royal prerogative.

The dramatic events which occurred at the Palace of Westminster on 5 November, gave many in Scotland great hopes that, at last, James would realise that the real threat to his crown came from Catholics and that, accordingly, he would take a more tolerant view of the activities of presbyterian ministers in Scotland and of their Puritan brethren in England. It was not to be. James VI and I was not concerned with belief, only with obedience. Whatever the opinion of a subject, if they disobeyed the king or tried to subvert his government or threaten his person, they were an enemy. Equally, whatever their opinions, if they were prepared to accept his rule without murmur, then they were the ideal subject. James even regarded the presbyterians as more of a threat than the Catholics because, although the latter sought his life, the former sought to deprive him of his crown by claiming to limit his authority.[55]

---

[53] Glasgow and Paisley Presbyteries, 1605, *passim*; RPC, vii, 52, 60, 66, 119, 130, 157.

[54] RPC, vii, 123; Calderwood, *History*, vi, 333–4, 339–40; Spottiswoode, *History*, iii, 160; Melville, *Diary*, 613.

[55] Melville, *Diary*, 617; Calderwood, *History*, vi, 376.

The synod of Lothian and Tweeddale tried to curry favour with the king by expressing heartfelt thanks for his deliverance from the gunpowder plot, a ploy also used in the supplications of the imprisoned ministers. With its additional request for the release of the imprisoned ministers, the letter was doomed to failure.[56] In January 1606, the trial of those who had attended the Aberdeen Assembly of 1605 took place at Linlithgow. In the previous October, the warded ministers, already in gaol for about three months, had been brought before the Privy Council and given the opportunity to confess that the fault was theirs. On that occasion, 17 ministers appeared before the Council and ten 'declarit that they wer resolved and perswadit that the said pretendit assemblie was not ane lauchfull Generall Assemblie' and they were permitted to return home. The other seven 'declarit ... that the said pretendit assemblie wes a very lawfull General Assemblie' and were therefore warded in the castles of Stirling, Doune and Dumbarton. A further six, those whom the crown regarded as the ringleaders, remained in ward in the state prison of Blackness Castle.[57] Three weeks later, all 13 were brought before the council with one other, Robert Youngson, minister of Clatt, who renounced the declaration he had made at Perth three weeks previously acknowledging the unlawfulness of the Assembly. First they tried to decline the jurisdiction of the Council who, rather predictably, 'all in ane voce, fand thaimselfis judges competent'. The Assembly was again declared to have been illegal and the 14 ministers were deemed to deserve punishment 'in thair persons and guids', with the sentence being remitted to the king. The 13 were returned to their wards and Youngson was sent to Edinburgh Castle.[58]

On 10 January 1606, the six ministers in Blackness were to appear before an assize at Linlithgow. Over the few days before, they had contacted a number of advocates and, on 9 January, one came to them to persuade them to submit to the king's mercy but they would not. They were joined by a number of ministers from Fife and Lothian who had come to give them advice and moral support. On the day appointed for the trial, the ministers were taken from Blackness to Linlithgow where they found, contrary to one recent assertion, that another 40 had come to encourage them.[59] Three of the Lords of Session again tried

---

[56] Calderwood, *History*, vi, 268; SRO, 'The copie of ane supplicatione send to his Majestie', Morton Papers, GD150/1797/3.

[57] *RPC*, vii, 128–9.

[58] *RPC*, vii, 134–7.

[59] For detailed accounts of this trial see Forbes, *Records*, 451–96; R. Pitcairn, ed., *Criminal Trials in Scotland from 1488 to 1624*, 3 vols (Edinburgh 1833), ii, pt ii, 494–50; M. Lynch, 'Preaching to the Converted? Perspectives on the Scottish Reformation', in eds, A.A. MacDonald et al., *The Renaissance in Scotland: Studies in Literature, Religion,*

unsuccessfully to persuade them to drop their declinature. They were tried for treason before the Lord Justice Depute and a large number of Privy Councillors for flouting the charge not to meet at Aberdeen and for having rejected the authority of the Privy Council, in breach of the act of Parliament of May 1584, declaring that all estates were subject to the king, under the pain of treason.[60] At length, after much fruitless debate, the trial proceeded. The jury was packed with the 'kinred and freindschip' of the Earl of Dunbar, now in control of implementing crown policy, who had also made the desired verdict clear to the judges. The king's advocate admitted that, if the assize had not been packed, 'that haill purpose had failled'.[61] The jury retired and returned to announce that it had reached a guilty verdict. Sentence was deferred until the king's pleasure was known and the ministers were sent back to Blackness at nine in the evening having been brought out early that morning.

Thus, in spite of misgivings on the part of the Bishop of Ross and the Earl of Dunfermline and the Archbishop of Glasgow's fears that harsh treatment of them could make the king's 'designe in the erecting of Bischops the more hatit', little lenience was shown, short of not hanging them.[62] That many of those convicted of treason or warded did not come from areas where opposition might have been expected is significant. Of the 15 ministers from the north of Scotland who attended the Assembly, only one had been to an Assembly before.[63] The Aberdeen Assembly had been quite unexpected both in its size and its consequences and the government's reaction to it was extreme. Since it had underestimated the depth of opposition, it was believed that harsh, exemplary punishment would be sufficient to remove the problem.

The level of discontent with the state, its failure to allow a General Assembly to meet and its lack of action against Catholics, was epitomised at the beginning of 1606 by David Lindsay, minister of St Andrews.

History and Culture Offered to John Durkan (Leiden, 1994) suggests that only 30 came to support them. The six ministers were: John Forbes (Alford); John Welsh (Ayr); Robert Durie (Anstruther); Andrew Duncan (Crail), Alexander Strachan (Creich); John Sharp (Kilmany).

[60] *APS*, iii, 292–3

[61] Sir Thomas Hamilton to James VI, 11 Jan. 1606, *State Papers and Miscellaneous Correspondence of Thomas, Earl of Melrose*, ed. J. Maidment, (Abbotsford Club, 1837), i, no. xi.

[62] PRO, Dunfermline to Lord Salisbury, 8 Jan. and same to same, 21 Jan. 1606, SP14/18 nos 8 and 31 (the latter shows that the verdict was guaranteed by packing and bribing the jury.); SRO, Balmerino to James VI, 19 Dec. 1606, Elphinstone Muniments, GD156/6/2/53, recounted the eventual departure of the six ministers; *RPC*, vii, 105, 260; Archbishop of Glasgow to James VI, 26 Dec. 1605, *Ecclesiastical Letters*, i, no. xv.

[63] MacDonald, 'Ecclesiastical Politics', Appendix i, (a) and (b).

He was the royal placeman, appointed in 1597 along with George Gledstanes to replace David Black and Robert Wallace and could be expected to have been obedient. In the winter of 1605–06, he began to criticise from his pulpit the crown's lack of effort against Catholics. His erstwhile parochial colleague, Archbishop Gledstanes, advised the king to move him to a less influential charge.[64]

King James's resolve to control the Kirk was stiffening. At the end of 1605, he had sent Patrick Galloway to Scotland to instruct the synods to meet in the following February and, in January 1606, he again commanded the synods of Aberdeen and Moray to stop acting against the Earl and Countess of Huntly. According to one source, he had decided to 'try the patience and constancy of the rest of the ministrie' – those who had not been at the Aberdeen Assembly. Galloway was to write to all the synods informing them of certain articles which the king wished them to discuss. The records of the presbytery of Haddington, where on 5 February the moderator of the last synod told them of the king's letter, show that Galloway did as he had been commanded.[65] Just over a week later, a royal proclamation was issued by the Privy Council, proclaiming supremacy of the king over all estates, citing the 'Black Acts' of 1584, reasserting the illegality of the 1605 Assembly and emphasising the danger of criticising the king.[66] The king's articles were remarkably radical and would have confirmed the fears of any that there was a drive towards Anglo-Scottish ecclesiastical conformity. He wanted nothing to be done to alter the acts of assemblies which he had attended; bishops were to have full jurisdiction over the ministry in their dioceses and were to be responsible to him alone; the commissioners of the General Assembly were to remain unchanged with no appeal from them to the General Assembly; and the king was to be acknowledged as the supreme head of the Kirk under Christ.[67]

James Melville, too ill to attend the synod of Fife, wrote to it from his sickbed. He expressed astonishment at what he called the 'plaine papistrie' of the articles and urged the synod to reject them and not to remit them to the General Assembly for, if it did, Parliament would simply enact them as law. None of the synods approved the royal articles but it is not clear how many rejected them outright and how many remitted them to a future General Assembly.[68] Many synods may

---

[64] NLS, Gledstanes to James VI, 9 Feb. 1606, Wodrow Folio, 42, no. 56.

[65] Patrick Galloway to James VI, 1 Jan. 1606, Ecclesiastical Letters, i, no. xvii; 'Ryseing and Usurpation', 18; Haddington Presbytery, ii, fo. 132r.

[66] RPC, vii, 179; Melville, Diary, 631–2; Calderwood, History, vi, 397–8.

[67] Melville, Diary, 627; Calderwood, History, vi, 391–2.

[68] Melville, Diary, 628–9; Calderwood, History, 396.

have felt that it was better to pass matters of such import to a General Assembly rather than challenge the king individually. Yet this scheme was not acceptable to the Kirk and James was angry.[69] The synod of Aberdeen was as concerned with its own problematic relations with the king as with his articles. It wrote to him in February, bemoaning the plague of Jesuits, the lack of support from the civil power against the Catholic nobility and, pointedly, its continued frustration at being forbidden to deal with Huntly and Errol.[70] The synod of Lothian complained to the Privy Council about a proclamation exhorting people to haul seditious ministers from their pulpits and bring them before the council. Presenting their protest in writing early in March, they were rebuffed with citations of the 'Black Acts' of 1584 and other acts of Parliament and Convention against seditious speeches.[71]

In May, the king called eight ministers to come to court in September. He wrote of his fear that the next Assembly might overturn things which had been recently established and of his concern about clerical opposition to his ecclesiastical policy. He wished to know what the problems were and how best they could be resolved. The letter implied that James wanted to see them before an Assembly met. This would have confirmed any fears which they may have had that the July in which it was to meet would not be in 1606.[72]

Plans for the restoration of a powerful episcopate were now firm. As a result of the appointments of John Spottiswoode to Glasgow, James Law to Orkney, Alexander Forbes to Caithness (Gledstanes was translated to St Andrews), Gavin Hamilton to Galloway, Andrew Knox to the Isles and Alexander Douglas to Moray, by the end of 1605, nine commissioners of the General Assembly were bishops.[73] If none but the bishops assembled, they could form a quorate meeting of the commission, acting with its full power with no appeal to the Assembly. As with those laymen he elevated to the higher nobility, King James rewarded those who had loyally served as commissioners of the Assembly by making them bishops. What better way of providing the episcopate with powers which did not require ratification by Parliament or General Assembly? Episcopacy with teeth was thus not reintroduced at a

---

[69] Melville, *Diary*, 635; James VI to William Scot, 21 May 1606, *Ecclesiastical Letters*, i, no. xxvi.

[70] Synod of Aberdeen to James VI, 20 Feb. 1606, *Ecclesiastical Letters*, i, no. xxvi.

[71] *RPC*, vii, 186.

[72] James VI to William Scot, 21 May 1606, *Ecclesiastical Letters*, i, no. xxxi. The eight were James Balfour, John Carmichael, Adam Colt, Andrew Melville, James Melville, William Scot, Robert Wallace and William Watson.

[73] MacDonald, 'Ecclesiastical Politics', Appendix 6, (a) and (b) which lists the commissioners of the General Assembly, indicating which were bishops; Watt, *Fasti, passim*.

stroke; it was drip-fed into the system via the commission of the General Assembly and ecclesiastical representation in Parliament. By the spring of 1607, 11 of Scotland's 13 bishops were commissioners and, of the exceptions, one, the Bishop of Argyll, was not even a cleric, having inherited the see from his father.[74] Bishops sat in Parliament and on the Privy Council, and royal articles to the synods had shown that James wished them to be his lieutenants in the Kirk. The synods had rejected this but, as James Melville had warned, what they remitted to the General Assembly was enacted by Parliament. It met at Perth in July 1606 and commissioners from 20 or more presbyteries converged on the town to lobby the legislature.[75] They presented petitions both from and in favour of the warded ministers and Robert Bruce, now in Inverness, to the commissioners of the General Assembly who flatly refused to pass their requests to Parliament. The delegates from the presbyteries then made a written protest against the 'Act anent the restitutioun of the estate of Bischoppis', stating that episcopacy was contrary to the 'Negative Confession' of 1581 because it had been abolished in that year by the Assembly. It asserted that the confession had also endorsed presbyterianism and, inaccurately, that the 'Golden Act' of 1592 had abolished the 'Black Acts' of 1584. The protest was subscribed by more than 43 ministers from at least 19 presbyteries concentrated around Perth but ranging from as far away as Wigtown in the South West, Jedburgh in the South East and Ellon in the North East.

The commissioners of the Assembly assured the ministers gathered in Perth that any alleged breaches of the episcopal 'caveats' and that a protest against the increase in episcopal power which this Parliament was to consider would be judged by the General Assembly, scheduled to meet in August after the Parliament. They refused to judge Archbishop Spottiswoode for his occupation of both a civil and ecclesiastical office – he sat on the Privy Council as well as representing the Kirk in Parliament. Their intransigence was largely caused by a letter from the king to Patrick Galloway, moderator of the commissioners, instructing him to ensure that nothing would happen which could interfere with the king's service or make his plans for the Parliament more difficult.[76]

---

[74] MacDonald, 'Ecclesiastical Politics', 127.

[75] Stirling Presbytery, iv, 25 June 1606; Aberdeen Presbytery, fo. 177v (which mentions the ministers from Ellon too); see also MacDonald, 'Ecclesiastical Politics', Appendix 7 listing those who signed the protest against episcopacy. The figure of 20 presbyteries was obtained from adding Aberdeen to the 19 from which identifiable ministers subscribing the protest came. Five names have not been linked to presbyteries because they are not in Scott, *Fasti*.

[76] Melville, *Diary*, 638–40; Calderwood, *History*, vi, 492, 539; Scot, *Apologetical Narration*, 158–9; SRO, James VI to Patrick Galloway, 4 June 1606, Rattray of

At this Parliament, the bishops received the return of the full patrimony of their dioceses; the 1587 'Act of Annexation' was thus repealed. The 'Act anent the restitutioun of the estate of Bischoppis' restricted itself to finance and the confirmation of the bishops as crown-appointed parliamentarians.[77] Their ecclesiastical role was left for the General Assembly to establish but, crucially, the 'caveats' were omitted from the legislation. The secular status of the ecclesiastical element of Parliament thus bore no relation to its spiritual status. If the Kirk deposed a bishop from his spiritual function as a minister, there was nothing it could do to prevent him from continuing to sit in Parliament as a bishop, since Parliament, in ignoring the 'caveats', had not recognised any ecclesiastical right in that sphere. This Parliament also drove the final nail into the coffin of the ostensible scheme, drawn up before the union, to restore all the prelacies to the Kirk by granting them to ministers. Every diocese now had a bishop for the first time since 1586 but no abbacies were held by the clergy. It is clear that the nobility simply would not have accepted 51 ecclesiastical parliamentarians, all of them royal appointees. This would have deprived many of monastic property and would have severely curtailed their influence in Parliament which rarely consisted of many more than 100 members. As it was, the nobility were not particularly happy about the institution of 13 new crown placemen in Parliament and it took 'continouall caire and exceiding paynis' on the part of the officers of state to get the act through.[78] To reassure the nobility and to persuade them into voting for the restoration of the episcopate, 17 of the abbacies which were in the hands of noble families were erected into temporal lordships and the possibility of their ever being given to ministers vanished. The ecclesiastical estate in Parliament was limited to 13 bishops, all of whom owed their positions to the king and would be used as a means to control an increasingly hostile Kirk. They also acted as a solidly loyal royalist group in parliaments and on the Privy Council in a parallel policy to James's enhancement of the role of the English episcopate in government.[79]

Craighall Rattray Muniments, RH4/126/2/2 (microfilm); Glasgow University Library, 'The protestation drawn up by Mr Patrick Simson minister at Stirline, offered to the estates convened in Parliament at Perth ... July 1606', MS Gen. 1216, Wodrow's Biographical Collections, Appendix vol.ii, no. 211; see also MacDonald, 'Ecclesiastical Politics', Appendix 7.

[77] APS, iv, 281.

[78] Privy Council to James VI, 4 July 1606, State Papers and Miscellaneous Correspondence, i, no. xiv.

[79] A. Foster, 'The Clerical Estate Revitalised', in ed., K. Fincham, The Early Stuart Church 1603–1642 (London, 1993), 139–160, at 142–3.

At the rising of the Parliament, the Assembly was prorogued for a further year, ostensibly so that matters in dispute could be resolved before it met. The eight ministers who had been called south would thus have left expecting to return in time to attend.[80] That they were prevented from doing so is testament to the fact that the Kirk had lost all confidence in the crown over the period since their king had left for England. The teething problems of remote government in a multiple-state monarchy had been painful, a fact which the only major work on the government of James VI does not really acknowledge.[81] Uncertainty and even diffidence reigned, with the government suffering a sudden loss of clerical confidence. In the years leading up to 1603, an increasingly confident government headed by a determined monarch had overcome the basic difficulties of church–state relations. After that, with power and responsibility dissipated, fear appears to have set in, a fear which would not allow general assemblies to meet or perfectly reasonable agreements which had been reached to be adhered to. There was confusion in government, with different messages reaching the king and conflicting advice being sent south.

Conflicting advice was not a novelty of the union of 1603 but its effects were entirely different. When the king had been in Scotland, he could evaluate in a much more informed manner the information and advice which he received. This was no longer possible and to describe James's government of the Kirk after 1603 as 'an able combination of tenacity and dexterity' is very wide of the mark.[82] Attempts to pursue different policies began to emerge at the centre. Chancellor Dunfermline's desire to steer a middle course with the Kirk failed and was instrumental in his temporary fall from grace, largely because of what the king felt about 'unquiet spreitis' among the ministry. James was disposed to believe what Lauriston told him and pursue a policy accordingly. In the matter of the ministers who were imprisoned for holding the Aberdeen Assembly, the commission of the General Assembly appears to have desired more lenience than the Privy Council, if the sentiments of the bishops of Ross and Glasgow discussed above are any guide to the former body's views. Again, the group taking a more narrow and negative view of the problem prevailed. The Privy Council saw those ministers as criminals and wanted to make an example and this was very much in tune with the king's views. The bishops and commissioners of the assembly were much more familiar with their clerical colleagues and, like Dunfermline, they took a broader view of

---

[80] Calderwood, *History*, vi, 592–3; *RPC*, vii, 219.
[81] Lee, *Government by Pen*, ch. 2.
[82] G. Donaldson, *Scotland: James V–James VII* (Edinburgh, 1971), 204.

the ecclesiastical situation. They feared the consequences of being too harsh but their pleas for moderation were ignored. In the second half of 1606, that governmental freefall came to an abrupt end.

CHAPTER SIX

The new autocracy, 1606–10

By the summer of 1606, James VI and all those advising him had realised that their ecclesiastical problems were worse than most of them had previously thought. The reaction to the 1605 Assembly, to the harsh treatment meted out to those who had attended it and to the enhancement of episcopal power beyond anything suggested before 1603 was now understood. Yet the king decided it was too late to retreat and, instead of trying to undo the problems which had caused dissent, he resolved to tighten the crown's grip on the Kirk, a grip which would go far beyond the transformation of the episcopate into an ecclesiastical privy council.

By the end of August, the clerics who had been called south were in London. Although superficially similar, this was not a Scottish version of the Hampton Court Conference of 1604.[1] There was no desire to investigate grievances or to negotiate; the king resolutely favoured one viewpoint and was not interested in what the ministers had to say. A brief and amicable introductory meeting took place on 20 September, the king allowing them all to kiss his hand and dismissing them 'with a very guid countenance'.[2] On the following day, a Sunday, they were subjected to a sermon in favour of episcopacy by the Bishop of Rochester, which James Melville condescendingly noted was delivered from a 'lytle buik, quhilk he had allwayis in his hand, for help of his memorie'. Meetings with the king began in earnest on 22 September with only Scots councillors present. King James asked the ministers how the Kirk could be set at peace and what they thought of the 1605 Assembly at Aberdeen. To ensure a united front, the eight appointed James Melville to speak for them and sought time to discuss their answers. The next day, they heard another sermon in the king's chapel, this time by a royal chaplain. It was based on Paul's letter to the Romans, chapter 13, verses 1–7, enjoining absolute obedience to the powers that be and, in his sermon, Dr Buckeridge equated the usurped power of the Pope with that of presbyteries. It was becoming clear that the whole exercise was conceived as a demonstration of royal

---

[1] K. Fincham and P. Lake, 'The Ecclesiastical Policy of James I', *Journal of British Studies*, 24 (1985), 170–88; F. Shriver, 'Hampton Court Revisited: James I and the Puritans', *Journal of Ecclesiastical History*, 33 (1982), 48–71.

[2] For detailed accounts of the meetings see: Melville, *Diary*, 653–78; Scot, *Apologetical Narration*, 167–78; Spottiswoode, *History*, 177–81.

power and of the king's resolution to make the Kirk conform more closely to its English counterpart. When they were admitted to his presence in the afternoon, they were not only greeted by familiar faces but also by the Archbishop of Canterbury, other English bishops and a number of prominent English noblemen.

The king began by asking the seven Scottish bishops, commissioners of the General Assembly and Lauriston for their opinion of the 1605 Assembly. To nobody's surprise, they condemned it. The ministers refused either to condemn or condone it, insisting that only a free General Assembly had the power to judge. Their natural frankness with the king greatly impressed the English audience 'quho wer not accustomit to heir the king so talkit to and ressounit with'. This meeting ended heatedly with Andrew Melville crossing the king. The ministers were charged not to return to Scotland or come near the court without special licence. When they were recalled, it was to hear another sermon, this time by the Bishop of Exeter, who declared that the power to convene and discharge assemblies lay exclusively with the king.

On Monday 28 September, after witnessing a service in honour of St Michael, they were called before the Scottish council. They were questioned separately but gave similar answers. On the Tuesday, they heard another sermon, by Dr King, another royal chaplain who railed against presbyteries, crying 'Doune! Doune with thame all!' The ministers were then kept waiting into November and, in the interim, lived together, kept a weekly exercise of doctrine and received like-minded English guests, or 'britherin of the best sort,' just as the 1584 exiles had done. On 13 November, they were each warded in the house of a different bishop and, at the end of the month, Andrew Melville was called before the English Privy Council for verses critical of the St Michael's service. He admitted they were his and did himself no favours by bursting out like 'inclossit fyre in watter', taking hold of Archbishop Bancroft's white sleeve, as he had done with his king in 1596, and declaring his vestments 'Romish ragis, and a pairt of the beastis mark'. Melville was warded in the Dean of St Paul's house and, in the following March, he was sent to the Tower. He was never to return to Scotland, eventually being allowed to live out his life in exile in France. His nephew James was confined to Newcastle and then Berwick, while the other six were allowed to return to Scotland but confined to their parishes.

Meanwhile, the six ministers convicted of treason for attending the Assembly in 1605 were banished. On 26 September, the king ordered their departure from his dominions, portraying this as a lenient commutation of the death sentence they deserved.[3] They were given a month to

---

[3] Forbes, *Records*, 556–8.

leave and were forbidden to return on pain of death. They embarked at Leith on 7 November while the other eight who had stood by the legality of the assembly were warded in various parts of the Highlands and Islands.[4] In the words of James Melville, 'The specialis of the ministrie being now exilit, wairdit, and confynit, they thought to mak ane essay of a General Assembly, quherby to proceid one step forward.'[5] Seeing them as some sort of ecclesiastical leadership without which there was no opposition to the crown, Maurice Lee has claimed that, 'With the removal of these men the heart went out of the clerical resistance' but this is not sustained by the evidence.[6] Perhaps James felt that, by the banishment, warding and imprisonment of over 20 ministers, he had removed the leadership of a movement, without which it would crumble. Some of those in ward, such as James Melville, Andrew Melville and William Scot, were the 'usual suspects', persistent troublemakers since 1596. Yet others had no history of opposition to the crown. Failure to allow assemblies to meet in 1604 or 1605 and the treatment of those who held one in defiance of the crown, combined with lack of support from the state for ecclesiastical action against Catholics had led to a growth in opposition. The crown's attempts to deal with this disquiet failed. If they had not, there would have been no need to pack the next national meeting of the Kirk.

In late November and early December 1606, royal letters were sent to the presbyteries naming ministers to meet at Linlithgow on 10 December.[7] Letters were received by the presbyteries of Aberdeen, Deer, Dunfermline, Ellon, Haddington and Jedburgh.[8] Not all presbyteries got the opportunity to send delegates. In 1607, the presbytery of Melrose protested that it had not heard of the Assembly, so had sent no commis-

---

[4] Scot, *Apologetical Narration*, 178; A.R. MacDonald, 'Ecclesiastical Politics in Scotland, 1586–1610' (unpublished Edinburgh PhD dissertation, 1995), Appendix 5.

[5] Melville, *Diary*, 683. 'They' were probably the king, the bishops, Dunbar and Lauriston.

[6] M. Lee, *Government by Pen: Scotland under James VI and I* (Urbana, 1980), 67. As on so many other occasions, this was not a coherent group. Previous historiography would have called them the 'Melvillians' but this suggests an organised, self-aware group stirring up opposition, without whom there would have been an acquiescent Kirk and that was not the case.

[7] Scot, *Apologetical Narration*, 177; Melville, *Diary*, 683; Calderwood, *History*, vi, 601–2.

[8] *BUK*, iii, 1020; Aberdeen Presbytery, fos 187v, 189v; Deer Presbytery, i, fo. 82v; Ellon Presbytery, i, fo. 139v; Glasgow Presbytery, i, fo. 137v; Haddington Presbytery, ii, fo. 144v; Jedburgh Presbytery, i, fo. 8r. The records of Glasgow are too damaged to tell if it received a letter – even under ultra-violet light. Although there is nothing specific in the records of Aberdeen and Deer, conflation of their records with Ellon shows that they met together to deal with the royal letters.

sioners to Linlithgow.[9] It is impossible to say how many presbyteries were left in ignorance but those who were not permitted to send commissioners were probably those in which the crown could not find obedient ministers. As far as the other groups attending were concerned, a similar process was used. One letter sent to a member of the landed classes survives but copies of the formula letters to Privy Councillors and barons are extant, as is a sederunt list of 33 nobles and barons who attended. The letter to Ogilvy of Inverquharity, dated at Whitehall on 1 November, announced that 'We have ... appointit ane meitting of sum of oure nobilitie and counsall with ane greit number of the mini[sterie] ... best affected to quyetnes and gude ordoure.' Although he was ordered to come 'all excuses set asyde', he failed to comply![10] The presbyteries were led to believe that the meeting would prepare the ground for a trouble-free General Assembly by resolving differences.[11] The only presbytery for which any suspicion was recorded is Haddington and, although it voiced misgivings about the meeting, it evidently believed that it was not to be a General Assembly since it told its commissioners to request that one be allowed to meet.[12] Like the assembly at Perth in February 1597, it was not called as a General Assembly and the next appointed date had not been publicly changed. Unlike the Perth Assembly, it was not even constituted as such.

Even with an entirely packed meeting, all did not go smoothly. Patrick Galloway, one of the king's own ministers and the moderator of the commissioners of the General Assembly, refused to make the opening exhortation. In the previous summer, he had warned that the 'caveats' must be kept while his fellow commissioners refused to judge any alleged breaches. He refused to take the moderator's chair for an opening exhortation because he had been moderator of the last General Assembly, in November 1602. It was normally the duty of the previous moderator to open proceedings with a sermon. To have done so might have provided grounds for declaring it, at a later date, to have been a General Assembly. He did, however, agree to chair the meeting.[13] The bishops, commissioners of the General Assembly and officers of state, unwilling to arouse any further suspicion, ensured that there was no examination and renewal of the commissions of the commissioners of

[9] Melrose Presbytery, fo. 2v.

[10] SRO, James VI to Ogilvy of Inverquharity, 1 Nov. 1606, Ogilvy of Inverquharity Papers, GD205/1/26; SRO, 'Copie to the presbiteries and uthers for sending and cumming to the generall assemble', CH8/57; BUK, iii, 1022.

[11] BUK, iii, 1020; Glasgow Presbytery, i, fo. 137v; Jedburgh Presbytery, i, fo. 8r; 'Ryseing and Usurpation', 20.

[12] Haddington Presbytery, ii, fo. 145r.

[13] BUK, iii, 979, 1023; Melville, Diary, 639, 683; Calderwood, History, vi, 605.

the Assembly. It seems that the crown had decided to see how amenable the hand-picked ministers were to the meeting being declared a General Assembly. When it became clear that they were not, no further action was taken for fear that it might jeopardise its success.

As on many previous occasions, financial promises were made by the crown and, in response to a request from some ministers, it was conceded that a General Assembly would meet in the following July. It was agreed that each presbytery should appoint an agent to monitor Catholicism and receive £100 per annum for this task. The king also asked them to endorse constant moderation of presbyteries as an interim measure to create stability within the Kirk and to help deal with Catholics, the ostensible reasons given for the gathering in the first place. Where a presbytery included a bishop's seat, the bishop was to be moderator. As with the bishops, certain 'caveats' were drawn up for the constant moderators. They were to be answerable to the synod in which the presbytery lay, that body having the power to depose them; presbyteries might appoint two commissioners to general assemblies in addition to their moderator; and the presbytery could reject the appointed moderator and choose another. It was agreed that the bishops, who had just surreptitiously obtained *ex officio* membership of general assemblies, were to be subject to their presbyteries for their ministry. For the sake of tidiness, the role of anti-Catholic agent and constant moderator were combined, elevating at a stroke constant moderators above their brethren in financial terms. Now that the state had rediscovered its enthusiasm against Catholicism, concrete means were provided for the Kirk to act. Proceedings closed with the reassurance that assemblies were to be allowed to elect their moderators and to meet as before, before *what* was not specified.[14]

Immediately afterwards, the king's commissioners wrote to James VI, calling the meeting a General Assembly.[15] Not once, in the letters of summons or during the meeting, had this been suggested, indeed, the letters explicitly stated that it would lay the ground for an Assembly. One person who would not have been surprised by this was King James. It had always been his intention to reinvent it as a General Assembly because useful precedents could be set. His right to nominate an Assembly's entire membership was established, as was his right to be the arbiter of what was an Assembly and what was not. The commissioners stated that, in spite of some opposition, the 'Assembly' had been successful, the ministry was satisfied with his good intentions and all

---

[14] *BUK*, iii, 1023–33.

[15] King's commissioners to the General Assembly to James VI, 16 Dec. 1606, *Letters and State Papers*, no. 1.

there had asked them to thank him. Once more, the narrow channels of communication are exposed. The heavy tone of reassurance and flattering exaggeration of goodwill towards James provided him with an inaccurate impression of the state of the Kirk and left him ill prepared for what was to come.

The king's secretary, Lord Balmerino, also wrote to him, praising the Earl of Dunbar for his 'wyis and secreit prosequuting' of what had been achieved and noting that 'his dexteritie in the leading of this turne has gone beyond all mennar of expectatioun'.[16] It was alleged elsewhere that this involved the distribution of 40 000 merks (£26 666 13s. 4d.), for it was 'notoriously understood and manifestly knowen, to the wysest, that the earle of Dunber ... distributed amongst the most needy and clamorous of the ministrey to obtaine their ... suffrages'.[17] The king and his advisers had felt it necessary to pack the 'Assembly', which was misled and possibly even bribed. Not only was it declared to have been a General Assembly after its dissolution but also its minutes were falsified. Spottiswoode and the official record suggest that constant moderators for synods were also agreed to but the furore over this issue which arose in 1607 indicates otherwise. William Scot alleged that 'two noblemen' were refused sight of the acts and a text of the act on synods was not produced until months later.[18] Many synods had opposed the crown over the previous few years. That might be eased by episcopal moderation. The falsified act stated that bishops were to moderate and, in their absence, the moderator should be elected from among the constant moderators of its presbyteries. The moderators of synods were to be subject to the General Assembly, of which they were to be members *ex officio*.

Dunbar and the bishops, expecting opposition, ensured that royal commissioners attended the synods in April.[19] The crown tried to avert

---

[16] SRO, Balmerino to James VI, 19 Dec. 1606, Elphinstone Muniments, GD156/6/2/54.

[17] Balfour, *Works*, ii, 17–18. It has proved impossible to verify or disprove this assertion because the MS Treasurer's Accounts are missing for this period: SRO, E21/78 covers the period Jan. 1604–Aug. 1605 and E21/79 covers from April 1610 to July 1611.

[18] Spottiswoode, *History*, ii, 183–5; *BUK*, iii, 1030; Calderwood, *History*, vi, 622–4; Melville, *Diary*, 685; Scot, *Apologetical Narration*, 184; G. Donaldson, *Scotland: James V–James VII* (Edinburgh, 1971), 205; D.G. Mullan, *Episcopacy in Scotland: the History of an Idea 1560–1638* (Edinburgh, 1986), 108; W.R. Foster, *The Church before the Covenants* (Edinburgh, 1975), 112. Not until eight months later was the 'act' produced. A detailed account of the reception given to constant moderators is provided here because previous works, operating on the assumption that there was little opposition in this period, have not explored the issue.

[19] *RPC*, vii, 343.

resistance before the synods met by prorogation and negotiation. Unlike the conferences on parliamentary representation, these talks were signally unsuccessful. The synod of Perth and Stirling met on 7 April, having been ordered by the king not to criticise the acts of Linlithgow. Criticise them it did not, nor did it obey them. The synod elected a moderator without the consent of the king's commissioner, Lord Scone, a beneficiary of the recent erections of temporal lordships from ecclesiastical lands.[20] He forced them to put the constant moderators of presbyteries on a leet for the election of a moderator but they protested that constant moderation of synods had not been agreed to. On the following day, he threatened to discharge the synod and brought in James Nicolson, Bishop of Dunkeld, to foster obedience. The synod voted to disregard the innovation, demanding freedom to act according to the acts of the General Assembly and Parliament. They requested sight of a copy of the act but were refused. Scone again threatened to discharge the synod which then claimed the authority of Christ, provoking Scone's intemperate response: 'Thair is no Jesus heir!' Chaos ensued. Henry Livingstone was elected moderator. Scone lunged into the moderator's chair to prevent him from taking office. He ordered his men to remove the moderator's desk and the stools. The synod met standing up. The bailies of Perth refused to eject the ministers who, after a recess, returned to find themselves locked out. Undaunted, they continued outside, drew up a supportive letter to the eight ministers warded in England, appointed three from each presbytery as commissioners to the General Assembly which was still scheduled to meet in July, and four to await on the Privy Council since Scone had threatened to charge them.

The government's response was swift. On 9 April, the Privy Council ordered the ministers of the synod to answer for obstructing Scone, for refusing to accept a constant moderator and for refusing to impose one on Auchterarder presbytery. Some ministers were summoned and the presbyteries of the synod were ordered to disregard its ordinances. The four ministers called before the council were put to the horn for failing to appear and one of them, William Row, went into hiding.[21] When the king heard of all this, he commanded the Privy Council to charge the synod to elect Alexander Lindsay, to imprison Henry Livingstone and William Row in Blackness Castle, and he ordered that the synod should be forbidden to meet until he was satisfied. On 11 June, Row and

[20] Calderwood, *History*, vi, 645–53; Spottiswoode, *History*, iii, 190; Melville, *Diary*, 701–5; Stirling Presbytery, iv, 8 April 1607; *RPC*, vii, 385; *Scots Peerage*, viii, 191–6.

[21] Melville, *Diary*, 701–5; Calderwood, *History*, vi, 645–53; *RPC*, vii, 347.

Livingstone were summoned and the synod did not meet again until August 1610, having failed to satisfy the king.[22]

Fearing the spread of opposition, on 23 April the Privy Council prorogued the synod of Fife until 2 June. The ministers met in the open air at Dysart, adjourning until 2 June and complaining to the Privy Council.[23] Further prorogations culminated with all synods being ordered to meet on 4 August to choose two of the 'most godlie, peiceable, wise, grave [and] of the best experience' to meet at Holyrood on 27 August with the commissioners of the Assembly and some Privy Councillors.[24] The synod of Fife met at the beginning of June, regardless, and three royal commissioners urged its acceptance of Gledstanes as constant moderator. It denied that there ever was an act for constant moderators of synods and the royal commissioners refused to produce a copy of it. They threatened horning if the synod did not adjourn and the synod threatened to excommunicate Gledstanes if it was horned! On 4 June, the Privy Council ordered them to accept Gledstanes.[25] On 23 July, the council charged all synods to accept constant moderators and, on 12 August, it forbade the synod of Perth and Stirling from meeting.[26] In August, the synod of Fife had the dubious honour of receiving four royal commissioners to impose Gledstanes as moderator. William Cranston, minister of Kettle, opening proceedings as the outgoing moderator, was commanded to silence but insisted that a greater lord than the king commanded him to speak. The archbishop and three of the royal commissioners left and, when it came to the examination of the presbytery of St Andrews, the synod censured Gledstanes for poor attendance at the weekly exercise. It then elected its own moderator and, after eight months' delay, the 'act' of Linlithgow was produced, only to be summarily rejected. The synod prorogued itself until 29 September but was forbidden to meet again without royal consent.[27] On 6 September, the king ordered the warding of four ministers for their behaviour at the synod.[28]

---

[22] *RPC*, vii, 521–3; Calderwood, *History*, vi, 666–7; Stirling Presbytery, iv, 15 July, 26 Aug. 1607, 6 April, 7 Sept. 1608, 12 April, 30 Aug. 1609, 25 April, 29 Aug. 1610.

[23] *RPC*, vii, 357; Melville, *Diary*, 714–15; Calderwood, *History*, vi, 653, 658.

[24] Melville, *Diary*, 713; Calderwood, *History*, viii, 295; *RPC*, vii, 412, 525; Haddington Presbytery, ii, fo. 150v; Privy Council to Cupar Presbytery, 21 May 1607, *Ecclesiastical Letters*, i, no. liv.

[25] *RPC*, vii, 380; Melville, *Diary*, 715–16; Calderwood, *History*, vi, 664–6.

[26] *RPC*, vii, 412, 416, 427.

[27] *RPC*, vii, 430, 440, xiv, 19; Archbishop of St Andrews to James VI, 8 Sept. 1607, *Ecclesiastical Letters*, i, no. lxvii; Melville, *Diary*, 716–20; Calderwood, *History*, vi, 666, 674–6.

[28] *RPC*, vii, 441, 539, viii, 26; Calderwood, *History*, vi, 678. The four were John Colden, William Cranston, John Dykes, John Scrimgeour.

The synod of Lothian and Tweeddale met on 18 August at Dalkeith. The outgoing moderator, in his opening address, criticised constant moderation. His sermon took as its text Genesis 42:21–4. Verse 21 reads: 'We are very guilty concerning our brother, in that we saw the anguish of his soul, when he besought us, and we would not hear; therefore is this distress come upon us,' a reproach to any ministers reluctant to defend the Kirk or support their warded brethren. In an attempt to buy time, constant moderation of synods was referred to the General Assembly.[29] Meeting again in October, the synod rejected constant moderation by 47 votes to 17. Because no bishop had his seat in the synod, they elected Patrick Galloway, the king's minister, in the hope that this would be seen as a compromise. It was rejected and the synod was adjourned *sine die* by Thomas Hamilton, the king's advocate, who ordered Galloway to demit only to be opposed by the outgoing moderator.[30]

On 24 July, the Earl of Abercorn, elevated to his earldom in 1606, attended the synod of Clydesdale as royal commissioner. On 18 August, he produced the fabricated act of Linlithgow and told the ministers to accept Archbishop Spottiswoode as moderator. Some asserted that only presbyteries were to have constant moderators but Abercorn forced the issue by asking any individual to gainsay constant moderation and refusing requests for postponement for further consideration. He declared that he had been commanded by the king to see the act obeyed or to denounce them as rebels. According to one source, he used 'menaces and threats' to ensure Spottiswoode's acceptance. The earl's own account, suggests that, to give this a veneer of compromise, he allowed a leet to be drawn up for the election of a moderator, as long as they elected Spottiswoode. All but two voted for the archbishop.[31]

In the South East, resistance was stronger. In April, the presbytery of Jedburgh nominated a minister to the leet for the moderator of the synod of the Merse and Teviotdale, in accordance with normal practice there, strengthening the assertion that constant moderation of synods had not been approved at Linlithgow.[32] In October, the synod refused to accept a constant moderator and discharged all constant moderators

---

[29] NLS, 'A Sermon at the synod of Lothian, Dalkeith', 18 Aug. 1607, Wodrow Quarto, 84, no. 1; Calderwood, *History*, vi, 673.

[30] Melville, *Diary*, 720; Calderwood, *History*, vi, 680, vii, 65.

[31] There is no record of a letter having been received by the presbytery of Paisley, the only one in the synod for which records are extant from this date – see Paisley Presbytery, fos 80–82; SRO, 'Extract from the records of the synod of Cliddisdaill, accepting John, archbishop of Glasgow, as moderator', CH8/59; Balfour, *Works*, ii, 22; Earl of Abercorn to James VI, 26 Aug. 1607, *Letters and State Papers*, no. lxiii; *Scots Peerage*, i, 46–7.

[32] Jedburgh Presbytery, i, fo. 15v; Melrose Presbytery, fo. 11v.

of its presbyteries. Five ministers were summoned before the Privy Council on pain of rebellion, two being ordered to enter ward in Blackness Castle. They refused and were put to the horn.[33]

According to Calderwood, only Angus and the Mearns put up no resistance. It is unclear how the other synods reacted but even Archbishop Spottiswoode admitted that all synods were 'forced' to obey.[34] The fact that he devoted only one page to constant moderation of synods is testament to his discomfort with their reception. Only the synods of Fife and Lothian had regularly created difficulties in the past but, by the latter half of the first decade of the seventeenth century, even Moray and Aberdeen caused problems. Tighter control was necessary but the heavy-handed methods used to impose constant moderators caused more problems than they solved. Opposition had reached such a level by 1606 that the king was convinced that only by the restoration of ecclesiastical jurisdiction to the episcopate could it be tackled. This resulted in a policy which was more extreme than was necessary and caused some ministers who had not previously shown dissent to do so.

The repercussions of the events of 1607 were felt into 1608. In March, the king appointed the provost of Glasgow as commissioner to the synod of Clydesdale. He was to ensure that no acts of general assemblies were questioned, especially that at Linlithgow in 1606, and to act on the advice of Archbishop Spottiswoode.[35] Afterwards, the provost reported that it had been an orderly meeting, that the archbishop's moderation had been skilful and that 'evin the adverse partie ... have now thair mouthis stoppit, and ar compellit to praise God for your hienes ... provident care in the redressinge of their former confusion'.[36] The letter does not give the impression that the 'adverse partie' were happy to obey. Tighter control was also evident in Fife, where Gledstanes reported that 'your honest servandis ... exceid the seditious', commenting that, if this once 'most seditious province' can be controlled, the rest would be easy. His confidence was exaggerated, for a group calling themselves 'the brethren of Fife', anticipating a General Assembly, wrote to the presbyteries of Fife in an attempt to create a united front against the crown. Royal control of the assembly had reached such a level, however, that this was to no avail.[37] The Merse and Teviotdale

---

[33] Calderwood, *History*, vi, 680; *RPC*, vii, 453, viii, 4, 9.

[34] Calderwood, *History*, vi, 677; Spottiswoode, *History*, iii, 189.

[35] James VI to Provost of Glasgow, 20 March 1608, *Ecclesiastical Letters*, i, no. lxxviii.

[36] Provost of Glasgow to James VI, 19 April 1608, *Ecclesiastical Letters*, i, no. lxix.

[37] Archbishop of St Andrews to James VI, 17 April 1608, *Ecclesiastical Letters*, i, no. lxxx; Melville, *Diary*, 749–52. It is impossible to say who 'the brethren of Fife' were or how many of them there were.

continued to resist. On 17 February 1608, the presbytery of Jedburgh received a letter from Melrose intimating a royal command for the synod to meet in March to answer for its misbehaviour.[38] On 24 March, the synod was discharged by the Privy Council for fear of unruliness and, when it finally met in June, the principle of constant moderators for presbyteries, but not synods, was agreed to. Indeed, later in that year and in April 1609, the presbytery of Melrose continued to nominate candidates to leets for the approaching synod's moderator.[39] Simmering discontent continued and, at a conference at Falkland in June 1608 involving representatives of synods, bishops and commissioners of the General Assembly, requests were made for the restoration of the synods' former liberties. They were resisted then and in 1609 when the bishops and commissioners of the General Assembly refused to debate in writing and the representatives of synods refused to debate orally, so *impasse* was reached.[40]

Constant moderators for presbyteries had been approved at Linlithgow, so resisting them was more difficult. The first to be pressed to accept one was Edinburgh. Surprisingly, Walter Balcanquhal, a veteran of 1584, agreed but others alleged that the act had allowed the presbytery to veto the nominee and appoint its own. Threatened with the abolition of presbyteries, they accepted John Hall but only until the next Assembly, scheduled for July. The fact that Hall was to hold office only until then suggests that decisions made at Linlithgow were not regarded as binding. The presbytery of Dalkeith refused to accept a constant moderator and others followed suit.[41] The king was told and he wrote to the Privy Council expressing fear that 'sum ... prisbitereis [were] ... too much addicted to ... anarchie and confusioun'. He ordered them to charge dissident presbyteries to obey on pain of horning. The charge was sent to every presbytery, save those of Argyll and the Isles, which existed in little more than name.[42] Since few presbytery registers survive, it is difficult to gauge the level of obedience but, in the spring of 1607, widespread efforts were made to impose them, suggesting that many were, initially at least, hostile.

In March, Lord Roxburgh, a Privy Councillor and a local landowner, charged the presbytery of Melrose to accept John Knox as moderator. Roxburgh's messenger was told that they had never heard of such a

---

[38] Jedburgh Presbytery, i, fo. 32r.

[39] *RPC*, viii, 68; Melrose Presbytery, fos 23r, 27r, 36r; Jedburgh Presbytery, i, fo. 37r.

[40] *BUK*, iii, 1045, 1069; Calderwood, *History*, vi, 732–5; Melville, *Diary*, 746.

[41] Calderwood, *History*, vi, 627–9; A.R. MacDonald, 'The Subscription Crisis and Church–State Relations 1584–1586', *RSCHS*, 25 (1994), 227–8.

[42] *RPC*, vii, 299–302.

thing, for they had not been asked to send commissioners to Linlithgow. Changing tack, the messenger asked Knox to accept the post and left, having charged the presbytery to admit Knox within 24 hours, 'quhilk was thoucht ... to be hard and precipitant deilling'. They protested to the Privy Council since they had had no commissioners at Linlithgow.[43] A week later, they were charged to accept their moderator but they appointed another. Lord Roxburgh arrived on 21 April and the presbytery agreed to accept Knox before the last Tuesday of July, the day appointed for the assembly. He expressed willingness to serve but insisted that he could not undertake the task because he was ignorant of its nature. Two weeks later, Roxburgh rejected this but the presbytery elected a new moderator, Alexander Justice. On 19 May, it was ordered to admit Knox and, 'The presbyterie ... for obedience of his Majestie ... admittit ... Mr John Knox moderator ... for ane tyme.' In October, another moderator was appointed in the usual fashion, after the synod. The affair continued into 1608 with the provincial visitor, Bishop Law of Orkney, ordering Knox's readmission in March. In April, Law returned and the presbytery promised to account for their disobedience. Two weeks later, George Byres was appointed moderator but, on 5 July, he demitted in favour of Knox. The issue did not arise again until 1610 when, in a mild gesture of defiance, the presbytery formally 'continewed Mr John Knox in the office of moderator to the nixt [synodal] assemblie'.

The neighbouring presbytery of Jedburgh also mounted resistance, linked to the synod of Merse and Teviotdale's own opposition to constant moderation.[44] In April 1607, the laird of Fernihurst and Sir Robert Kerr of Ancrum commanded the presbytery to adopt its moderator within a week. It refused and, on 17 June, Fernihurst returned with another charge. The presbytery said that it would consider this and the nominee, Thomas Abernethy, asked to see the act of Linlithgow. On 8 July, Fernihurst gave the presbytery another week to accept its moderator on pain of horning and he returned to charge it to appoint Abernethy 'for a certaine tyme' – the phrase used in the act to suggest that constant did not mean permanent. The presbytery relented, although two ministers, David Calderwood and George Johnstone, protested because 'thair names wes not contenit in the letters of horning'. In spite of this apparent acquiescence, another moderator was elected in October and, in February 1608, it resolved that whoever led the weekly exercise of doctrine would moderate. In March, Bishop Law ordered Abernethy's

---

[43] For a full account of this episode, see Melrose Presbytery, fos 2v-23r and 58r; *Scots Peerage*, vii, 341–8.

[44] For details of this section, see Jedburgh Presbytery, i, fos 17r-37r; Melrose Presbytery, fo. 8r.

admission but was unable to produce written authority for this command. Not until July 1608, as with Melrose, did Jedburgh admit its constant moderator. The other presbyteries in the synod, Duns and Chirnside, put up equally staunch resistance. In November 1607, their illegal moderators were summoned and commanded to demit by the Privy Council. They revealed that the synod had co-ordinated resistance and 'thair presbiteryis had layed that charge upoun thame'. On 10 December, both produced acts of their presbyteries confirming their demission but Duns, at least, continued to resist for, in June 1608, the Privy Council ordered it to accept its constant moderator.[45]

The synod of Perth and Stirling also directed the resistance of its presbyteries. In April 1607, it forbade the acceptance of constant moderators. The Privy Council ordered them to ignore their synod.[46] In spite of a token acceptance by the presbytery of Perth, in August, the Privy Council charged the commissioners responsible for it to force it to receive its moderator within a week.[47] The lack of further proceedings may indicate acquiescence, yet evidence from Stirling might suggest otherwise. After the synod met in April, that presbytery elected its own moderator. Two local lairds immediately appeared and charged it to accept Patrick Simson as moderator but it protested that he was old and ill.[48] The lairds ordered it to choose another but it refused. No further action was taken and the presbytery continued to elect a new moderator biannually.[49] This may have been the beginnings, in a localised way, of latitude being given to those who disobeyed, a tendency which became more widespread in the closing years of the reign.

The presbyteries of Glasgow and Paisley both accepted their moderators. On 26 March, the Earl of Abercorn, asked Paisley to accept John Hay, 'Unto the quhilk ... the haill brethrein ... maist willingly accepted.'[50] On 10 April, Abercorn came to Glasgow with Archbishop Spottiswoode and the principal of the university, Patrick Sharp was admitted but 'only for obedience of his majestie' and not without dissent from some who 'had not sein the [act and] could not give thair voitt'.[51] In Lothian and

[45] RPC, viii, 12, 20, 102.

[46] Calderwood, History, vi, 653; Melville, Diary, 705; RPC, vii, 347.

[47] RPC, vii, 431–2.

[48] Stirling Presbytery, iv, 15 April 1607; this, and the case of Deer below, refutes Foster's assertion in one place that resistance ended in the summer of 1608 and, in another, that it was over 'by 1608', see W.R. Foster, 'The Operation of Presbyteries in Scotland, 1600–1638', RSCHS, 15 (1963), 21–33, at 24 and his, Church before the Covenants, 93.

[49] Stirling Presbytery, iv, passim.

[50] Paisley Presbytery, fo. 77r.

[51] Glasgow Presbytery, i, fo. 329r.

Tweeddale, the picture is uncertain. The presbytery of Haddington is the only one for which contemporary records survive. On 11 March, two lairds ordered it to appoint James Carmichael as moderator. Sight of the act was refused but Carmichael was accepted because the presbytery of Edinburgh had acquiesced. Some doubts surround this for, in July, the lairds returned for written proof that Carmichael was moderator. He was absent, so none was provided but Carmichael was recorded as moderator in the following January.[52] As noted above, the presbytery of Dalkeith refused to accept its moderator but for how long is unknown. Calderwood stated that, by April 1607, three of the six presbyteries in Lothian and Tweeddale (Edinburgh, Dunbar and Linlithgow) had accepted moderators. He also noted that the synod refused to impose a constant moderator on one presbytery. By 1610, they had all acquiesced.[53]

In the North East, the response varied. In April 1607, two lairds charged the presbytery of Ellon to admit John Reid. It answered that 'inrespect the said suit was groundit upon the act ... than thai culd give thair answer ... [only] ... after the sicht thairof'. After this initial resistance, it accepted its moderator.[54] On 26 March, the presbytery of Deer recorded David Robertson as moderator although Abraham Sibbald had been nominated as constant moderator. In 1608, its defiance continued and it elected new moderators in 1609 and 1610.[55] Since it was already defying the crown in allowing Charles Ferme, warded for attending the 1605 Assembly, to sit on the exercise, its resistance to constant moderation is no surprise.[56] The presbytery of Aberdeen was not ordered to accept its moderator, yet its proceedings in the spring of 1607 suggest that at least a token stand was taken. In April, a new moderator was elected, an unusual move because it was normal for the synod to appoint them, but, in the following July, Bishop Blackburn was accepted as moderator and continued in that post during subsequent years.[57]

There is very little data from the South West. In February 1607, two ministers of the presbytery of Irvine were summoned before the privy council for resistance to their moderator but they were at variance with their brethren in this protest.[58] In June 1608, Dumfries was charged to accept its moderator even though the commissioners assigned to

---

[52] Haddington Presbytery, ii, fos 148r, 150r, 154r; RPC, vii, 784.
[53] Melville, Diary, 686–7; Calderwood, History, vi, 645, viii, 64; Scot Apologetical Narration, 233.
[54] Ellon Presbytery, ii, mistakenly placed at fo. 211, 1627.
[55] Deer Presbytery, i, fos 87r, 100r, 119r, 130v; BUK, iii, 1036.
[56] See Deer Presbytery, i, from fo. 87 onwards.
[57] Aberdeen Presbytery, fos 12v, 195v, 211r.
[58] RPC, vii, 312.

Dumfries had reported its acquiescence in 1607. In June 1607, the commissioners responsible for Wigtown and Kirkcudbright were horned for failing to provide evidence that these presbyteries had accepted constant moderators.[59] The crown's use of lairds in their own localities to impose its decrees is of some significance. Many were patrons of parishes, so their influence with the clergy was guaranteed. It also demonstrates the crown's desire to increase its power in the localities, arguably another example of the state's absolutist ambitions. The examples of the presbyteries of Galloway, however, suggest that attempts to use lairds as the hand on the end of the long arm of the law were not always successful.

It is hard to make sense of the varied pattern of obedience and resistance. The synod of the Merse and Teviotdale led resistance to all forms of constant moderation, as did Perth and Stirling. The presbyteries of Clydesdale acquiesced, while those in the North East and in Lothian and Tweeddale were divided. It is surprising that there is so little evidence in Fife for resistance to a concept which could not have been expected to be welcomed there. That resistance was widespread and enduring, at least during 1607, is suggested by a charge by the Privy Council in June to its commissioners to ensure that 33 presbyteries, from Sutherland to Wigtown, admitted their moderators. Many had not reported 'thair diligence in the executioun of thair ... commissioun' and were ordered to do so 'undir pane of rebellioun'. If nothing else, this demonstrates a distinct lack of local enthusiasm to enforce an unpopular measure. Later that month, acts of the presbyteries of Chirnside, Duns, Haddington, Dunbar, Stirling, Dumbarton, Ayr, Hamilton, Dumfries and Peebles signifying obedience were presented to the council.[60] Yet, since Duns, Chirnside, Stirling and Dumfries continued to resist, the significance of this is hard to gauge.

Opposition to constant moderators meant that the Assembly, intended to meet at Linlithgow in July 1607, was moved to Dundee and scheduled for 24 November. Fearing a repetition of 1605, it was declared that any keeping the original diet would be punished. At Parliament in August, Archbishop Gledstanes affirmed the king's right to call and control general assemblies.[61] Continued opposition to constant moderators led to conferences being held in an attempt to resolve the matter but agreement proved impossible. Because of the continuing unrest in the Kirk and an expected royal visit, the Assembly was prorogued until

---

[59] *RPC*, vii, 400–401, viii, 102.

[60] *RPC*, vii, 376–7, 397, 400–401.

[61] *RPC*, vii, 370; Melville, *Diary*, 711–14; Calderwood, *History*, vi, 661, 669–70; The Bishops to the Earl of Dunbar, 8 June 1607, *Ecclesiastical Letters*, i, no. lv.

July 1608.[62] Conferences continued; in June 1608, the bishops, commissioners of the General Assembly and some ministers met at Falkland. The ministers called for: the 'caveats' to be upheld; a guarantee of the security of presbyterianism; the freedom of synods and general assemblies to meet; and the restoration of banished and confined ministers. The bishops claimed to be sympathetic but suggested that these articles should be put to an Assembly, which could not meet until the king was satisfied that it would do so peaceably. Five compromise articles were sent to the king. They stated that differences should be set aside until an Assembly; that the king should be asked if it could meet in July; that it would concern only 'the commoun effairis of the Kirk' and action against Catholics; and that disagreements would be dealt with only in the privy conference. The fifth article asked for the release of the warded ministers and was retained to gain consent for the other four.[63] James Melville alleged that the ministers acquiesced, fearing the overthrow of presbyterianism by Dunbar, sent from court with money and three English divines to persuade the Scots of the virtues of episcopacy and royal supremacy.[64] The bishops, in preventing a true indication of the level of disquiet from reaching James, demonstrated that the pen which directed government was indeed wielded in Edinburgh not Westminster.

Although the members of the Assembly of 1608 were not nominated as those of 1606 had been, commissioners were not elected freely. In October 1607, the visitors of Stirlingshire and Perthshire were ordered to choose two or three from each presbytery who would be amenable to the king's policies. Similar letters were probably sent to those with responsibility for other parts of Scotland. It is stretching a point beyond the bounds of credibility to say that the ministers 'were chosen in the customary way' rather than by 'the methods employed for ... Linlithgow'.[65] The records of the presbytery of Stirling suggest that it nominated its own commissioners, so it either defied the visitors' nominations or formally appointed them.[66] The visitor for Teviotdale, Bishop Law of Orkney, influenced the choice of commissioners from Melrose and Jedburgh.

---

[62] Calderwood, *History*, vi, 681–6; *RPC*, vii, 451, viii, 25.

[63] Melville, *Diary*, 746–8; Calderwood, *History*, vi, 733 ff.

[64] Melville, *Diary*, 748; Calderwood, *History*, vi, 735; SRO, James VI to Patrick Galloway, 14 June, 1608, Rattray of Craighall Rattray Muniments, RH4/126/2/6 (microfilm) in which James asked Galloway to help the English divines, including George Abbott, Dunbar's chaplain and later Archbishop of Canterbury, and John King, later Bishop of London.

[65] James VI to John Caldcleuch and James Martin, 18 Oct. 1607, *Ecclesiastical Letters*, i, no. lxxi; Lee, *Government by Pen*, 91.

[66] Stirling Presbytery, iv, 20 July 1608.

David Calderwood, a minister in the latter, asserted that Law nominated commissioners in spite of some resistance.[67] Since Aberdeen, Ellon and Deer were in a synod moderated by the Bishop of Aberdeen, and since it was normal for that synod to appoint commissioners to assemblies, episcopal control was easily exercised there. A similar state of affairs probably prevailed in Glasgow and the other presbyteries of the west under the influence of Archbishop Spottiswoode. Of the presbyteries with surviving records, Haddington is the only clear exception. It 'did by electioune appoynt' commissioners, an unusual phrase which may indicate an assertion of defiance.[68] Some ministers in Fife tried to persuade the presbyteries there to elect independent commissioners but Archbishop Gledstanes reported a qualified success, claiming to be answerable for nine of the 12 commissioners.[69] The same ministers tried to prevent the attendance of nobles and barons without commissions from presbyteries but all the barons were appointed by the crown.[70] There is evidence that at least some burgh commissioners were also royal appointees. The council of Glasgow was ordered to send a commissioner and, although the letter did not specify a name, one of the bailies, archiepiscopal appointees, was chosen. The king also ordered the provost of Glasgow to attend, to aid in the resolution of disputes in the Kirk and to assist in the suppression of 'Contrarie professors'.[71] The burgh commissioners from Fife were also nominated by the crown.[72]

The Assembly began on 26 July and James Law, Bishop of Orkney, was elected moderator. Again, there were allegations that the votes of the 'best sort' were split by allowing more than one of them onto the leet for moderator and by the votes of 40 laymen swinging the decision.[73] Since the Assembly was substantially packed, the election of a moderator hostile to the king's policy would have been unlikely. This was not a freely elected Assembly and was not a 'happy example' for

---

[67] Jedburgh Presbytery, i, fos 33–4, 37r; Melrose Presbytery, fo. 21v; Calderwood, *History*, vi, 712.

[68] Haddington Presbytery, ii, fo. 159r.

[69] Calderwood, *History*, vi, 735; Melville, *Diary*, 749 ff; Archbishop of St Andrews to James VI, 17 April 1608, *Ecclesiastical Letters*, i, no. lxxx.

[70] Scot, *Apologetical Narration*, 201–2; Melville, *Diary*, 753–4; Calderwood, *History*, vi, 751.

[71] *Extracts from the Records of the Burgh of Glasgow*, 11 vols (Scottish Burgh Records Society/Glasgow Corporation, 1876–1916), vol. 1573–1642, 270, 286; James VI to the Provost of Glasgow, 14 June 1608, *Ecclesiastical Letters*, i, no. lxxxv. 'Contrarie professors' probably meant Catholics but the ambiguity is interesting! See also James VI to Provost of Glasgow, 24 Nov. 1608, *Ecclesiastical Letters*, i, no. c, showing that James wrote to the provost after the Assembly to thank him.

[72] Melville, *Diary*, 753.

[73] *BUK*, iii, 1046; Calderwood, *History*, vi, 751–2; Melville, *Diary*, 755.

the future.[74] It was becoming clear that the crown needed to subvert the wishes of the ministry to achieve its ends. The king wrote to the Assembly declaring that he had allowed it to meet out of zeal against Catholicism and his desire for an orderly Kirk. Free debate would be allowed but 'disorderlie speeches' falsely based on inspiration of the spirit would not, for that was 'the ordinary alleged ground of all the foolish new ... sects in Europe'. He expressed the hope that they could now combat the common enemy and acknowledged that assemblies had been prevented in previous years because 'factious' ministers had justified the 1605 assembly.[75] This, of course, did not explain the lack of assemblies in 1604 and 1605.

For years, the Kirk had criticised the crown's failure to deal with Catholics, now the Earl of Dunbar promised action. Huntly was excommunicated and the presbyteries of Glasgow and Perth were told to proceed to the excommunication of Angus and Errol respectively. It is hard to believe that this was anything other than a ploy by the crown in order to gain favour from a disillusioned Kirk. Once James had gained the English crown and secured peace with Spain, and after the flight of the Catholic earls from Ireland in 1607, he neither required their services, nor did he fear an alliance with their Irish counterparts.[76] He was free to further his ecclesiastical policies by giving in to years of anti-Catholic pressure. This is borne out by a letter of 1610 from Dunbar and the bishops of Orkney and Galloway to the king. They suggested that the confinement of Errol and Huntly would incline ministers to obedience, which augured well for the forthcoming Assembly.[77]

The commissioners of the General Assembly declared that they were unable to provide a written account of their actions since their last examination in 1602, so they requested oral criticism. Since none raised his voice, their proceedings were approved. Even James Melville admitted that they were good at their job but, since he saw that as subverting the Kirk's freedom, it was something of a backhanded compliment. The Assembly raised the commission to 30 with a quorum of 11, the number of bishops on the commission.[78] A token request for the release of the

---

[74] G.C. Wadsworth, 'The General Assembly of 1610' (unpublished Edinburgh PhD dissertation, 1930), 64.

[75] James VI to the General Assembly, 20 July 1608, *Ecclesiastical Letters*, i, no. lxxxvi.

[76] K.M. Brown, *Kingdom or Province? Scotland and the Regal Union, 1603–1715* (London, 1992), 89.

[77] *BUK*, iii, 1047–50; NLS, Earl of Dunbar and Bishops of Orkney and Galloway to James VI [1610?], Wodrow Folio, 42, no. 67.

[78] *BUK*, iii, 1057–8; Scot, *Apologetical Narration*, 203–4; Melville, *Diary*, 759; A.R. MacDonald, 'Ecclesiastical Politics in Scotland, 1586–1610' (unpublished Edinburgh PhD dissertation, 1995), Appendix 6(a) and (b).

warded ministers was made and, before the Assembly dissolved, the last Tuesday of May 1609 was set as the date for the next Assembly. Articles concerning Catholics were sent to the king and the commissioners of the Assembly were to meet in November to discuss his replies which did not come until the end of January 1609. James gave the bishops the principal role in combating Catholicism, a role later confirmed by Parliament. Thus the civil authority enhanced a spiritual aspect of episcopal power without reference to the Kirk.[79]

The excommunication of the three earls and the warding of Huntly and Errol are testament to the new policy of allowing action against recusants.[80] The presbyteries of Glasgow, Stirling, Aberdeen, Ellon and Deer were all allowed freedom to act against Catholics during 1608 and 1609. This is significant because it has been suggested that bishops were more effective than presbyteries in this respect. The coincidence of increased episcopal power and renewed action against Catholics is offered as evidence for this.[81] Undoubtedly, the bishops were happy to support such action but the effective work was done by presbyteries. The presence of bishops, giving the crown ecclesiastical control, was responsible for the relatively free rein given to the Kirk. The principal reason for the novel effectiveness of anti-Catholic action, however, was the crown's willingness to support the Kirk with civil sanctions. The previous ineffectiveness of the presbyteries had not been due to inherent weakness but to the crown's failure to support them.

After the 1608 Assembly, the bishops told the king of its success, praising Dunbar for suppression of opposition: 'Nevir ... wes more travell takin be our adversaries to disapoint your Hienes service.'[82] This may have been an exaggeration to impress James, but it may reflect the strength of opposition demonstrated in the Assembly's refusal to grant bishops *ex officio* rights of visitation in their own dioceses. The king's reply shows his pleasure with the Assembly, which demonstrated 'the good fructis that weill licenced and lawfullie convened assemblies will produce'.[83] The Assembly intended for May 1609 never met because

---

[79] *BUK*, iii, 1062–6; *RPC*, viii, 173; *APS*, iv, 410 ff.

[80] See NLS, Letters to Errol and Angus to James VI in Denmilne Papers, Advocates Manuscripts 33.1.1, i-iii; *BUK*, iii, 1047–56; Edinburgh Presbytery to James VI, 15 Nov. 1608, *Ecclesiastical Letters*, i, no. xcviii.

[81] M. Lynch, 'Preaching to the Converted? Perspectives on the Scottish Reformation', in eds, A.A. MacDonald et al., *The Renaissance in Scotland: Studies in Literature, Religion, History and Culture Offered to John Durkan* (Leiden, 1994), 305–6.

[82] Archbishops and bishops to James VI, 31 July 1608, *Ecclesiastical Letters*, i, no. lxxxvii.

[83] Melville, *Diary*, 760; *RPC*, viii, 172.

further conferences between bishops and representatives of the ministers failed. They agreed that all Acts of legal assemblies were unassailable but they could not agree upon a definition of a legal Assembly. They also concurred on the grounds of disagreement: constant moderators and the episcopal 'caveats'. The Assembly was prorogued until May 1610 for further discussion which never took place. In the light of these continuing difficulties, the view that, by the end of 1608, controversy had died down is hard to sustain.[84]

The years after 1606 saw an increasingly prominent role for the bishops *per se*. Most letters by the commissioners of the General Assembly were signed exclusively or predominantly by bishops who acted increasingly as an episcopate rather than as commissioners who happened to be bishops.[85] They were prominent in the packing of general assemblies and, in June 1607, after a meeting of the commissioners of the Assembly, they remained in Edinburgh with the Earl of Dunfermline and agreed to divide Scotland up so that 'everie ane ... sal have ane secreit oversight ... of ane several part'. They also arranged to meet every six weeks to 'frustrat the plattis and purposis of the turbulent'.[86] The increasingly episcopal commission continued to operate as an ecclesiastical executive, planting ministers in principal towns, proroguing general assemblies, imposing constant moderators and meeting with ministers to try to resolve differences. In January 1609, their powers became even greater when a Convention of the Estates authorised them to examine the religion of tutors and the sons of nobles whom they taught, when leaving for study abroad and on returning. They were also empowered to exclude from inheritance previously excommunicated people by being the sole certificators of their absolution.[87] In June, Parliament confirmed those powers and returned to the Kirk, in the persons of the bishops, commissariat jurisdiction with power over the confirmation of wills which had been secularised in the 1560s. The bishops' livings were also augmented by the restoration of the feudal

---

[84] *BUK*, iii, 1069–77; Melville, *Diary*, 770–9; 'Ryseing and Usurpation', 26; Foster, *Church before the Covenants*, 21–2, 205. Foster asserted this to support his thesis that the mixed polity was acceptable to the Kirk. His personal inclination to modern presbyterian-episcopalian union (205) should be noted.

[85] See *Ecclesiastical Letters*, *passim*, for example no. lv, The bishops to the Earl of Dunbar, June 1607, subscribed 'Ross, Cattnes, Sanctandois, Breichin, An[drew] Isles', no. lx, The Archbishop of St Andrews to James VI, 20 July 1607, which is subscribed 'Sanctandrois', and no. lxii, The Archbishops and bishops to James VI, Aug. 1607, which is subscribed 'Murray, Sanctandrois, Galloway, Glasgow, Dunblanen, Abirdein'.

[86] The bishops to the Earl of Dunbar, 3 June 1607, *Ecclesiastical Letters*, i, no. lv.

[87] *APS*, iv, 405–7; Spottiswoode, *History*, iii, 201; Melville, *Diary*, 769; Calderwood, *History*, vii, 4–5.

casualties of their sees.[88] Bit by bit, the episcopate was enhanced without reference to the Kirk.

On 13 February 1610, the Privy Council passed 'Ane act anent the deserting of the general assembly' – it was prorogued indefinitely.[89] Soon after, two archiepiscopal courts of High Commission were established, with the power, as in England, over all ecclesiastical causes. The Archbishop of St Andrews' jurisdiction covered the dioceses of St Andrews, Orkney, Caithness, Ross, Moray, Aberdeen, Brechin, Dunkeld and Dunblane, while that of the Archbishop of Glasgow covered Glasgow, Galloway, Argyll and the Isles. They had the power

> To call before them anie person dwelling within their provinces whom they hold to be scandalous. And if they find them guiltie and impenitent they sall command the preacher of that parish where they dwell to proceed with excommunication which if their command be not obeyed, they sall conveene [the] minister before them and proceed in censuring him by suspensioun, deprivatioun, or wairding.[90]

They might also judge the speeches of ministers, school and university teachers and deal with them if they were deemed to be seditious, to have brought the conclusions of recent assemblies into question or to have spoken in favour of warded or banished ministers.

It was decided that a General Assembly should give this a gloss of clerical approval. Spottiswoode doubted the wisdom of this, believing that many ministers feared the abolition of presbyteries but his colleagues disagreed, declaring that even those once 'most refractarie', would 'suffer thingis to proceed and be quyet'.[91] Had they really believed that, they would not have obtained royal letters nominating the ministers to be commissioned. The assertion that 'There is no evidence that any ministers of note were deliberately excluded' is simply absurd.[92] Bishop Law of Orkney personally delivered the presbytery of Jedburgh's letter and ensured the attendance of ministers from Orkney and Caithness. The presbytery of Ellon, as well as receiving a royal letter, was called to Aberdeen by Bishop Blackburn for commissions to be dispensed. The presbytery of Turriff was commanded by a royal letter to accept the bishop's nominees and the presbyteries of the diocese of St Andrews were told to accept the names given to them by Archbishop

---

[88] RPC, viii, 417–20; Melville, Diary, 746.

[89] RPC, viii, 413.

[90] RPC, viii, 418–19.

[91] RPC, viii, 417–20; Melville, Diary, 790; Archbishop of Glasgow to James VI, 12 March and Archbishops and bishops to James VI, Ecclesiastical Letters, i, nos cxli, cxlv.

[92] Donaldson, Scotland: James V–James VII, 206.

Gledstanes.[93] A full sederunt survives from the 1610 Assembly. Twelve of the 13 Bishops attended, only David Lindsay, bishop of Ross, was absent. Many presbyteries had more than three representatives, even discounting their moderators, and thus the act of 1598 had been ignored. For the first time, there were representatives from the Isles and ministers in appreciable numbers from Argyll, Caithness, Orkney and Galloway. The clerical contingent was entirely under the control of the crown and in the election of the moderator, only five ministers out of 138 opposed Archbishop Spottiswoode.[94]

As with the assemblies of 1606 and 1608, the landed element was summoned by the crown. A royal letter to William Stewart of Grandtully told him that he had been chosen 'inregarde of your knowne affectioun and love to the weill and peace of that churche, and of manie good proofes we have had of your forwardnes in our service'.[95] Unlike Ogilvy of Inverquharity in 1606, Grandtully went. Seven earls, seven lords and 13 lairds attended. Most notable among the barons at the assemblies of 1606, 1608 and 1610 were the new nobility. Of 16 earls, seven had been elevated to that status since 1603; of the 15 lords, eight had been given their titles since 1600 and another, Lord Torphichen, had his status confirmed by Parliament in 1606 because his father's charter of the lands of the Knights Hospitallers had not included the title of lord.[96] These new peers owed their recently enhanced status to the king and they were a useful tool in general assemblies. Using them in greater numbers than their older colleagues was part of a broader crown policy which attempted to increase central control by the creation of a client nobility and has been portrayed as further evidence of the king's 'absolutist' ambitions. This new nobility would be notably loyal in the Parliament of 1621, when 13 out of 15 voted in favour of the five articles of Perth.[97] Yet those who benefited from the erections of 1606 were to be at greatest risk from Charles I's revocation of 1625.[98]

---

[93] Jedburgh Presbytery, i, fo. 81v; Ellon Presbytery, ii, fo. 69r; see *Ecclesiastical Letters*, i, nos cxlii, cxliii, cli; 'Ryseing and Usurpation', 31–2; Scot, *Apologetical Narration*, 224.

[94] *BUK*, iii, 1085–91; Scot, *Apologetical Narration*, 223.

[95] James VI to the laird of Grandtully, 2 April 1610, in ed., W. Fraser, *The Red Book of Grandtully*, 2 vols (Edinburgh, 1868), ii, no. 80.

[96] The earls of Abercorn, Dunbar, Kinghorn, Linlithgow, Lothian (snr and jnr) and Wigtown and lords Blantyre, Buccleuch, Burntisland, Culross, Holyrood, Kintail, Loudoun and Scone. See *Scots Peerage*, i, 46–7, ii, 81–5, 232–3, 553–7, iii, 286–9, iv, 431–3, v, 443–6, 455–7, 458–60, 497, vi , 96–9, vii, 503–5, viii, 191–6, 291–4, 387–91, 545–7.

[97] J. Goodare, 'The Nobility and the Absolutist State in Scotland, 1584–1638', *History*, 78 (1993), 161–82; J. Goodare, 'The Scottish Parliament of 1621', *The Historical Journal*, 38 (1995), 29–51, at 39; Foster, *Church before the Covenants*, 30.

[98] A.I. Macinnes, *Charles I and the Making of the Covenanting Movement, 1625–1641* (Edinburgh, 1991), 54–7.

Again, English clerics came north with Dunbar as did 10 000 merks (£6 666 13s. 4d.), which the king ordered Dunbar to divide 'among suche personis as you sall holde fitting'.[99] It was given 'to such as served the king and the bishops under pretence of bearing their charges [as constant moderators] for such as voted contrair the act or voted *non-liquet* [literally 'not clear'] got no money'. Spottiswoode denied that anything underhand occurred but the king's letter clearly refutes this.[100] The Assembly began at Glasgow on 8 June and was the mostly tightly controlled yet.[101] Dunbar declared the king's desire for strong discipline and his belief that recent events had proved the folly of headless government – presbyteries without bishops. Spottiswoode's moderator's privy conference consisted of bishops, courtiers, nobles and 'some ministers' and it submitted articles to the Assembly to be accepted *en bloc*. Only five voted against them and a few more abstained. The Assembly of 1605 was declared null and the king's right to call general assemblies was acknowledged. Synods were to be moderated by bishops (admitting the forgery of the 1606 'Act'); the assembly could only *advise* the king to depose bishops; presentations, deprivations and visitations were to be conducted by bishops; and ministers were to swear obedience to king and bishop – royal supremacy by the back door. Protests were silenced by threats and flattery, according to Calderwood.[102]

Most significant of all was the fact that the commissioners of the General Assembly were not examined and their commission was not renewed. The boundaries of the pre-Reformation dioceses were restored and the synods became episcopal courts (see Maps 1 and 4 in the Appendix). The bishops were now the source of ecclesiastical power and that power flowed directly from the king. After 1596, the commission had been an effective organ of royal authority and a vehicle for the consensual reintroduction of episcopacy. Contrary to what Maurice Lee has argued, James did not reintroduce episcopacy because the commission failed to achieve control but because the control it had achieved was squandered.[103] The opposition provoked by failure to allow assemblies to meet directed its resentment at the commission, so it was

---

[99] See *Ecclesiastical Letters*, i, 425; Calderwood, *History*, viii, 70.

[100] 'Ryseing and Usurpation', 32; Spottiswoode, *History*, iii, 207; J. Perry, 'John Spottiswoode, Archbishop and Chancellor as Churchman' (unpublished Edinburgh PhD dissertation, 1950), 118–19 also accepts Spottiswoode's view, although presents no convincing argument to support it.

[101] For detailed accounts see *BUK*, iii, 1092–8; Melville, *Diary*, 793; Calderwood, *History*, vii, 95–101; Row, *History*, 273–9; Spottiswoode, *History*, iii, 205–8.

[102] Calderwood, *History*, viii, 71.

[103] M. Lee, 'James VI and the Revival of Episcopacy in Scotland: 1596–1600', *Church History*, 43 (1974), 57, 63.

superceded by the episcopate in an upward spiral of centralised power. In December, in London, apostolic succession was restored with the consecration of the Archbishop of Glasgow and the bishops of Brechin and Galloway by the bishops of Bath, Ely and London. To avoid any connotations of subjection, neither Canterbury nor York was involved. Once back in Scotland those three consecrated their brethren.[104]

On 19 June, the Privy Council proclaimed the 'grite harmonie and uniformitie of myndis' at the Assembly.[105] This fiction was revealed in the proclamation itself, which forbade criticism of the Assembly under pain of imprisonment. To portray this as the 'final completion of the task' for James is at odds with the evidence. The techniques used by the crown to gain approval for its policies are testament to their unpopularity. Dunbar's period as the principal conduit for royal power was characterised by tighter control than had been seen between 1603 and 1606: 'his function was to translate the royal wishes into accomplished facts'.[106] What the king wanted was done, without moderation by the Privy Council. This was control without consent and to suggest that, because the 1610 Assembly was geographically the most representative to date, it represented the 'vast majority' or the 'great majority' of ministers is not sustainable.[107] Had that been true, the act of 1598 limiting presbyteries to commissioning three ministers could have ensured that the Assembly expressed the will of the Kirk. Such distorted analysis has been taken up by English historiography where it has informed ideas about the consensual nature of James's English ecclesiastical policy. Perhaps both need to be reassessed.[108]

---

[104] Calderwood, *History*, vii, 150, 152, 154; Spottiswoode, *History*, iii, 208–9.

[105] *RPC*, viii, 616.

[106] Lee, *Government by Pen*, 61. His assessment of the autocratic rule of this period sits oddly with his statement about the acceptability of the crown's ecclesiastical policy noted below.

[107] M. Lee, *Great Britain's Solomon: James VI and I in his Three Kingdoms* (Urbana, 1990), 81; Foster, *Church before the Covenants*, 29; Donaldson, *Scotland: James V–James VII*, 207; M. Lynch, *Scotland: a New History* (London, 1991), 231 expresses a similar view.

[108] Fincham and Lake, 'The Ecclesiastical Policies of James I and Charles I', 30. The same discussion notes continuity with the policy of Elizabeth in England, which may be more relevant in this case, as may James's conduct as hands-on King of Scots before 1603 which was carried into his government of England.

CHAPTER SEVEN

New polity, new liturgy, 1610–25

In 1611, James Melville languished in Berwick, forbidden to return to Scotland. In the aftermath of the Glasgow Assembly of 1610, he wrote a poem, 'The Black Bastel', portraying the Kirk as a woman with a glass crown, forced to dress in garish clothes and with a heavy yoke around her neck. She was 'Rich in attire, yet sillie [i.e. weak], leane and poore'.[1] Above her sat a red lion on a throne and she was led by two foxes and 13 wolves. The lion was, of course, the king while the foxes were the earls of Dunbar and Dunfermline. The 13 wolves require explanation only by the fact that there were 13 dioceses. Beside her stood her shepherds, once bold but now heedless of her cries. Many of them were but 'huble buble sheepheards hir'd and thralled' who had participated in the Assembly at Glasgow.[2] On the prompting of the lion, the wolves' power increased, causing her to weep and to cry out that she had once been admired throughout Europe for her purity, discipline and learning but the coming and advancing of the bishops had reduced her to 'Babel's harlot'.[3] As well as expressing his disillusion in verse, Melville produced at about this time, a prose account of the Kirk's fortunes since 1596, tellingly entitled *A True Narratioune of the Declyneing Aige of the Kirk of Scotland*. After a brief preamble, he summarised the story.

> The age of the Church of Scotland since she was brought out of the darknes of poperie to the cleir light of the gospell hes beine nou a perfyte Jubilie of sevin sevins from the yeare of hir lords incarnation 1560 unto this present yeare 1610. The infancie quhairof was admirable, the grouth to full perfection incomparabill in any kingdome, and so this dolefull decay and almost dieing age most pitifull and lamentable.[4]

---

[1] 'The Black Bastel or a lamentation in name of the Kirk of Scotland, composed by Mr James Melvil when he was confined at Berwick anno 1611', in ed., D. Laing, *Various Pieces of Fugitive Scottish Poetry Principally of the XVIIth Century* (Edinburgh, 1853). A 'bastel' was a castle, with connotations of prison, being the same word as the French 'Bastille'.

[2] 'The Black Bastel', p. 5, stanza 8.

[3] 'The Black Bastel', p. 8, stanza 21.

[4] Melville, *Diary*, 503–804, esp. 505–6; but see also the MS catalogued at the SRO as 'Part of "The Second Declinatour of the King and Counsells judicatour in matters spirituall ... " by David Black', Clerk of Penicuik Muniments, GD18/3952 which contains a clearer reading of the passage quoted above than that in the printed edition. A.R. MacDonald, 'A Fragment of an Early Copy of James Melville's *A True Narratioune of the Declyneing Aige of the Kirk of Scotland*', *Innes Review*, 47 (1996), 81–8.

Melville looked back with the eyes of one experiencing exile for a second time. He had fled to England in 1584 to escape the government of the Earl of Arran. He now despaired because Arran's policy had been eclipsed in 1586 but, by 1610, the power of the crown, through a revived episcopate, was even greater than it had been under Arran. The 'declyne' was to continue, although Melville would die in 1614 with a remedy still far off. In 1612, Parliament ratified the acts of the 1610 Assembly, which were, 'under colour of explanation, inlarged and altered, so that in effect they were new'. Episcopal subjection to the General Assembly was omitted and new episcopal powers were introduced: the right to nominate a depute moderator of a synod and the power of collation, the former granted to the synod and the latter left with the presbytery in 1610. The original act had mentioned the continuation of the exercise of doctrine while the omission of this by the 1612 Parliament could have opened the way to presbyteries' abolition.[5] It became common, after 1610, for the word 'exercise' to supersede 'presbytery' and this may have been part of a move towards their loss of disciplinary powers and their reduction to the status which they held before 1581. That this did not happen was probably due to the bishops' awareness that it would have been unacceptable. That the episcopate intended to play a long game is indicated by the establishment, in April 1611, of a new 'exercise' at Forfar. In the following month, however, Archbishop Gledstanes informed the king that his son-in-law was teaching canon law at St Andrews 'as ane reddie way to bring out the Presbiterian Discipline fra the heartis of the young ones' training for the ministry.[6]

After 1610, a time of settlement was allowed by the crown, hoping that the new authority structures would bed down and this period was characterised neither by strong opposition from the ministers nor by crown authoritarianism. It was more than a coincidence that, with the death of Dunbar in 1611, went the authoritarian implementation of the crown's ecclesiastical policy. Dunbar may have been doctrinally a Calvinist, as his influence in the appointment of Abbot to Canterbury showed, but the fact that he was comfortable in the Church of England shows that he had no truck with Calvin's views on ceremonies, polity or ecclesiastical independence.

Opposition did continue, however. In June 1611, the presbytery of Cupar was cited by Gledstanes for admitting a minister without his

[5] APS, iv, 469–70; Calderwood, *History*, vii 165–6, 171–3.

[6] SRO, Record of the Diocesan Synod of St Andrews benorth Forth from September 1610 to April 1636, CH2/154/1, fo. 17v; Gledstanes to James VI, 3 May 1611, *Ecclesiastical Letters*, i, no. 166.

consent and their meeting place was moved to Falkland, so that the royal palace there might remind them who was boss.[7] In October, George Dunbar, minister of Ayr, was summoned before the Privy Council for praying for the ministers convicted of treason in 1606, warded in Dumbarton Castle and replaced by a royal appointee.[8] In the North East too, discontent remained. In the spring of 1611, Archbishop Gledstanes noted that the greatest opposition to episcopacy came from the north of his diocese while John Straiton, minister of Forres, was brought before the High Commission for criticism of the acts of the 1610 Assembly. He refused to acknowledge the bishops' authority to judge him and was warded in Inverness Castle.[9]

The most striking instance of opposition to the new system occurred in the presbytery of Deer. Just as presbyteries had gradually accrued presentations to benefices after 1586, so they lost them after 1609. By March 1610 all were directed to bishops, a typical example being to 'the rycht reverend father in God, John archbishop of Glasgow'.[10] In October 1613, the presbytery of Deer was summoned to Aberdeen to voice any criticisms they might have of a presentee. The ministers,

> considering of the novatioun of the forme that ane unknawin man never hard be the peple nor allowed be the presbyterie to that ministry suld be obtrudit forcably ... ather to the charge of Godis peple or to the fellowschip of the presbyterie contrar to the wontit forme of the admission of ministeries,

demanded that the 'wontit forme' (examination by the presbytery and preaching before the congregation) should proceed. If this were not granted, the presbytery asked its messenger to 'disasent from the admission'.[11] The right to receive presentations had been granted to bishops in 1610 but the right to examine the presentee was not. In 1612, they gained the right to give collation and now Bishop Blackburn was attempting to take on the whole process. The presbytery's messenger pressed their case and the bishop relented. After examining and hearing him preach, the presbytery assertively declared that the presentee's doctrine contained 'thrie or four gross errroures in the fundamentall grundes'. The bishop did not try to usurp the rights of the presbytery again.

---

[7] Gledstanes to James VI, 9 June 1611, *Ecclesiastical Letters*, i, no. 169. It was allowed to return in the following year, see SRO, synod of St Andrews benorth Forth, fo. 55r.

[8] *RPC*, ix, 258, 351; James VI to Spottiswoode, 10 April 1612, *Ecclesiastical Letters*, i, no. 174.

[9] Gledstanes to James VI, 3 May 1611, *Ecclesiastical Letters*, i, no. 166; Calderwood, *History*, vii, 160.

[10] SRO, Register of Presentations to Benefices, 1607–17, CH4/1/4, fos 31r, 82r, *et passim*.

[11] Deer Presbytery, ii, fos 153r-155v.

The rarity of such instances of opposition was due to the absence of Dunbar's forceful personality and also to attempts by the crown to recover the goodwill of the ministry through the rehabilitation of some of those warded and imprisoned between 1603 and 1610. In February 1611, William Row, minister of Forgandenny, suspended for misbehaviour at the synod of Perth and Stirling, was restored to the ministry. Two months later, four ministers confined in Glasgow were freed, having apologised for their opposition. In May 1612, Charles Ferme was allowed to return to Aberdeen and, in November, James Irving, another of those warded for attending the 1605 Assembly, had his confinement lifted, as did Robert Youngson, minister of Clatt in the presbytery of Alford, in March 1613. At the same time, David Calderwood and George Johnstone were released, having been warded in 1608 for resisting episcopal visitation. The presbytery of Jedburgh sent a messenger 'to mak intimatioun of the samyn and desyr thame to resort to the presbiterie'. In Fife, William Watson, John Carmichael, William Scot and John Scrimgeour were also relieved from their wards in 1613.[12] This clemency had its limits, however. In 1611 and 1612, the synod of St Andrews 'benorth Forth' received petitions from the parishioners of Kilrenny, requesting the restoration of their minister.[13] Archbishop Gledstanes agreed to ask the king but it was in vain for the minister of Kilrenny was James Melville.

Some rejected the liberty which they were granted. In 1612, the synod of St Andrews 'benorth Forth' noted that 'the brethren sometymes confyned be authoritie from the kingis majestie wer for the maist part absent'. Gledstanes made it clear that they had been authorised to attend and he would give them a warrant to that effect. William Watson and John Carmichael refused to come. The civil power had confined them so the civil power must release them. The synod called them before the High Commission to try 'the relevancie of thair excuses'.[14] They were absent again in May 1614, as were William Scot and John Scrimgeour, so a commission of the synod was established to examine them. Soon afterwards, a provincial synod, involving Archbishop Gledstanes and the bishops of Dunblane, Dunkeld, Moray and Ross, asked the king to permit their attendance at the courts of the Kirk and, in July, the Privy Council relieved all four. Meeting in October, the synod judged that their impediments were removed and ordered them

---

[12] *RPC*, ix, 140, 383, 498–9, 600–601, x, 5; Calderwood, *History*, vii, 181; Spottiswoode to James VI, 12 Oct. 1611, *Ecclesiastical Letters*, i, no. 172; Jedburgh Presbytery, i, 10 March 1613.

[13] SRO, synod of St Andrews benorth Forth, fos 15r, 55r.

[14] SRO, synod of St Andrews benorth Forth, fos 49v, 67r.

to attend. Scot, Carmichael and Scrimgeour did not, in spite of having run out of excuses.[15] The synod sent them the Privy Council's warrant and threatened to suspend them if they remained absent.

The reasons for their behaviour were probably the same as those given by George Johnstone, Calderwood's colleague. On 4 August, he explained that he did not attend the presbytery because the moderator presided in the name of the bishop, his liberty as published allowed him to attend only the exercise, not to participate in discipline, and he feared he would be accused of speaking against the king or the bishop (he could not help himself). His excuses were rejected. Archibald Oswald in the presbytery of Haddington took a similar view. In July 1613, it was noted that 'in great contempt of the presbiterie he withdrawis him self from ther societie and will not concurre with them in the censure'.[16]

Absenteeism was to became a serious problem and these instances were not isolated. Increasingly poor attendance is discernible throughout this period. In 1612, the presbytery of Melrose noted multiple and repeated absences. In the following year, the presbytery of Stirling observed a similar problem and wrote to those who were habitually absent, urging them to return and, in 1615, the presbytery of Linlithgow noted the persistent absence of one of its ministers.[17] That the discontented element kept away from presbyteries may be another explanation for the lack of vocal trouble in the courts of the Kirk. Many kept their disobedience to themselves.

There was one area in which concord was possible, the fight against Catholicism, for the bishops had as much enthusiasm against nonconformity as the ministers. The release from ward of Huntly and Errol in 1611 prompted allegations that their confinement in 1608 had merely been a device to aid the crown's ecclesiastical policy. They were released conditionally and confined within a few miles of their principal residences. Further liberty was granted to Huntly when he was permitted to travel outwith this confinement and, at the end of 1612, he was allowed to visit the king.[18] Below the level of the nobility, however, action

---

[15] *RPC*, x, 258; SRO, synod of St Andrews benorth Forth, fos 86v, 92v, 94v, 98r.

[16] Jedburgh Presbytery, i, 10 March, 4 Aug. 1613; Haddington Presbytery, iii, 28 July 1613.

[17] Melrose Presbytery, fo. 88r; Stirling Presbytery, iv, 16 June 1613; Linlithgow Presbytery, i, fo. 115r.

[18] Scot, *Apologetical Narration*, 253; *RPC*, ix, 117, 159–61, 162, 180, 514. Huntly was warded within 24 miles of Strathbogie and Errol within 12 miles of Errol. Under 20 000 merks' caution, they undertook to come to the Privy Council on 20 days' notice, to go to the kirk weekly, to be instructed by a minister, not to reset (harbour) priests, to have their children baptised and educated by Protestants.

against Catholics increased. In June 1611, the Bishop of Dunkeld, acting as an effective inter-presbytery link, informed the presbytery of Ellon that they should publicly intimate the excommunication, by Linlithgow presbytery, of a servant of the Countess of Errol. In July, the Bishop of Moray was commissioned by the Privy Council to execute laws against pilgrimages to wells and, in February 1612, the council proclaimed that bishops and ministers were to seek out Jesuits and other Catholic missionaries and report their names to the archbishops so that the High Commission could deal with them.[19]

While the Kirk welcomed this co-ordinated campaign, discontent with the lenience shown to Catholic figureheads soon became apparent. In April 1612, the synod of St Andrews 'benorth Forth' decided to investigate reports that the Earl of Dunfermline had a crucifix painted on his private pew in the kirk of Dunfermline. In September, the king made it clear that nothing should be done because the painting had been removed, so the synod diverted its vexation into complaining about the 'oversicht granted' to Huntly and Errol which made efforts against Catholicism in general futile. They had broken their conditions of release, so the synod called for the banishment of Huntly and his wife, closer confinement of Errol and fresh intimation of his excommunication. It was also demanded that all 'thair escheatis' (confiscation of their property to the value of their cautions) should be taken up. In the following April, the king replied that Huntly was at court being dealt with by the Bishop of Brechin and that others were appointed to speak to Errol.[20]

Unlike the king, the bishops would attack Catholicism irrespective of rank. During 1613, the presbytery of Linlithgow took up the case of the determinedly Catholic Countess of Linlithgow and received permission from Archbishop Gledstanes to proceed against her, taking the case to the verge of excommunication, referring it properly to the synod.[21] Episcopal unease was firmly demonstrated in the summer of that year when they wrote to the king lamenting the 'increase of papistry' which proceeded 'from the oversight gifin to the Marquis of Huntly'. They informed James that they would intimate Errol's excommunication again and give Huntly until November. They clearly felt that the king was out of touch, convinced that the Catholic nobles would get no favours 'did your Majestie understand the trew state of thingis'. They were being criticised by the ministry but their hands were tied. In November, Errol

---

[19] Ellon Presbytery, ii, fo. 85r; *RPC*, ix, 217, 331.
[20] SRO, synod of St Andrews benorth Forth, fos 50, 58v, 62r, 67r.
[21] Linlithgow Presbytery, i, fos 50r, 59. She was the same person as Lady Livingstone with whom the presbytery of Stirling had been dealing in 1596–97.

was warded in St Andrews and other Catholic nobles were also confined.[22]

The bishops were still not satisfied. In May 1614, Gledstanes and the bishops of Dunblane, Dunkeld, Moray and Ross asked that Huntly be given a final ultimatum. Since Catholics looked to him as their leader, they thought it 'meet for his majesties conscience' that the process be delayed no longer. They also urged that Errol, the Earl of Sutherland and the laird of Gicht should be banished if they failed to conform.[23] A frustrated Archbishop Spottiswoode, writing to Sir John Murray of Lochmaben in July, complained that Huntly's failure to conform made people think that the bishops encouraged the king to allow it 'and so our invy is the greater and the worke more difficil for his religion'. Huntly's own parish minister had counted three recusants in the parish before the suspension of Huntly's excommunication. There were now 73! Without protection, Catholics would at least conform. 'Surely his Majestie knowis not the worst', wrote Spottiswoode.[24] James was no longer aware, nor did he seem to care very much, especially when it came to old friends like Huntly. Two years later, Huntly was warded by the High Commission for refusal to subscribe the Confession of Faith. Less than a week later, he was released, by Chancellor Dunfermline and, intercepting a royal command for his return to ward, went to London where, on 8 July, he was absolved by the Archbishop of Canterbury and received communion. The Scottish bishops were angry but the king and Archbishop Abbot insisted that nothing had been done in prejudice of the Kirk. King James argued that the original excommunication had been recognised because absolution was given before communion and that the rights and authority of the Kirk had been explicitly reserved.[25] It is hard to see either what force this could have had or why it was absolutely necessary for Huntly to communicate. The bishops were left with no choice, short of creating a constitutional crisis, but to acquiesce and, at the General Assembly of 1616, Huntly was absolved.

At the end of 1614, the king was set up by the bishops. In October, Spottiswoode, having apprehended the Jesuit, John Ogilvie, urged exemplary punishment in a tone which betrayed worry that James might

---

[22] Archbishops and bishops to James VI, 23 June, 1613, *Ecclesiastical Letters*, i, 341–3; *RPC*, x, 169.

[23] SRO, synod of St Andrews benorth Forth (includes one provincial synod), fos 91v, 92r.

[24] Spottiswoode to Sir John Murray, 11 July 1614, *Ecclesiastical Letters*, ii, no. 215.

[25] Scot, *Apologetical Narration*, 240; Spottiswoode, *History*, iii, 230–33; *RPC*, x, 542, 580–81; James VI to Spottiswoode, Archbishop Abbot to Spottiswoode, July 1616, *Ecclesiastical Letters*, ii, nos 300 and 310.

be lenient. In November, it emerged that two Jesuits, Ogilvie and James Moffat, had been apprehended by Spottiswoode and Gledstanes respectively.[26] The king, who issued a commission for Ogilvie's trial, was inclined to have him banished as long as he did not assert the supreme authority of the Pope. Spottiswoode pressed this point in the hope that Ogilvie would relent and acknowledge the royal supremacy to save his life, as Moffat did. Ogilvie would not and he was tried in February 1615 and executed for treason.[27] John Ogilvie was a scapegoat. The ministers who attended the Assembly of 1605 had denied royal power over the Kirk and were convicted of treason but not executed. The bishops had a genuine desire to uproot Catholicism but had been thwarted by royal favour to Huntly. The ministry doubted their zeal, so a test case was required. Each archbishop arrested a token Jesuit and, somewhat unexpectedly, one refused to yield even under torture and was executed. Scores could have been apprehended and many trials might have occurred. That they did not shows that Ogilvie was the tragic victim of the bishops' need to prove that they meant business. No chances were taken. The king, having pressed for banishment if Ogilvie acknowledged his supremacy or death if he did not, was given no opportunity to grant last-minute clemency. In the morning, Ogilvie was found guilty and sentenced; three hours later, he was hanged.[28]

The widespread zeal against Catholicism was also turned to the crown's advantage as a vehicle for the liturgical innovations which would dominate ecclesiastical affairs for the rest of the reign. In March 1614, the Privy Council proclaimed that, to ensure universal receipt of communion and to expose Catholics, every minister should hold communion on Sunday 24 April.[29] A national communion on one Sunday was an excellent way of monitoring withdrawal from the sacrament but it did not need to be Easter Sunday. David Calderwood wrote that, 'The pretence of the charge was the tryall of Popishe recusants; but the true intent ... was to try how the people wold beare with alterations ... in the worship.'[30] Some presbyteries were already in a frenzy about Catholics, so when this opportunity to pin them down was presented, it was

---

[26] Spottiswoode to James VI, 5 Oct. 1614, *Ecclesiastical Letters*, ii, no. 235; *RPC*, x, 284.

[27] Spottiswoode, *History*, iii, 222–7; Calderwood, *History*, vii, 196. The 'political overtones' of Ogilvie's trial and execution have been acknowledged in J. Durkan, 'Two Jesuits: Patrick Anderson and John Ogilvie', *Innes Review*, 21 (1970), 157–61 but it would appear that this view of the events is new.

[28] R. Pitcairn, ed., *Criminal Trials in Scotland from 1488 to 1624*, 3 vols (Edinburgh, 1833), iii, 330–54.

[29] *RPC*, x, 215–16.

[30] Calderwood, *History*, vii, 191.

grasped with both hands. Communions were held and the names of those who did not attend were collected to be forwarded to the bishops. Even Calderwood and William Scot admitted that 'the most part' obeyed the command to hold this communion.[31] There is evidence, however, that some suspected an ulterior motive. At the synod of St Andrews 'benorth Forth' in May, each presbytery was told to forward a list of non-communicants with certification that every minister had held communion. At a provincial synod 12 days later, it was found that some had not and it was decided that the bishops should find out their names and proceed to suspension or even deprivation.[32] In 1615, the crown was more open about the nature of the communion when it was proclaimed that, in time coming, it would be celebrated 'ane day yeirlie, to witt Pasche day'. Stirling presbytery was told that this would ensure 'that all occasione of excuse may be taine away frome the recusants'. Calderwood ruefully observed that thus 'the king by his owne authoritie, without advise or consent of the Kirk, enjoyneth Kirk orders'.[33]

That was not far from the truth, for an idea from 1612, when a draft confession of faith was sent up from England, was revived in June 1615. Certain 'Articles required for the service of the Church of Scotland' were sent from court.[34] They proposed a set liturgy and prayers because extempore prayer could 'prove so often impertinent'; a confession of faith which agreed 'so neir as can be' with the English one; set forms for ordination, baptism, marriage and communion; canons of ecclesiastical law and confirmation of children by bishops. It was proposed that these should be accepted by a General Assembly which should be 'drawn to the form of the Convocation House heir in England'. Here is proof, if any were needed, that, although James did not desire absolute conformity between the churches, Anglocentric convergence was what he had in mind. In light of this and of events in years to come, it is hard to sustain an argument that this was not an attempt to Anglicanise the Kirk.[35]

---

[31] Linlithgow Presbytery, i, fos 85v, 86r, 88v; Dalkeith Presbytery, 28 April 1614; Glasgow Presbytery, ii, fo. 81v; Scot, *Apologetical Narration*, 238; Calderwood, *History*, vii, 191.

[32] SRO, synod of St Andrews benorth Forth, fos 88r, 91v.

[33] *RPC*, x, 316–17; Stirling Presbytery, iv, 8 March 1615; Calderwood, *History*, vii, 196.

[34] Articles required for the service of the Church of Scotland, June 1615, *Ecclesiastical Letters*, i, no. 275; Sir Alexander Hay to James VI, 4 July 1612, *Ecclesiastical Letters*, i, no. 180.

[35] J. Morrill, 'A British Patriarchy? Ecclesiastical Imperialism under the Early Stuarts' [sic], in eds, A. Fletcher and P. Roberts, *Religion, Culture and Society in Early Modern Britain: Essays in Honour of Patrick Collinson* (Cambridge, 1994), 209–37. The Anglocentric subtitle apart, Morrill portrays James's policy as more balanced than it really was.

The death of George Gledstanes in May 1615 led to the promotion of Spottiswoode to the primacy and of Bishop Law of Orkney to the vacant see of Glasgow. In December, the courts of High Commission were united under Archbishop Spottiswoode who thus attained to a position of considerable power and, on 18 July 1616, it was proclaimed that the first General Assembly since 1610 would meet in August. Surprisingly, there were no attempts to control absolutely the membership of this assembly as there had been in 1610, although the bishops and their appointees, the moderators of presbyteries, attended *ex officio* and the lay element was summoned by the crown once more. Surviving presbytery records do suggest that, apart from those restrictions, election was free.[36]

The Assembly, meeting in Aberdeen because of the strength of Catholicism in that area, dealt with a combination of royal articles and anti-Catholic measures.[37] Among the latter, the bishops were given powers to examine the young and admit them to communion. For this, it was agreed that a standard catechism should be composed. Effectively this introduced episcopal confirmation, although it does not seem to have been exercised.[38] It was also agreed, in accordance with the king's wishes, that ecclesiastical law should be codified in canons drawn from the acts of former assemblies, that a liturgy should be drawn up and that the Confession of Faith should be revised.

As a consequence of concentrating on measures against Catholics, this Assembly passed off relatively successfully. Soon after it had risen, the Bishop of Caithness sent word to court that all royal requests had been accepted. Flushed with this success, James sent north five articles which he wished to be inserted along with the canons.[39] This was in contravention of the General Assembly's agreement to draw up canons only from acts of former assemblies and Spottiswoode knew he could not oblige. He warned the king of the 'difficulty of admitting these articles' since they had not been 'motioned in the Church' and James agreed to wait until his trip to Scotland in 1617. Their reception was not to be warm.

---

[36] E.g., Haddington Presbytery, iii, 31 July 1616; Linlithgow Presbytery, i, fo. 150r; James VI to Sir Andrew Murray of Balvaird, 18 July 1616, *Ecclesiastical Letters*, i, no. 204.

[37] For accounts of this assembly, see *BUK*, iii, 1116–40; Calderwood, *History*, vii, 222–33; Scot, *Apologetical Narration*, 241–4.

[38] W.R. Foster, *The Church before the Covenants* (Edinburgh, 1975), 57; P.H.R. MacKay, 'The Reception Given to the Five Articles of Perth', *RSCHS*, 19 (1975–77), 185–201, at 194; G. Donaldson, *Scotland: James V–James VII* (Edinburgh, 1971), 207.

[39] Bishop of Caithness to Murray of Lochmaben, 17 Aug. 1616, *Ecclesiastical Letters*, i, no. 306; Spottiswoode, *History*, iii, 236–7.

Right from the planning stage, the king's only visit to Scotland after 1603 was an ecclesiastical public relations disaster. He may have been returning 'salmon-like' to Scotland but he had become so used to the ecclesiastical salt water of England that he had forgotten the very different taste of his native river. Indeed, in 1616, he had declared that the Church of England was the 'most pure and neerest [to] the Primitive and Apostolicall Church in doctrine and discipline'.[40] In August, the Privy Council hired Nicholas Stone of London to 'repair' the king's chapel in Holyrood Palace and, in October, organs, not used in Scottish worship since the Reformation, were sent up from England.[41] These 'repairs' were to involve erection of statues of the apostles. By the close of the year, rumours had reached such a level that the king wrote to the Privy Council insisting that there would be no alterations in religion 'which sall not tend to the glorie of God and the weele of that common wealth and all our good subjects therein'.[42] This did not preclude alterations per se and, in the following March, he wrote angrily to the Privy Council complaining that the Scots could not tell the difference between idolatrous images and decoration. He was, however, persuaded by a letter from the bishops that to insist on statues would be unwise. The Bishop of Galloway reassured Patrick Simson, minister of Stirling, that they had 'gotten them discharged' although they had received a 'sharpe rebuke' from James and Archbishop Abbott. Such an intervention outwith his jurisdiction by the English primate would have done nothing to endear him or any proposed ecclesiastical innovations either to the ministers or the Scottish bishops.[43] Soon after the king arrived in Scotland, he made his intentions for changes in worship clear. Communion was held at Whitsun in his chapel in Holyrood which had been fitted out with an altar, candles and an organ. Choristers sang in the service, the English liturgy was used and the bishops and nobles knelt to take communion.[44] Since the five articles were not yet public, the fears which such innovations caused would have been magnified. To the ministers and others, this form of worship was tantamount to Catholicism especially the kneeling which, to them, suggested worship of the sacrament, and therefore transubstantiation and idolatry.

---

[40] Quoted in Mullan, Episcopacy in Scotland, 151. This has notable echoes with his speech to the General Assembly of 1590, see below p. 44.

[41] RPC, x, 593–4; Calderwood, History, vii, 242.

[42] RPC, x, 685–6.

[43] James VI to the Privy Council, 13 March, Bishop of Galloway to Patrick Simson, 26 March 1616, Ecclesiastical Letters, ii, nos 314 and 315.

[44] Row, History, 307; Scot, Apologetical Narration, 246; Calderwood, History, vii, 246.

Parliament met at Edinburgh on 28 June and scores of ministers flocked there, leading to the suspension of many presbyteries' meetings.[45] The lords of the articles approved a vague royal act granting the king, with the advice of bishops and some ministers, power over 'indifferent' ecclesiastical matters. One of the ministers of Edinburgh preached against this, prompting an assurance that no innovations were intended. Fearing that this was untrue, a protestation asserting the right of freely elected assemblies to make all ecclesiastical decisions was subscribed by 55 ministers. Parliament, 'passed over' the act, because the king felt it unnecessary to define a particular aspect of his prerogative, but it reintroduced episcopal chapters with the right to 'elect' royal appointees to sees, restored to members of the chapters their manses and other property, and passed some acts relating to stipends.[46] In spite of the fact that the main target of the protestation was not enacted, Peter Hewatt, one of the ministers of Edinburgh, Archibald Simson, minister of Dalkeith, and David Calderwood were called before the High Commission for their parts in its composition and presentation. Hewatt was warded in Dundee and Simson in Aberdeen, while Calderwood, for defending the rights of the Kirk against the royal prerogative, was banished from Scotland. Presumably it was thought that such exemplary punishments would be enough, for when the other ministers of Edinburgh begged for royal forgiveness for their part in the protestation, they were pardoned.[47]

In July, the king's five articles were presented to the synods. Fearing one was not planned, they remitted them to a General Assembly to force the crown's hand. The king was reluctant to accede to this, even though it was supported by the bishops, reasoning that he would appear a tyrant if he was forced to impose the articles after their rejection by an Assembly. He relented, however, and the synods met in October for the bishops to choose commissioners to an Assembly which had yet to be proclaimed.[48] Before it met, Patrick Galloway, a minister to the royal household, was asked for his opinions on the articles which proposed confirmation by bishops; the celebration of holy days (Christmas, Good Friday, Easter Sunday, Ascension and Pentecost); private

---

[45] Linlithgow Presbytery, i, fo. 168r; Jedburgh Presbytery, i, 7 May 1617; Melrose Presbytery, fo. 138v; Peebles Presbytery, ii, fo. 147v; Dunblane Presbytery, 29 May 1617; SRO, synod of St Andrews benorth Forth, fo. 112v; Calderwood, *History*, vii, 249.

[46] *APS*, iv, 529–34; Spottiswoode, *History*, iii, 241–5; Calderwood, *History*, vii, 250–56.

[47] Scot, *Apologetical Narration*, 249; Calderwood, *History*, vii, 257–71; Row, *History*, 311–12.

[48] Scot, *Apologetical Narration*, 251; Row, *History*, 313; Calderwood, *History*, vii, 271–2, 284; Spottiswoode, *History*, iii, 247.

baptism; private communion; and kneeling to receive communion from the minister's hands. He began by stating that they were unnecessary and that the first had been enacted already, in 1616. He felt that holy days were indifferent, noting that several Reformed churches celebrated them, but advised that, since Scotland's only holy day had been Sunday since 1560, it might be best to celebrate them on the nearest Sunday. As far as baptism was concerned, he felt that it should be available publicly at any time of the day but not at night or in private since that might imply necessity for salvation. Private communion would be acceptable only for the long-term housebound but kneeling could not be countenanced. He was clear that communion should be taken sitting, observing that Innocent III had introduced kneeling in 1215 along with transubstantiation and insisting that 'Christis actione sould be oure institutione'.[49] This did not augur well for the General Assembly and a stark division of sentiment, with four articles acceptable in some form but kneeling strongly opposed, was mirrored in the Kirk at large. It has been observed that such misgivings as were expressed by Galloway 'ought to have moved a wiser or clearer mind to step back from the brink'.[50]

The Assembly met at St Andrews on 25 November and records suggest that most of those who attended were appointed by the bishops. There were also many amenable nobles and officers of state present, in fact the Court of Session had to be suspended because so many Lords of Session were at the Assembly![51] In spite of these preparations, and a royal letter threatening the use of the prerogative if they did not accept the articles, all did not go well for the crown. Even the privy conference, appointed by Archbishop Spottiswoode, did not accept the articles. The Assembly agreed only to two things: private communion on 24 hours' notice, with six others present and on condition that the recipient testified to terminal illness; and to the minister giving communion directly from his hand with the communicants sitting round a table, thus rendering kneeling impossible.[52] The Assembly was thinly attended, with no ministers from seven dioceses and not even the bishops of two of them. This was used as an excuse to remit the final decision to another Assembly.

---

[49] Patrick Galloway to James VI, 5 Nov. 1617, *Ecclesiastical Letters*, ii, no. 322.

[50] D.G. Mullan, *Episcopacy in Scotland: the History of an Idea, 1560–1638* (Edinburgh, 1986), 153.

[51] Deer Presbytery, ii, fo. 216v; Ellon Presbytery, ii, fo. 134r; Dalkeith Presbytery, 20 Nov. 1617; Peebles Presbytery, ii, fo. 150v; SRO, synod of St Andrews benorth Forth, fo. 116; Lord Binning to James VI, 20 Nov. 1616, *Ecclesiastical Letters*, ii, no. 325.

[52] Calderwood, *History*, vii, 285–6; Scot, *Apologetical Narration*, 252.

The bishops and Lord Binning steeled themselves and wrote to the king. Binning portrayed it as a hard-won victory by pointing out that the ministers had wanted everything remitted to further consideration but, rather than dissolve the assembly with nothing achieved, two things were agreed. The bishops insisted they had done their best: 'we haif left nothing undone that lay in us to haif your majesties articles passed … and thocht we haif done litle, yet a way is made to al'. James was furious: 'We thinke this … a disgrace no less than the protestation' presented to Parliament in June. He reminded them to preach at Christmas, which they duly did and insisted that, at the annual modification of stipends in November, they should give no augmentation to ministers opposing the articles. In January, the bishops had to plead with him to allow payment because this condition would have left too many without money.[53]

True to his threat that he would use his prerogative if the articles were rejected, on 14 January 1618, James ordered the Privy Council to command observation of the holy days. Good Friday was kept in Edinburgh by a command to the provost and bailies; it was also observed in Stirling and 'many touns'. On Easter Sunday, the bishops tried to enforce kneeling at communion. The Bishop of Galloway, remaining in Edinburgh, gave communion to the officers of state in the royal chapel at Holyrood on both days. He reported that many did not come, expressing 'reluctance', and only six complied.[54] The synod of St Andrews 'benorth Forth' met in April and those who had not celebrated communion at Easter were ordered to do so in future on pain of deprivation. In accordance with Patrick Galloway's advice of November 1617, and against the king's wishes, Ascension was celebrated on the following Sunday in Edinburgh. Fewer than 50 received communion kneeling. Observation of Whitsun was restricted to the Privy Council which was ordered to take communion at Holyrood again.[55] The cost of obtaining sufficient bread and wine meant that communion was normally held once a year in rural parishes and twice in the burghs. Virtually no parish kirk could have held three communions in such quick succession: in 1618, Easter Sunday was 5 April, Ascension was

---

[53] Lord Binning to James VI and Archbishops and bishops to James VI, both 28 Nov. 1617, James VI to the bishops, 6 Dec. 1617, *Ecclesiastical Letters*, ii, nos 326, 327, 328; Calderwood, *History*, vii, 288; Row, *History*, 314; Spottiswoode, *History*, iii, 251; Dunblane Presbytery, 25 Dec. 1617.

[54] *RPC*, xi, 296–7; Row, *History*, 315; Scot, *Apologetical Narration*, 253–4; Calderwood, *History*, vii, 290, 297; James VI to Privy Council, 14 Jan. 1618, Bishop of Galloway to James VI, [April 1618], *Ecclesiastical Letters*, ii, nos 333, 345.

[55] Calderwood, *History*, vii, 298; Bishop of Galloway to James VI, [May/June 1618], *Ecclesiastical Letters*, ii, 348; SRO, synod of St Andrews benorth Forth, fo. 117r.

14 May and Whitsun 24 May. In succeeding years, therefore, the crown's efforts to ensure obedience concentrated on Easter.

Although the date for the last General Assembly before 1638 was not proclaimed until July, it had been made clear in April that one was to meet. At the synod of St Andrews 'benorth Forth', the presbyteries were told by Spottiswoode to appoint 'wise and discreit' commissioners who would satisfy the king regarding the five articles. It is not clear how many were appointed by bishops, although those from Perth, Dunblane and Glasgow, where bishops moderated, certainly were. The strength of opposition to the articles in the Assembly itself would suggest that, in spite of allegations that the bishops prepared amenable ministers at the stipend commission and at the synods, many presbyteries appointed hostile commissioners.[56] The king had been persuaded to allow an Assembly only after reassurances that it would approve his articles. In a letter to it, he wrote that he had once been 'fully resolved never ... to have called any more assemblies' because of 'the disgrace offered' to him in November 1617. He declared that he would be happy only with 'a simple and direct acceptation of these articles'.[57]

The Assembly at Perth on 25 August was engineered as a powerful display of royal authority. Writing to the Privy Council in July, the king named his commissioners, stating that it was his 'forder pleasour that ye gif order to the Capitane of oure guaird with his horsemen to attend oure commissionaris during ... the said assemblie'. In 1613, the gerrymandered Irish Parliament had sat in Dublin Castle with an armed guard to intimidate it into accepting the crown's programme. The General Assembly of 1617 had resisted the king's plans for the Kirk, so the technique was transferred to Scotland.[58] The ministers were forced to stand while the bishops, officers of state, nobles and lairds sat. Proceedings began with the king's letter being read out twice, just to make sure. Archbishop Spottiswoode, moderating for the third time in a row without election, predicted the overthrow of 'the whole estate and order of *our* Kirk' (my italics) if the articles were

---

[56] *RPC*, xi, 419–20; Scot, *Apologetical Narration*, 255; Calderwood, *History*, vii, 303–4; Perth Presbytery, 7; Dunblane Presbytery, 13 Aug. 1618; Glasgow Presbytery, ii, fo. 133v; Deer Presbytery, ii, fo. 223v; Dalkeith Presbytery, 19 Aug. 1618; Jedburgh Presbytery, i, 29 July 1618; Melrose Presbytery, fo. 145v; Haddington Presbytery, iii, 22 July 1618.

[57] Spottiswoode, *History*, iii, 252–4.

[58] James VI to the Privy Council, 27 July 1618, *Ecclesiastical Letters*, ii, no. 352; A. Clarke and R. Dudley-Edwards, 'Pacification, Plantation and the Catholic Question', in eds, T.W. Moody, et al., *A New History of Ireland*, vol. iii, *Early Modern Ireland, 1534–1691* (Oxford, 1976), 213.

not accepted and threatened deprivation and banishment for any voting against them. He declared that none of this was his doing for it was the king's desire alone 'and if ye call him a persecutor, all the world will stand up against you'. Spottiswoode nominated the privy conference which, after hearing the king's letter again, spent the rest of the first day and the whole of the next debating the articles which were approved in a vote. On Thursday 27 August, the full Assembly reconvened and Spottiswoode pleaded for approval of the articles, hinting that they would not be strictly enforced. Some requested postponement for further discussion but this was denied. In the debate that ensued, those favouring the articles were allowed to speak at length, while those opposed were 'cutt off and sowrlie rebuked'. The Bishop of Brechin admitted, paradoxically trying to gain approval for the articles, that he knew of nothing in 'Scripture, Reasone, nor Antiquitie that inforceth kneeling', the article to which, as Patrick Galloway had predicted, there was most opposition. The bishop argued that, since they were indifferent and nothing was 'more expedient for the weill of our Kirk, than to keepe peace with our ... soveraigne', they should be accepted.

After the rejection of a written protest, the king's letter was read yet again, Spottiswoode announced that the names of those voting against the articles would be given to the king and, when each member's vote was sought, he was told to 'Have the king in mind'.[59] Having assured James that things would go smoothly, the bishops were desperate to deliver and went to great lengths to ensure success. The five articles of Perth were passed *en bloc* with 86 voting in favour, 41, 45 or 47 against, according to different sources, and three abstaining.[60] All but two of those who opposed were ministers. Even accepting the lowest estimate, given the number of bishops and laymen who were there, a majority of parish ministers probably voted against. The voice of the Kirk had not been heard because, in the words of the presbytery of Dalkeith, to their 'heavie displeasour ... the kingis majestie and the bishops hade gottin all thair will be pluralitie of such votes as wes lede to the purpose'.[61] In October, the Privy Council ratified the Five Articles of Perth, proclaimed them publicly and made every effort to ensure that

[59] Calderwood, *History*, vii, 304–32; Scot, *Apologetical Narration*, 255–63.

[60] Scot, *Apologetical Narration*, 263; Calderwood, *History*, vii, 332; Lord Binning to James VI, 27 Aug. 1618, *Ecclesiastical Letters*, ii, no. 355; M. Lynch, 'Preaching to the converted? Perspectives on the Scottish Reformation', in eds, A.A. MacDonald et al., *The Renaissance in Scotland: Studies in Literature, Religion, History and Culture Offered to John Durkan* (Leiden, 1994) 318 fails to take this factor, and the unprecedented level of intimidation, into account in describing this 'protest vote' as 'modest'.

[61] Dalkeith Presbytery, 2 Sept. 1618.

Christmas was kept with a number of presbyteries receiving letters commanding obedience to the articles. Resistance began early. Archbishop Law faced opposition at synods in Glasgow and Peebles, an order to ministers to intimate the articles from their pulpits was widely disregarded and, in Edinburgh at least, on 25 December, attendance at the kirk was poor.[62]

The period from Christmas 1618 until the king's death in 1625 witnessed repeated, ultimately futile, attempts to enforce obedience to the articles and these are well documented.[63] Under certain conditions, private baptism and private communion were acceptable and confirmation was not practised. Of the holy days, serious attempts were made to enforce observance only of Good Friday, Easter Sunday and Christmas and even then, obedience was hard to enforce. The presbytery of Dalkeith met on 25 December 1623, rendering it impossible for its ministers to preach in their own kirks on that day.[64] The only one which was strongly enforced was kneeling at communion. Most ministers did not want it, the bishops would rather not have had it and only on the grounds of obedience to the king could they justify it even to themselves. It became increasingly clear that enforcement was impossible. Many ministers were called before the High Commission for preaching against the articles, for refusal to enforce kneeling, for actively preventing it by holding communion seated round a table, and for willingly administering communion to people from other parishes who wished to avoid kneeling. One writer claims 48 ministers were called before the High Commission between 1610 and 1625 but a glance through Calderwood's History provides 43 names as well as 'others' summoned before the Commission for refusal to conform to the new style of communion between 1618 and 1625 alone.[65] More than 30 were warded, suspended or deposed but that was the tip of an iceberg. In April 1619, 36 ministers at the synod of St Andrews 'benorth Forth' had failed to conform and a further 17 were absent, at least some of whom had not

---

[62] Scot, *Apologetical Narration*, 266; Calderwood, *History*, vii, 337–41; Spottiswoode, *History*, iii, 257; Archbishop Law to Ayr Presbytery, 30 Nov. 1618, *Ecclesiastical Letters*, ii, no. 363; *RPC*, xi, 454; Linlithgow Presbytery, ii, 23 Dec. 1618; Dalkeith Presbytery, 24 Dec. 1618; Perth Presbytery, 12; Haddington Presbytery, iii, 16 Dec. 1618; Peebles Presbytery, ii, 17 Dec. 1618; Glasgow Presbytery, ii, fo. 136v.

[63] MacKay, 'The Reception Given to the Five Articles of Perth'; I.B. Cowan, 'The Five Articles of Perth', in ed., D. Shaw, *Reformation and Revolution* (Edinburgh, 1967), 160–77, at 174; G.I.R. McMahon, 'The Scottish Courts of High Commission, 1610–38', *RSCHS*, 15 (1966), 193–209, at 200.

[64] Dalkeith Presbytery, 25 Dec. 1623.

[65] Foster, *Church before the Covenants*, 48; Calderwood, *History*, vii, 352–614; SRO, synod of St Andrews benorth Forth, fo. 125v.

conformed.[66] By 1620, Spottiswoode was reduced to summoning the moderators of presbyteries from the Merse on behalf of their ministers. They were told merely to be quiet and not to encourage others to disobey.[67]

The king remained insistent that kneeling must be enforced. In November 1619, he commanded that all who disobeyed should be deposed, promising to provide as many English clerics as were necessary to replace them.[68] Such an unfeasible and provocative proposition demonstrated that James VI was increasingly out of touch with Scotland. The bishops tried to instil some moderation by suggesting that, if he wanted to resolve his ecclesiastical problems, he should 'shew ... more vehemencie in correcting and repressing the ... receptors of Jesuits and priests, then in urging conformitie to ceremonies'.[69] This impertinent advice went unheeded because James's goal was not peace with the Kirk; he had a wider agenda, including peace with Spain which might be cemented by marrying Prince Charles to the Infanta. That required domestic favour to Catholics which made the Scottish bishops' jobs all the more difficult. What seemed to be a pro-Catholic foreign policy was all the more likely to raise fears in the Kirk since, with the outbreak of what was to become the Thirty Years War on the Continent, Protestantism seemed to be under the hammer once more.

The royal desire to maintain pressure on non-conforming ministers continued at the Parliament of 1621, although 'an unprecedented level of management' was required to ensure the approval of the Five Articles. Parliament, called to raise money for military support to the Elector Palatine in the Thirty Years War, was also used to reinforce the articles which, although ratified by the Privy Council in 1618, continued to be disobeyed. To an extent they took over, Parliament being prorogued so that 'great dealling' could be done to ensure their approval, efforts being made 'either [to] reconquer the opposites ... or persuade or compel them ... to be absent'. Many ministers came to Edinburgh to lobby against the articles and with some success. A delegation went to the burgh commissioners and, after Parliament rose, it was reported that some of the smaller burghs had broken promises to vote with the crown. So alarmed was the crown by the presence of so many ministers

---

[66] SRO, synod of St Andrews benorth Forth, fos 119r–120v. That is well over half the ministers. Foster, *Church before the Covenants*, 187–8 argues for a 'collapse' in opposition in Fife. The figure of nine he provides for 1620 does not include absentees or those who bought time by declaring themselves 'purposed to conform'.

[67] Scot, *Apologetical Narration*, 278; Calderwood, *History*, vii, 425.

[68] James VI to Spottiswoode, Nov. 1619, *Ecclesiastical Letters*, ii, no. 387.

[69] Bishop of Aberdeen to James VI, 4 July 1620, *Ecclesiastical Letters*, ii, no. 396.

that they were commanded to leave Edinburgh unless they had episcopal permission to be there.[70] Although the articles became law, they were passed even more narrowly than they had been by the Assembly. As Ian Cowan observed, 'Had it not been for the votes of the bishops and the officers of state and the liberal use of proxies, the articles might well have failed to gain ratification.' Indeed, the opposition, concentrated within 'a line drawn roughly around Dumbarton, Ayr, Dunbar and St Andrews', mirrored very closely the areas of most intense opposition to kneeling at communion. Parallel divisions were opening up within the political nation.[71]

If the reintroduction of a powerful episcopate led to a number of ministers refusing to attend presbyteries and synods, the Five Articles of Perth exacerbated the problem. Increasingly, the records of presbyteries recorded persistent absenteeism. In 1624, in the presbytery of Linlithgow 'the moderatour protested he wold lay doun his moderatioun at the feet of the [synodal] assembly because of the brethrein quha for the maist pairt be continuall absence misregairdis thair dayis of meiting and so shaikis loos their discipline'. In the same year, a new minister in the presbytery of Dunblane was admitted only after promising to attend presbytery.[72] The only complete record of absences comes from the synod of St Andrews 'benorth Forth'. In April 1616, only 12 ministers were absent out of a possible total somewhere in the region of 100. By October 1622, that number had risen to 33 in addition to those who were warded or deprived for disobedience. There was a reduction in absences after this, probably resulting from a reduction in enforcement of holy days and kneeling, yet in Lothian, in November 1624 one-third of ministers failed to attend the synod and, in October 1625, a new commission was appointed by the synod of St Andrews 'benorth Forth' to cite persistent absentees.[73] Opposition and obedience to the Five

---

[70] Scot, *Apologetical Narration*, 284; Row, *History*, 328–9; Earl of Montrose to James VI, 3 Aug., same to same, 4 Aug. 1621, *Ecclesiastical Letters*, ii, nos 412, 414; Ellon Presbytery, ii, fo. 163r; Perth Presbytery, 63; Peebles Presbytery, ii, fo. 162v; K.M. Brown, *Kingdom or Province? Scotland and the Regal Union, 1603–1707* (London, 1992), 96.

[71] J. Goodare, 'The Scottish Parliament of 1621', *The Historical Journal*, 38 (1995), 29–51, which is a detailed analysis of the Parliament; Cowan, 'The Five Articles of Perth', 176; Mullan, *Episcopacy in Scotland*, 158.

[72] This is evident in most of the presbyteries for which records survive. See Linlithgow Presbytery, *passim* (quote is from 19 May 1624); Dunblane Presbytery, 15 April 1619, 9 Aug. 1621, 18 Feb. 1624, Glasgow Presbytery ii, fo. 167r; Dalkeith Presbytery, 21 Nov. 1622, 3 June 1624, Haddington Presbytery, iii, 16 June 1624; Perth Presbytery, 114.

[73] SRO, synod of St Andrews benorth Forth, fo. 148v, *et passim*; Calderwood, *History*, vii, 625; Foster, *Church before the Covenants*, 189–90 where he notes the reduction in enforcement.

Articles of Perth, or at least the two which were seriously enforced, varied geographically, there being little disobedience to them in the North East and much more in Fife and Lothian. Yet, where opposition was strong, an ecclesiastical crisis occurred. Discipline began to crumble and the basic functions of the courts of the Kirk ceased to operate effectively in numerous areas. The number of discipline cases dealt with by presbyteries plummeted. This, as well as a genuine lack of enthusiasm for the articles themselves, may have been significant in the episcopate's increasing lack of enthusiasm to ensure obedience.

What made attempts to enforce kneeling at communion entirely different from any ecclesiastical innovation since the Reformation, however, was widespread lay resistance. Although Edinburgh saw the greatest opposition, with prominent people being dealt with by the courts for their refusal to kneel and where there were the most enduring attempts to enforce obedience, there is evidence for considerable resistance elsewhere. According to John Row, obedience to Easter communion was, at best, patchy. He wrote that, in 1619, 'in some parts all the people went out of the kirk and left the minister alone; in other parts the minister and people fell in disputing'. In May, the Privy Council issued a proclamation noting that 'in divers congregationis of this kingdome thair hes bene litill obedience gevin to the saidis actis', and that many stayed away from kirks or refused to communicate.[74] This resulted from a royal letter which noted disobedience only in Edinburgh but the Privy Council knew opposition to be much more widespread and they were not giving their king an account of its true level. In April 1620, a minister in Fife said his parishioners refused to communicate kneeling and, in the summer, the Privy Council instituted fines for those who failed to communicate properly: earls were to be fined £100, lords 100 merks, lairds £40 and craftsmen and husbandmen £10.[75] These hefty fines were not imposed. The weight of cases would have been too great; the level of nonconformity meant that exemplary punishments would fail and the Privy Council lacked the will for enforcement.

That lay nonconformity was an intractable problem can be partly explained by the resistance of the ministers themselves. One, however, the minister of Kinghorn in Fife and a crown placeman, sought the removal from his session of people who refused to kneel in 1622 but Archbishop Spottiswoode refused to help.[76] In the North East and the South West, there is evidence for Protestant nonconformity, in the sense that people refused to take communion in the new form. In 1620, the

---

[74] Row, *History*, 321; *RPC*, xi, 579–81.
[75] Calderwood, *History*, vii, 443; *RPC*, xii, 279–81.
[76] Calderwood, *History*, vii, 563.

synod of Aberdeen tried to prevent the laity from going to other parishes to take communion, presumably to avoid kneeling. The same policy was attempted in Fife and Angus in 1624. In 1622, the parishioners of Mauchline in Ayrshire were prosecuted for refusing a presentee unless he promised not to enforce kneeling, while in 1623, the Bishop of Galloway found 'proofe of contempt of our authoritie' in Catholic and Protestant nonconformity.[77] One of the greatest problems created by concentration on obedience to kneeling at communion was the confusion of Catholic and Protestant disobedience. Although the king regarded the two as equally dangerous, the ministers and the bishops did not.[78] Yet, the widespread nature of Protestant resistance to kneeling meant that, after 1618, it became extremely difficult to disentangle the Catholics who would not take communion because it was Protestant from the Protestants who would not take it because it was idolatrous. The Kirk's relatively successful efforts against Catholicism after 1610 were thus undone.

The capital witnessed the most concerted attempt at enforcement of kneeling at communion and, as a result, the most vociferous and persistent opposition to it. As an example to the people of Edinburgh, at Easter 1619, the Privy Council, the Court of Session, all advocates and the town council were ordered to communicate kneeling but 'there were sundrie that came not'. The earls of Roxburgh and Linlithgow excused themselves on the grounds of illness but Sir James Skene of Curriehill, a Lord of Session, was called before the Privy Council for attending a kirk where there was no kneeling. In November 1621, the king ordered the Privy Council to declare its own obedience to the articles and to enforce an oath of obedience on public office-holders. Even as late as the autumn of 1624, he had to command the attendance of Privy Councillors and members of the court of session at Christmas communion and was unable to obtain promises of conformity from the council of Edinburgh.[79]

Whatever example the privy councillors, judges, advocates and town councillors gave, its effect on the populace was negligible. Before the articles had been passed by the General Assembly, attempts to introduce them had been largely ignored by the people of Edinburgh. After their

---

[77] Deer Presbytery, ii, fo. 244v; SRO, synod of St Andrews benorth Forth, fo. 143v; *RPC*, xii, 728–9; Bishop of Galloway to Archbishop Spottiswoode, 11 Dec. 1623, *Ecclesiastical Letters*, ii, no. 467.

[78] *RPC*, xii, 79–81, which is a royal letter of November 1622 in which the king equated 'papist' and 'puritan' nonconformists.

[79] Row, *History*, 320, 337; *RPC*, xi, 595, 598, 635–6, xii, 597–8; Calderwood, *History*, vii, 628.

enactment, active and determined opposition developed. In February 1619, a number of townspeople were called before the Privy Council for having worked on Christmas day. That Easter, and in succeeding years, thousands deserted Edinburgh to take communion outside the city where no efforts could be made to enforce kneeling. The minutes of the presbytery of Dalkeith reflect the strain this put upon their resources by describing approaching Easter communions as 'the weightie burden hanging on thair shoulders the nixt Sabboth day'. A number of the inhabitants of Edinburgh were warded, some were even banished to distant parts of Scotland but too many were of like mind for this to be effective.[80]

In 1619, Archbishop Spottiswoode warned the presbytery of Perth that the failure of ministers to accept the articles and their tendency to preach against them threatened ecclesiastical schism. In the following year, his fears were realised when, for the first time since before 1560, 'privie meetings of ministers and other good Christians' took place. Some ministers who had been deposed for refusal to conform went to Edinburgh and were conducting clandestine religious services.[81] The king was making unreasonable demands of his agents in Edinburgh and, in 1623, the Earl of Melrose wrote to him with the news that 'the nomber of communicants wes small' that Easter and of those who did attend one Edinburgh kirk, 'verie few of them kneeled'. He assured James that it was neither the fault of the bishops nor of the ministers of Edinburgh and urged that time, rather than harsh punishment, was required to heal this wound. Soon afterwards, Spottiswoode noted 'ane obstinat purpose and resolution in that people to hearken to no persuasion'. He also noted that, in 1624, William Rig, one of the bailies of Edinburgh and a prominent lay dissident, had warned that everyone would forsake the Kirk unless 'the old form of ministering the holy communion' was reinstated.[82]

The bishops had made it clear all along that they had no affection for the Five Articles, or for their enforcement. As early as May 1619, Archbishop Law resisted the deprivation of three ministers 'for these indifferent things' and, in November of the same year, Spottiswoode

---

[80] Calderwood, *History*, vii, 348, 359; Lord Binning to James VI, 29 March 1619, *Ecclesiastical Letters*, ii, no. 372; Dalkeith Presbytery, 18 March 1619; MacKay, 'The Reception Given to the Five Articles of Perth', 198–9; McMahon, 'The Scottish Courts of High Commission', 207.

[81] Row, *History*, 328; Calderwood, *History*, vii, 449; *RPC*, xii, 517, 519–20, 578, 582–3; D. Stevenson, 'Conventicles in the Kirk, 1619–1637: the Emergence of a Radical Party', *RSCHS*, 18 (1974), 99–114, at 101–5.

[82] Melrose to James VI, 16 April, Spottiswoode to Annandale, 11 May 1623, *Ecclesiastical Letters*, ii, nos 352, 467; Spottiswoode, *History*, iii, 268.

declared that he would have been happy had they never been introduced but that the king must be obeyed. They were in an awkward position indeed. The Bishop of Aberdeen pressed a minister to obey because the articles were indifferent. The minister responded by asking why he was being pressed so hard if that was so and the bishop was forced to admit that the episcopate would allow toleration but the king would not have it. He and Spottiswoode promised Lord Scone that they would tell James that Scone had done his duty in executing a royal commission in ecclesiastical affairs as long as Scone, in return, gave a sanitised report of the level of nonconformity to the king. When, in 1620, Spottiswoode declared that 'the king is pope now!', it was as much in exasperation with the commands coming up from court as an attempt to intimidate a recalcitrant minister. According to Calderwood, the bishops finally decided, at St Andrews in April 1623, that further pressure for conformity was futile and that they should ease off.[83]

In England in 1623, James was considering to tolerate Catholics or at least to allow the Spanish Infanta, if she were to marry Charles, freedom of worship. He even ordered the trial of any Scots who criticised the laxity shown to English Catholics in the cause of the Spanish marriage.[84] Yet he pushed more and more strongly for conformity to the Five Articles of Perth. In the summer of 1624, he urged 'extremitie' against those who would not obey. He wanted communion to be held at Christmas in Edinburgh but an outbreak of disease there thwarted this desire. As Easter 1625 approached, he demanded, once more, that all ministers should give communion to kneeling recipients and that all who would not do so should be deprived.[85] His death on 27 March rescued the bishops from what might very well have become an extremely awkward situation. Had James lived for even a few years longer, it would have been difficult to keep from him the latitude given to nonconformists.

---

[83] Row, *History*, 323; Scot, *Apologetical Narration*, 270–71, 273–8; Calderwood, *History*, vii, 397–9, 403, 406–7, 571.

[84] Calderwood, *History*, vii, 570–71; Spottiswoode, *History*, iii, 265–8.

[85] Row, *History*, 338; Calderwood, *History*, vii, 615.

CHAPTER EIGHT

Conclusion

As is obvious from the preceding pages and from any reading of other secondary works, the influence of late sixteenth- and early seventeenth-century narrative historians on modern views of the Jacobean Kirk can only be immense. They enhance the official record of both Kirk and state, providing details which would otherwise have perished. The seminal work was James Melville's *Diary*, completed in 1602, and his *True Narratioune of the Declyneing Aige of the Kirk of Scotland*, written in 1610. The degree to which his writings influenced anti-episcopalian historiography of Jacobean Scotland is difficult to overestimate. His works influenced and were heavily borrowed by later writers such as David Calderwood, William Scot and John Row.[1] Calderwood's *History of the Kirk of Scotland* is the most heavily used source for the period, drawing upon Knox's *History of the Reformation in Scotland* for its early passages and upon Melville for the period between the 1570s and 1610. Much of Calderwood's text is taken almost verbatim from these earlier works and he fleshed out the rest from personal experience and an impressive collection of contemporary letters, tracts and official papers. The work of Archbishop John Spottiswoode, although he wrote from a very different perspective from that offered by the so-called 'presbyterian historians', has served only to bolster the impression of the period given by James Melville and his followers. That is because Spottiswoode used very similar frames of reference to those employed by his opponents. As a result of the personal fortunes of James Melville and John Spottiswoode, and of their respective political opinions, a misleading picture of Jacobean ecclesiastical politics developed. The use, by these writers, of such terms as 'the better sort' or 'the wiser sort' to describe different groups of ministers has given the impression of factions or parties within the Kirk and later writers have interpreted them in this way. What they actually appear to have denoted was the group of ministers which agreed with the author's

---

[1] Calderwood, *History, passim*; Scot, *Apologetical Narration, passim*. The extent of the influence of Melville has been noted in D.G. Mullan, *Episcopacy in Scotland: the History of an Idea, 1560–1638* (Edinburgh, 1986), 78 and recently by M. Lynch in 'Preaching to the Converted? Perspectives on the Scottish Reformation', in eds, A.A. MacDonald et al., *The Renaissance in Scotland: Studies in Literature, Religion, History and Culture Offered to John Durkan* (Leiden, 1994), 302.

viewpoint in a particular vote or concerning a particular issue at a particular time, or in hindsight. James Melville wrote, for instance, that the General Assembly of February and March 1597 at Perth was 'esteemed by the best and most godly' to have been invalid.[2] Describing the events of November 1596, John Spottiswoode suggested that 'the wiser sort' wanted to take a more moderate course of action than those who prevailed.[3] This was an attempt by Spottiswoode to distance himself, at the time of writing in the 1620s, from the upsurge of opposition at the end of 1596 and thus from his dissident past. The inference that these designations referred to groupings which were not ephemeral and were in any way distinct is a mistaken notion which bears little relationship to the Kirk in late sixteenth- and early seventeenth-century Scotland.

The difficulties in the relationship between the Kirk and the crown from the 1570s onwards, most notably after c. 1581, have thus led to a belief, observable in current and recent historiography that a group which have been called the 'Melvillians' dominated the Kirk before 1597 through coercion and vociferous persuasion of those who attended general assemblies.[4] It has recently been acknowledged that the word 'Melvillian' requires some reassessment, yet the frames of reference, of entrenched factions, remain the same. In the context of the universities, the word has been put in quotation marks by James Kirk, the foremost recent writer on the 'Melvillians'.[5] Michael Lynch has recently noted that:

> The dynamic – or the spectre – of a Melvillian party in the Kirk has absorbed many historians' attentions. The history of the post-Reformation Church in its vital second and third generations, between the 1580s and the 1620s, has, as a result, often become focussed on a struggle between contending parties within the Kirk ... .[6]

---

[2] Melville, *Diary*, 410.

[3] Spottiswoode, *History*, iii, 7.

[4] G. Donaldson, *The Scottish Reformation* (Cambridge, 1960), 217; G. Donaldson, 'The Scottish Church 1567–1625', in ed., A.G.R. Smith, *The Reign of James VI and I* (Aylesbury, 1973), 45; Lynch, 'Preaching to the Converted?', 315–16 where the same idea of unrepresentative power of the 'Melvillians' lost after 1596 is implied; R. Mason, 'George Buchanan, James VI and the Presbyterians', in ed., R. Mason, *Scots and Britons: Scottish Political Thought and the Union of 1603* (Cambridge, 1994), 114, 122.

[5] J. Kirk, '"Melvillian" Reform in the Scottish Universities', in eds, A.A. MacDonald et al., *The Renaissance in Scotland: Studies in Literature, Religion, History and Culture Offered to John Durkan* (Leiden, 1994), 276–300. The word is given thus, primarily because Melville's university reforms were actually Ramist, but also perhaps because it has connotations of the introduction of presbyterianism by Melville in the 1570s. There is, however, no rejection of the idea of a presbyterian 'movement' or party in the Kirk; see also J. Kirk, 'The Development of the Melvillian Movement in Late Sixteenth Century Scotland' (unpublished Edinburgh PhD dissertation, 1972).

[6] Lynch, 'Preaching to the Converted?', 314.

Although this comes closer than almost any other writer to the thesis proposed here, it goes on to discuss the subject of the actual process of Protestantisation. This is examined in terms of a challenge which faced the Kirk as a whole regardless of individuals' views on polity or jurisdiction but the very premiss of the existence of a 'Melvillian party' in the sphere of ecclesiastical politics is not questioned. As a result, such phrases as splits 'within Melvillian ranks' and 'the standard Melvillian protest vote' were still used.[7]

The simple fact of the existence of a group of ministers, supposedly centred on Andrew Melville, remains unquestioned, in spite of the fact that evidence to support Andrew Melville's leadership of a group, or even of his peculiar prominence in the Kirk, is severely lacking. Indeed, the historiographical consensus has recently been neatly summed up as follows: 'First came the Union of the Crowns when James VI and his governments were locked in a protracted struggle with the Melvillians. Then followed the era after 1603 when the king overcame his religious adversaries and episcopacy triumphed over Presbyterianism.'[8] Historians have been approaching their sources with too many preconceptions. They have looked for 'Melvillians' in circumstances where such people might not be found. Indeed most of them have failed to define what it was to be a 'Melvillian' let alone who the members of this supposed party were.[9] The only attempt to come up with answers to these points can be found in James Kirk's 'The Development of the Melvillian Movement in Late Sixteenth Century Scotland' which includes 'A Census of Melvillian Preachers' numbering 155.[10] The criteria for inclusion, and therefore the definition of a Melvillian, appear to be that an individual had to have some record against their name of action in support or defence of presbyterianism or the separation of civil and ecclesiastical

---

[7] Lynch, 'Preaching to the Converted?', 316, 318.

[8] G. Hewitt, 'Reformation to Revolution', in eds, I. Donnachie and C. Whatley, *The Manufacture of Scottish History* (Edinburgh, 1992) 21–2.

[9] This is found in the work of most historians of the period: Mullan, *Episcopacy in Scotland*, 63 'the Melvilles and their friends', 86 'the presbyterians'; Donaldson, *Scottish Reformation*, 217 'the Melvillian achievement'; G. Donaldson, *Scotland: James V-James VII* (Edinburgh, 1971), 198 'Melville and his associates', 200 'Melville's resolute party'; Mason, 'George Buchanan, James VI and the Presbyterians', 114 'the Melvillian presbyterians', 122 'Melville and his colleagues'; W.R. Foster, *The Church before the Covenants* (Edinburgh, 1975), 17 'the presbyterian party'; Lynch, 'Preaching to the Converted?' devotes a section to 'The Melvillian Party'; J. Dawson, 'Anglo-Scottish Protestant Culture and Integration in Sixteenth Century Britain', in eds, S.G. Ellis and S. Barber, *Conquest and Union: Fashioning a British State, 1485–1725* (London, 1995), 87–114, at 92, 98, 99 where emphasis is placed on 'two mutually antagonistic ecclesiastical parties'.

[10] Kirk, 'The Development of the Melvillian Movement', 559–665.

jurisdictions. A significant number were not ministers and some had only one such instance of 'Melvillian' activity against their names. Moreover, had such ministers as David Lindsay and Peter Blackburn died at the beginning of 1597, they would probably have made it onto the list on the strength of their activities before that date, yet they went on to become bishops. John Spottiswoode, on the other hand, in spite of becoming Archbishop of Glasgow in 1603 and of St Andrews in 1615, was surprisingly included, as was Patrick Forbes of Corse who became Bishop of Aberdeen in 1618.

It seems fair to say that there was, in England, a 'Puritan movement', a self-aware group of ministers and lay folk who verged on religious nonconformity and sometimes overstepped its bounds. They were people who wanted a presbyterian polity in the Church of England, or at least a significant simplification of dress and liturgy, and Patrick Collinson has shown that they were organised and self-conscious.[11] Perhaps, in an attempt to find a similar phenomenon in Scotland, a 'movement' has been posited. There is, however, no evidence of a coherent, self-aware band of ministers pursuing an ideological goal. Had the 'Black Acts' of 1584 been fulfilled, leading to a sustained period of powerful episcopacy sponsored by the crown and, crucially, enforced by a subscription, such a movement might have emerged but, before 1606 there was no meaningful episcopate or objectionable polity against which to organise. It should be noted that when, in the later years of the reign, there was a settled polity which was abhorrent to a sufficient number of ministers, nonconformity, both clerical and lay did develop and it was perceived as a genuine threat to ecclesiastical and royal authority. The nonconformity may be better explained, however, by a reaction to the liturgical innovations. In England, as in Scotland, 'voluntary religion' can be seen to have emerged in response to attempts to enforce ceremonies, modes of dress and subscription to articles of faith.[12] An English cleric could refuse to wear the cap or the surplice but, before 1618, there was really nothing that a Scottish minister could refuse to do and it is to that period that historians should look if they are seeking a Scottish nonconformist presbyterian 'movement'.

The prevailing historiographical frames of reference are mistaken and can be misleading. Loose, ill-defined labels are picked up and used without critical appraisal. To ask 'Which ministers were Melvillian?' or 'Was he Melvillian?' begs the question so blatantly, yet no satisfactory

---

[11] P. Collinson, *The Elizabethan Puritan Movement* (Oxford, 1967).

[12] Collinson, *Elizabethan Puritan Movement*, esp. ch. 3. The use of the term 'movement' can be traced to Donaldson's *Scottish Reformation*, ch. 8, 'The Rise of the Presbyterian Movement'.

explanations are provided because generalised labels are easier. Analysis of the Jacobean Kirk, or of any institution or group of people, needs to look behind and beyond such labels because they represent simplistic answers to complex questions. An analysis of attendance patterns at general assemblies and shifting waves of obedience and opposition to the policies of the crown urge that such interpretations should be fundamentally revised. Similar ideas of the centrality of party are being challenged in English ecclesiastical history where the terms Anglican and Puritan 'have been dethroned'; it is time that the terms 'Melvillian' and 'episcopalian' were challenged in Scotland.[13]

The term 'Melvillian', or more accurately 'Melvinian', was indeed one which was coined during the period under investigation, yet the earliest instance of its use dates from 1610.[14] Describing the recent meeting of the diocesan synod of St Andrews 'benorth Forth', Archbishop Gledstanes told the king that 'some of the old Melvinian brude that remains here' had caused trouble. Since this statement was made four years after Andrew and James Melville had left Scotland for the last time, and since it applied only to Fife, its application to the period as a whole and to any wider geographical context lack substance. Alexander Hume, in 1609, also wrote that the ministers were, at that time, 'devydet in twa factionis or opinionis' but this referred only to the split between those who favoured the form of episcopacy introduced after 1606 and those who opposed it, and cannot be applied to the whole reign.[15]

The analysis given here attempts to explain the misinterpretations, while offering a new interpretation of the course of ecclesiastical politics in Jacobean Scotland. As has been demonstrated in detail above, the minority of James VI saw a number of attempts to establish the Reformed Kirk with new systems of ecclesiastical oversight and financial provision, sometimes resulting in extreme controversy. The adult reign, which adopted some of the approaches of the minority, began with another such experiment. The first 11 years of James's personal rule were dominated by opposition to the broader religious policy of the crown because, although it tolerated the independent development of a presbyterian polity, it involved too much tolerance of the activities of

---

[13] P. White, 'The *via media* in the Early Stuart Church', in ed., K. Fincham, *The Early Stuart Church, 1603–1642* (London, 1993), 217, where it is noted that many English clerics 'did not naturally fall into either category' (Arminian or Puritan); see also Fincham's 'Introduction', 8 in the same work and N. Tyacke, 'Anglican Attitudes: Some Recent Writings on English Religious History, from the Reformation to the Civil War', *Journal of British Studies*, 35 (1996), 139–67.

[14] NLS, 'Memories to the King his sacred Majestie', Oct. 1610, Wodrow Folio, 42, no. 68.

[15] Hume, 'Ane afold admonition', in *Wodrow Miscellany*, i, 569.

the Catholic earls. This provided a unifying force and a cause behind which the Kirk was able to unite against the king. That the ecclesiastical politics of the later 1580s and early 1590s were not dominated by any doctrinaire party line, however, is demonstrated by the lack of opposition or controversy surrounding the compromise polity of 1586. In Scotland in this period, the atmosphere was laced with the constant fear of Spanish, and therefore Catholic, invasion. Zealous Catholic posturing by the Earl of Huntly, continental counter-Reformation activity and the state of international politics meant that Protestantism, especially Calvinism, felt acutely threatened at home and in much of mainland Europe. In The Netherlands, Spanish power was a constant threat into the last years of the sixteenth century and beyond. In France, uncertainty was almost endemic. Repeated civil wars and uneasy compromises throughout the 1560s, 1570s and 1580s were followed by the conversion to Catholicism of Henri IV and the end of any hope for national Reformation there. Most alarming of all, for international Calvinism, was the threat to the mother-church of Geneva from Savoy.[16] In this atmosphere, it was a desire to see Catholicism at home decisively confronted which was the foremost unifying factor in the Kirk prior to 1597.

Alignments within the Kirk were not fixed; they shifted as new issues came to the fore and old ones retreated. Opposition to the king's lack of firm action against particular Catholics and against Catholicism in general reached a peak at the end of 1596. The return of the earls of Huntly and Errol without having satisfied the Kirk and the trial of David Black led to a point at which such a shift occurred. Passionate clerical anxiety over the potential consequences of royal favour to Catholics became entangled with ecclesiastical claims of freedom from civil jurisdiction. The king feared a challenge to royal authority and constitutional order. The royal reaction to this challenge, and to the alleged riot which resulted, was so strong and decisive that a new agenda emerged and there was a realignment of clerical opinion. The foremost issue became obedience to the monarch and the cementing of the relationship between the Kirk and the crown through a new system of ecclesiastical representation in Parliament. Only a minority of ministers continued to resist royal policy and to use frames of reference which had been the currency of 1596. As a result, those ministers have

---

[16] Koenigsberger et al., *Europe in the Sixteenth Century*, 2nd edn (London, 1989) ch. 12; G. Lewis, 'Calvinism in Geneva in the Time of Calvin and Beza (1541–1605), in ed., M. Prestwich, *International Calvinism, 1541–1715* (Oxford, 1985); M. Greengrass, 'France', in eds, B. Scribner, R. Porter and M. Teich, *Reformation in National Context* (Cambridge, 1994).

been identified as a 'party', as a supposed core group which had co-ordinated opposition over the previous ten years and more but was now suddenly visible because they had been left behind by the others, just like those imprisoned or exiled for resistance to the Arran regime of 1583–85.

From these episodes comes the view that, behind any ecclesiastical opposition to the crown after about 1575, the 'Melvillians' were pulling the strings. The prominence in opposition, prior to 1597, of David Lindsay, John Spottiswoode, Adam Bellenden, Peter Blackburn, Patrick Galloway, James Nicolson and many others who would later be impor-tant instruments of royal power in the Kirk undermines this notion severely.[17] It may also be observed that alignments shifted in both directions. At the time of James VI's absence from Scotland in 1589–90, Robert Bruce, later to be deprived of his charge in Edinburgh and banished to Inverness, was trusted with a prominent role in govern-ment. James Melville himself appears to have been one of the ministers most close to the court in the early 1590s but his face ceased to be welcome there after 1595 when his 'court grew les'. In later life, he was clearly ashamed of how close he had been to court and he began to play down his 'courting' by saying that he had 'sought it nocht' and that he had done it only so that 'Kirk and polecie might go right and weill fordwart'.[18] Implicit within the idea that the 'Melvillians' were defeated after 1596 is the assumption of the rigidity of clerical opinion. This sits very shakily indeed alongside the fact that arguments, issues, circum-stances and allegiances changed quite dramatically in 1596–97.

Events changed minds – in both directions across the supposedly rigid divide. While, on the one hand, a number of ministers who had previ-ously been involved at the forefront of opposition became agents of the crown within the Kirk, those who continued to oppose the policies of the king effectively found that the ground had shifted beneath them and they had to move quickly to keep standing. During the 11 years after 1585, the theory of two kingdoms was rarely aired. The issue of parlia-mentary representation provides clear evidence of that. Throughout the period from 1585 until 1596, as well as in the years before, the views expressed in general assemblies and elsewhere were firmly in support of

---

[17] The closest a recent historian has got to grasping this is Mullan, *Episcopacy in Scotland*, 114–16, 123 (discussing David Lindsay), 125–6 (discussing Patrick Forbes) where he virtually admits that it is not a question of parties but of changed views. Most of those listed became bishops; e.g., Adam Bellenden, victimised by Lord Livingstone in 1597 (see p. 79) became Bishop of Dunblane.

[18] On Bruce, see SRO, Royal letters presented by Mr R.J. Bruce of Elmhurst Farm, Sussex, GD1/240/1–4; Melville, *Diary*, 328–9.

some form of ecclesiastical representation in Parliament. Even that supposed 'Melvillian' manifesto, the *Second Book of Discipline*, advocated a place in Parliament for the Kirk.[19] In 1596, James Melville described a plan which involved ministers as commissioners from presbyteries representing the Kirk in Parliament as 'the best and maist exact that ever was devysit or sett doun, and wald, sum litle things amendit, [haiff] bein glaidlie receavit be the breithring of best judgement'.[20] Within two years of this, however, the theory of two kingdoms, of the separation of the civil and ecclesiastical spheres, was being applied to this issue by Melville and others for the first time. Suddenly, ecclesiastical representation in Parliament had become an intolerable mixing of the two jurisdictions.[21] The mainstream of clerical opinion remained in favour of parliamentary representation but certain individuals changed their minds because circumstances had altered.

Contrary to the assertions of contemporaries, which have been taken on board without question by subsequent historians, there were no significant changes in the composition of general assemblies after 1596. There was no influx of 'Northland ministers', there was no eclipse of a dominant party by royal gerrymandering of general assemblies. The king, as a result of events in the last few months of 1596, devoted much more time to ecclesiastical affairs. Indeed, he was more able to do this because of the political stability which prevailed in comparison with the first 11 years of his personal reign. The Earl of Bothwell was in exile. Spain's ambitions to invade Britain had waned, so the earls of Huntly, Errol and Angus had neither the opportunity nor the desire to rise in arms and the king's secretary, John Maitland of Thirlestane, the relatively low-born object of much noble resentment after 1585, was dead. What resulted, largely by careful negotiations and consultation, was a crown policy, albeit a much more interventionist one, which was acceptable to a majority of the ministry, as was shown by the demonstrable successes for the crown at freely elected assemblies between 1597 and 1602. This policy involved the possibility of financial benefit to the Kirk, attractive in such times of economic instability, through the revival of the ecclesiastical estate in Parliament. Those sitting as representatives of the Kirk would bring with them the revenues of prelacies to pay for the upkeep of parish kirks, schools and universities and to provide poor relief, but would have strictly circumscribed powers. A *via media* was found and, when James VI went south to take up

---

[19] *Second Book of Discipline*, 226.
[20] Melville, *Diary*, 343–4.
[21] Melville, *Diary*, 435–6, 446–59; Calderwood, *History*, v, 746–62.

his new throne in 1603, he believed, with some justification, that he had left a Kirk at peace.[22]

Recent work on James's English reign has begun to revise the largely negative assessment his ecclesiastical policy had previously received from English historiography.[23] The general assessment is that, in his southern kingdom, he tried to pursue a policy of accommodation which was generally acceptable and excluded only the extremes of Puritanism and Catholicism. In the sense that it steered this middle course and was as consensual as possible, this policy was fundamentally similar to that which he had pursued in Scotland between 1597 and 1603. The accessibility and consultation which had characterised Scottish kingship before the regal union was something which James applied to his new kingdom, albeit within the confines of the more rigidly formalised English court structure. The very fact that he held the Hampton Court Conference of 1604 was a radical departure from the aloof approach of his predecessor. His personal investigations of its effects while on a prolonged hunting expedition in late 1604 and early 1605 were quite unprecedented. Through contact with the English Puritan clergy and gentry, he discovered that they were largely 'free from the taint of presbyterianism' and so he eventually adopted a more moderate drive for conformity in England than he had originally intended.[24] When the backlash against his post-union Scottish policy came in 1604–05, Scottish dissident clergy were thus, however, made to seem all the more dangerous and subversive. James had transferred a successful policy from Scotland to his new kingdom. The crucial nature of the personal involvement of the monarch was thus lost in Scotland. It may well have been that factor which was of primary importance in the collapse of consent for his Scottish ecclesiastical policy.

After he had travelled south, James put his energies into dealing with matters at hand and these, inevitably, were English. As a result of his belief that ecclesiastical affairs were settled before he had left, he began

---

[22] See e.g., NLS James VI to William Scot, 21 May 1606, Wodrow Folio, 42, no. 48 where he expressed the desire to see the Kirk at peace as it had been in 1603; NLS, 'Report of the conference at Hampton Court in September 1606', Wodrow Folio 42, no. 49(a), fo. 130r where the same desire was reported; Devine and Lythe, 'The Economy of Scotland under James VI', esp. 94.

[23] K. Fincham and P. Lake, 'The Ecclesiastical Policy of James I', *Journal of British Studies*, 24, (1985), 170–88; F. Shriver, 'Hampton Court Revisited: James I and the Puritans', *Journal of Ecclesiastical History*, 33 (1982), 48–71; B. Quintrell, 'The Royal Hunt and the Puritans', *Journal of Ecclesiastical History*, 31 (1980); White, 'The *via media* in the Early Stuart Church', 211–30; C. Durston, *James I* (London, 1993), esp. ch. 6.

[24] Quintrell, 'The Royal Hunt and the Puritans', esp. 45.

to pay attention to the Kirk in Scotland only when it stood in his way by objecting to his new policies or when it wanted to adhere to agreements which had been made prior to 1603. The Parliament of 1604, for which the Kirk had not been allowed to advise its episcopal representatives by holding a General Assembly, may have been as crucial a turning point, albeit a less dramatic one, as the last few months of 1596. Fear of an incorporating union with England, continued lack of royal action against the leaders of Scottish Catholicism and repeated prorogations of the General Assembly which were really attempts by the crown to brush ecclesiastical problems under the carpet, led to increased opposition. By 1606, an illegal Assembly had been held at Aberdeen and the level of support for those who had attended it, as well as general discontent, was high. James therefore called to Hampton Court eight of the most prominent churchmen opposed to his policies, held them in England as virtual prisoners without charge and staged an entirely packed meeting of ministers which was not described as a General Assembly until after it had met.[25] From that time onwards, the intervention of the crown in the conduct of the Kirk at every level reached unprecedented levels and, in the sphere of constant moderation of synods and presbyteries, it had the effect of increasing, rather than stifling, clerical hostility.

With opposition reaching levels even greater than those of 1596, the crown was able to maintain control only by the enhancement of the spiritual power of the episcopate and by the warding, imprisonment and even banishment of ministers who were vociferous in their opposition. The royal desire for firm, even absolute, authority was clear in many spheres. Attempts to enhance central power under James VI, by the increased scope and amount of parliamentary legislation, taxation and intervention with Parliament itself, as well as in the Kirk, reached unprecedented levels.[26] The crown also provided itself with loyal servants

---

[25] NLS, James VI to William Scot, 21 May 1606, Wodrow Folio, 42, no. 48. The letter called Scot to meet the king at Hampton Court in September. James wrote of the lack of peace in the Kirk, of 'maliciously disposed persons' defying his authority and of others who justified their actions from the pulpit and criticised both himself and the Privy Council. He also complained that synods disregarded his requests not to discuss certain matters. The impression given is that James felt that things were getting seriously out of control.

[26] J. Goodare, 'Parliament and Society in Scotland, 1560–1603' (unpublished Edinburgh PhD dissertation, 1989), esp. 9–10 and ch. 9; and by the same author, 'The Nobility and the Absolutist State in Scotland, 1584–1638', History, 78 (1993), 161–82 and 'Parliamentary Taxation in Scotland, 1560–1603' SHR, 68 (1989), 23–52. The idea that James VI was 'absolutist' can be found in P. Hume Brown, History of Scotland to the Present Time, 3 vols (Cambridge, 1905), ii, book vi, chs 1 and 2. See also SRO, James VI to the Earl of Mar, 7 June 1609, Mar and Kellie Papers, GD124/10/90 in which James asked Mar to record the way those in Parliament voted so that they could be rewarded or not. There is a

through the creation of new aristocratic titles and the elevation of ministers to bishoprics. In the Kirk, the king sought control via the Privy Council, members of the new nobility and the commission of the General Assembly, which was gradually eclipsed by the episcopate which emerged from it. Intervention in the operations and affairs of the Kirk from 1606 onwards was exhibited in a number of crucial areas: general assemblies were effectively nominated by the crown, in the form of the episcopate; moderators of synods and presbyteries were either the bishops or their appointees; stipends were under episcopal control after 1607; in 1610, the two archbishops, heading their Courts of High Commission, became the supreme court of appeal, above the General Assembly, for all cases of ecclesiastical discipline. A structure was set in place which allowed the Kirk to operate without regular assemblies. With the exception of 1584, 1585 and 1599, the General Assembly met at least annually until 1603. After that date, there were only six further assemblies before 1638 and two of those, the assemblies of 1617 and 1618, met solely to approve the Five Articles of Perth. As an absentee king, James did not want the ministers of the Kirk running their own show, so he effectively transferred that power to the episcopate, obviating the administrative need for general assemblies. In a similar process, Parliament met far less frequently with only three parliaments between 1610 and 1625.[27]

The development of the commission of the General Assembly itself provides further insight into the accruing of patronage and power by the crown and into the attitudes of the ministry as a whole. Many of those who were commissioners of the General Assembly after 1596 had been involved in its predecessor. A substantial number of those who had stood to the principle of two kingdoms and had continually pestered the king for action against Catholicism in the later 1580s and early 1590s, became his most trusted ecclesiastical advisers. Some were even rewarded with bishoprics – of the 18 appointments to sees between 1600 and 1618, all but three had been on James VI's commission of the General Assembly.[28] Conversely, ministers who have been portrayed by subsequent historians, and occasionally by themselves, as radical doctrinaire firebrands, such as James Melville and Robert Bruce, were part of the mainstream of clerical opinion in the former period and it was only after 1596 that they became anathema to the king.

---

heated debate over how absolutist the crown was able to be under James VI but the point in this context is that he sought absolute power, even if its achievement was impossible.

[27] *BUK*, iii, *passim*; *APS*, iv, *passim*.

[28] Mullan, *Episcopacy in Scotland*, 123; MacDonald, 'Ecclesiastical Politics in Scotland, 1586–1610' (unpublished Edinburgh PhD dissertation, 1995), Appendix 6 (a) and (b).

When, in 1597, matters reached the stage of a choice between loyalty to the Kirk and loyalty to the king, the majority took the latter course. Circumstances, though, were to dictate that the pendulum would swing the other way and when it did, and opposition re-emerged in the years after 1603, the loyalty to the crown of most of the commissioners of the General Assembly was entrenched. They had a vested interest in their new positions and more and more were made bishops. Of those who were not, however, a number were to lose their loyalty to the crown after 1610 when liturgical innovations were added to the episcopal polity.[29] In the game of musical chairs which was ecclesiastical politics in Jacobean Scotland, the distribution of radicals and moderates changed quite markedly each time the music stopped.

The episcopate as it had stood in 1602 was acceptable to the majority of ministers in the Kirk but it is difficult to argue the same for that of 1610. Episcopacy *per se* is impossible to define and, therefore, the search for an 'episcopalian' minister is as difficult and fruitless as the search for a 'Melvillian' one. There was episcopacy in Scotland before the Reformation which did not abolish episcopacy and, in the Concordat of Leith in 1572, a new form of episcopate was agreed upon by representatives of the Kirk and the crown and later approved by the General Assembly. In 1584, the Arran regime demonstrated a desire for a powerful episcopate but that regime fell and episcopacy atrophied, but only after some experimentation in oversight vested in individuals had failed. For almost a decade after that, the subject of episcopacy disappeared, only to be revived by James VI in the later 1590s. The form it initially took was acceptable to the Kirk but the flouting of agreed limitations of its power, the level of oversight it accrued after 1603 and the policies it was involved in implementing undermined its initial acceptability. It was not so much a question of 'Episcopacy: good or bad?', rather it was one of 'Episcopacy: how strong and how accountable?' As Jenny Wormald has pointed out, episcopacy would exist in the Reformed Kirk in Scotland only as the result of the crown's initiative.[30] The Kirk would accept it, but only on its own terms.

---

[29] MacDonald, 'Ecclesiastical Politics in Scotland, 1586–1610' (unpublished Edinburgh PhD dissertation, 1995), Appendix 6 (a). According to Calderwood, *History*, vi, 425, 443, John Clapperton and William Cranston were summoned to the High Commission for resisting the Five Articles of Perth. Clapperton served on the commission for its entire duration (1597–1608). The important point here is not that they objected to the Five Articles (most ministers and even the bishops did) but that, in spite of having served on the king's commission, they were prepared to oppose them actively and even face deprivation.

[30] J. Wormald, 'No Bishop, no King: the Scottish Jacobean Episcopate, 1600–1625', in ed., B. Vogler, *Bibliotheque de la Revue d'Histoire Ecclesiastique: Miscellania Historiae Ecclesiasticae VIII* (Louvain, 1987), 263.

Many current and recent historians have portrayed the ecclesiastical policy of James VI between 1603 and 1610 as having been acceptable to the 'vast majority' of the clergy in contrast to the new policy of liturgical innovation after 1610.[31] It is undeniable that there was a great deal of opposition to those later innovations, yet the difference was quantitative rather than qualitative. The crown's ecclesiastical policy was already unpopular; the Five Articles of Perth did little more than add the bishops to those who were unhappy with it. The evidence presented here suggests that a widespread and entrenched opposition to the ecclesiastical policy of James VI can be traced from as early as 1604 or 1605. Contrasts between the changes in polity of the first decade of the seventeenth century and the liturgical innovations of the second, and the manner of their reception, have their origins in confessional historiography rather than the reign of James VI.[32] The General Assembly of 1638 certainly saw no significant discontinuity in 1610, tracing the origins of the problem to no later than 1606 by annulling all assemblies from that year onwards, not just those of 1616, 1617 and 1618.[33]

The continuity which is identified in royal policy from 1603 onwards and the rejection of a significant discontinuity after 1610 compels a British perspective to be adopted in the analysis of the Scottish ecclesiastical policy of James VI. Even before the Anglo-Scottish regal union of 1603, James VI had anticipated an expansion of his dominions. The fact that he was increasingly inclined towards an episcopal polity in the later 1590s was at least partially related to this. John Morrill has suggested that, after 1603, James did not intend to Anglicise, or 'Anglicanise', the Kirk, but that he wanted to bring the two nations together with a policy of 'congruity'.[34] Morrill argued that, although

---

[31] M. Lee, *Great Britain's Solomon: James VI and I in his Three Kingdoms* (Urbana, 1990), 81; W.R. Foster, *The Church before the Covenants* (Edinburgh, 1975), 29, 199–200; Donaldson, *Scotland: James V–James VII*, 207; Mullan, *Episcopacy in Scotland*, 197; M. Lynch, *Scotland: a New History* (London, 1991), 231.

[32] See Foster, *Church before the Covenants*, 205. Urging unity between presbyterian and episcopal churches, he wrote that 'The 1610 settlement ... can provide some very useful perspectives for those ... considering similar comprehensive schemes today.' He thus felt that the opportunity was squandered by the imposition of the Five Articles.

[33] *Acts of the General Assembly of the Church of Scotland 1638–1842*, ed. G. Peterkin (Edinburgh, 1843), 6–7.

[34] J. Morrill, 'A British Patriarchy? Ecclesiastical Imperialism under the Early Stuarts' [*sic*], in eds, A. Fletcher and P. Roberts, *Religion, Culture and Society in Early Modern Britain: Essays in Honour of Patrick Collinson* (Cambridge, 1994), esp. 216; K. Fincham and P. Lake, 'The Ecclesiastical Policies of James I and Charles I', in ed., K. Fincham, *The Early Stuart Church, 1603–1642* (London, 1993) 27, 49; B.P. Levack, 'Religious and Ecclesiastical Union', in ed., B.P. Levack, *The Formation of the British State: England, Scotland and the Union, 1603–1707* (Oxford, 1987), 103–13 for an alternative view, emphasising the fact that the *idea* of ecclesiastical union was important.

the English Church was seen to be closer to the ideal, it was not the model and that such things as the promotion of preaching, which was relatively neglected in England, is evidence for this. It must be acknowledged that James VI and I was much more enthusiastic about preaching than Elizabeth who had felt that there was no need for more than three or four preachers in any county. James did indeed promote preaching in England. He did not, however, attempt a radical overhaul of the polity and the form of worship there. He took to the Church of England much as he found it. It was, for him, closer to the way a church should be and he made no bones about that when he enhanced the power of the Scottish episcopate, introduced the courts of High Commission, attempted liturgical reform in Scotland and brought choristers, organs and the English service with him on his 1617 visit to Scotland. He even had to be dissuaded by the bishops from erecting statues of the apostles in his chapel in Holyrood Palace.

It is true that James did not explicitly seek an ecclesiastical union in the way that he sought legal and parliamentary unions but the inescapable conclusion seems to be that he wanted religion to be uniform throughout his dominions. The union plans of 1604–08 were careful to avoid references to ecclesiastical union, in spite of the fact that it was 'unanimously regard[ed] ... as essential for general union and that, for decades, Scots had emphasised that a shared religion made alliance with England the obvious choice'.[35] The fact that, in spite of some doctrinal common ground, the two nations did not share much more in polity, liturgy or relations with the state than independence from Rome had to be glossed over in this context.[36] Also, possession of a common language was another alleged example of similarity, ignoring the fact that there remained clear differences between Scots and English, let alone the fact that around half of the population of Scotland were monoglot Gaels. It seems likely that ecclesiastical union was not attempted because of the hostility to the concept in both realms, outstripping even the fundamental disinclination to any further civil union upon which James's scheme foundered.

James's policy of toleration of moderate Catholics and moderate Puritans or presbyterians, born before 1603, was carried into England and seems to have had more success there than it did in Scotland. The language question was answered for him before he came to his multiple

---

[35] B. Galloway, *The Union of England and Scotland, 1603–1608* (Edinburgh, 1986), 43.

[36] Levack, 'Religious and Ecclesiastical Union', 107; B.R. Galloway and B.P. Levack, *The Jacobean Union: Six Tracts of 1604* (Scottish History Society, 1985), xxxix–xl; Dawson, 'Anglo-Scottish Protestant Culture and Integration in Sixteenth Century Britain', 101.

monarchy. Wales had been under English rule since the thirteenth century and administrative convergence had been completed under Henry VIII. Although the Reformation there suffered from economic difficulties and a stouter recusancy than in England, the adoption of the Welsh language as the medium for evangelism as early as the 1560s made a significant difference. In 1563, the English Parliament ordered the publication of a Welsh Bible and, by 1567, both the prayerbook and the New Testament were available in the language. Perhaps because Wales had been part of the English polity for so long, its Celtic language did not carry the connotations of Catholicism, barbarism and lawlessness which were attached to Irish and Scots Gaelic and thus Wales presented 'a striking contrast with the situation in Ireland and Scotland'.[37] The Kirk itself had mixed views of the cultural differences between Lowlands and Highlands. In 1625, the synod of Moray ordered the ministers of the presbytery of Inverness not to wear 'uncomly habitts such as bonnats and plaids', yet the need to have ministers with Gaelic was clearly appreciated since the same meeting lamented that two ministers had none.[38]

The similarities between Ireland and the Scottish *Gaidhealtachd* are obvious. Both lay largely outwith the reach of effective central control and were thus viewed with fear and suspicion by the central authorities. Relatively little effort was put into providing Protestant material in Gaelic in either country. Indeed, because of the Scots and English speaking peoples' attitudes to the Gaels and their language: 'In the new British state, the Gaelic language in both its Irish and Scottish homelands would be subjected to the cultural imperialism of the dominant Anglo-Scots vernacular.'[39] The eradication of Scots and Irish Gaelic was pursued by the state as part of a policy involving 'civilisation' and Protestantism, although the Kirk did make efforts to plant Gaelic-speaking ministers in Gaelic-speaking areas. As a result of this confused policy, however, the Catholic missionary efforts stole a march on the Protestants. The crown's anti-Gaelic, anti-Catholic policy was pursued with a unity of purpose across its Gaelic dominions. Attempts were made to plant Lowland Scottish Protestants in the Hebrides

---

[37] P. Jenkins, 'The Anglican Church and the Unity of Britain: the Welsh Experience', in eds, S.G. Ellis and S. Barber, *Conquest and Union Fashioning a British State, 1485–1725* (London, 1995), 115–28, at 118–26; C. Brady, 'Comparative Histories? Tudor Reform in Wales and Ireland', in ibid., 67–85; G. Williams, *Recovery, Reorientation and Reformation: Wales c.1415–1642* (Oxford, 1987), 471–8.

[38] SRO, Records of the synod of Moray, CH2/271–1, 7.

[39] J. Dawson, 'Calvinism and the *Gaidhealtachd* in Scotland', in eds, A. Pettegree et al., *Calvinism in Europe, 1540–1620* (Cambridge, 1994) 231–53, at 231.

(unsuccessfully) and in Ireland (successfully) and efforts were made to ensure the English or Scots education of the sons of the Gaelic aristocracy.[40]

James wanted a united kingdom but, contrary to what Jenny Wormald has recently argued, he became increasingly uninterested in tailoring policies to meet the peculiarities of his realms. He wanted law and order to prevail throughout his dominions and he favoured the unification of British laws and parliaments and, perhaps, ultimately, one parliament and law which included Ireland. To this end, he pursued linguistic and religious uniformity, with an increasingly Anglocentric focus. In 1616, he reassured the Star Chamber that he wanted to make Scotland conform to England, not *vice versa*.[41] By 1625, he was drifting away from Calvinism, reasserted in his support of the conclusions of the synod of Dort in 1618, towards favour to the growing anti-Calvinist tendency in the Church of England.[42]

As a result of the pursuit of a British policy, the 'British problem', the difficulty of drawing together historically antipathetic nations with different cultural and political traditions, was revealed. In Scotland in 1625, the Kirk was in crisis. Catholic nonconformity remained rife and a new Protestant nonconformity was increasing, fuelled by conventicling and by the importation from the Low Countries of dissident literature produced by exiled ministers.[43] By insistence on kneeling at communion, the king had more than doubled the number of lay nonconformists in Scotland and split the Kirk, since many ministers were of a mind with the dissident laity. The minister in Fife who, in 1620, agreed to conform only because, otherwise, he would not be allowed to preach, may exemplify a common tendency.[44] At Easter 1622, Patrick Galloway resorted to absurd contortions to avoid, at one and the same time, kneeling and disobedience to the king. He 'bowed the one legge, had the sole of his other foote upon the ground and satt withall upon the furme[bench]'.[45] Far more serious than overt disobedience to the Five

---

[40] A. Clarke and R. Dudley-Edwards, 'Pacification, Plantation and the Catholic Question', in eds, T.W. Moody et al., *A New History of Ireland*, vol. iii, *Early Modern Ireland, 1534–1691* (Oxford, 1976) ch. 7; M. MacCraith, 'The Gaelic Reaction to the Reformation', in eds, S.G. Ellis and S. Barber *Conquest and Union Fashioning a British State, 1485–1725* (London, 1995), 139–161; A.I. Macinnes, 'Gaelic Culture in the Seventeenth Century: Polarisation and Assimilation', in ibid., 162–94; J. Wormald, 'James VI, James I and the Identity of Britain', in eds, B. Bradshaw and J. Morrill, *The British Problem, c.1534–1707: State Formation in the Atlantic Archipelago* (London, 1996), 148–171, at 165–70.

[41] Wormald, 'James VI, James I and the Identity of Britain', 165, 170–71.

[42] Fincham and Lake, 'The Ecclesiastical Policies of James I and Charles I', 33–8.

[43] RPC, xiii, 668, the principal work being David Calderwood's *Perth Assemblie*.

[44] Synod of St Andrews benorth Forth, fo. 127r.

[45] Calderwood, *History*, vii, 547.

Articles of Perth, however, was the increasing absence of ministers from presbyteries and synods. Although parochial religion was not disrupted, in some places the organisational structure and system of discipline were severely undermined. The Kirk as a body of ministers united by the consistorial system was gone. It had been undermined by the failure of general assemblies to meet in all but six years after 1603 but it was destroyed when scores of ministers were forced out by the obstinacy of James VI in his desire to see convergence between his churches. James had not 'realised his mistake and learned his lesson' nor is it the case that 'he did not seek to enforce the changes' in liturgy. It is unfair to contrast a supposed climbdown 'in the face of fiercer resistance than he had anticipated' with his son's 'blunder on to catastrophe'. Others have observed more accurately that, because of the Five Articles of Perth, 'it may be seriously questioned whether the King ... left a Church at peace', and even that he 'left a Church divided as she had never been before'. Scott observed in *The Fortunes of Nigel*, that 'during that very reign, were sown those seeds of dissension, which, like the teeth of the fabulous dragon, had their harvest in a bloody and universal civil war'.[46] Whatever the failures of Charles I, and there were many, his father's ecclesiastical legacy was the worst start he could have been given. The genesis of the religious problems which were part and parcel of the Covenanting revolution of 1638, if Jacobean origins may be sought, should, however, be traced to the period immediately after the regal union of 1603 and not to the 1610s.[47]

---

[46] Donaldson, *Scotland: James V-James VII*, 210–11; Morrill, 'A British Patriarchy?', 220–21; I.B. Cowan, 'The Five Articles of Perth', in ed., D. Shaw, *Reformation and Revolution* (Edinburgh, 1967) 177; P.H.R. MacKay, 'The Reception Given to the Five Articles of Perth', *RSCHS*, 19 (1975–77) 200; Sir Walter Scott, *The Fortunes of Nigel*, ch. 5.

[47] A.I. Macinnes, *Charles I and the Making of the Covenanting Movement, 1625–1641* (Edinburgh, 1991), ch. 2, esp. 37–41 and 45. James VI was 'losing touch' and 'Charles I inherited a kingdom in which the crown had failed to maintain consensus', yet Macinnes still dated the problems to the period after 1610.

Maps

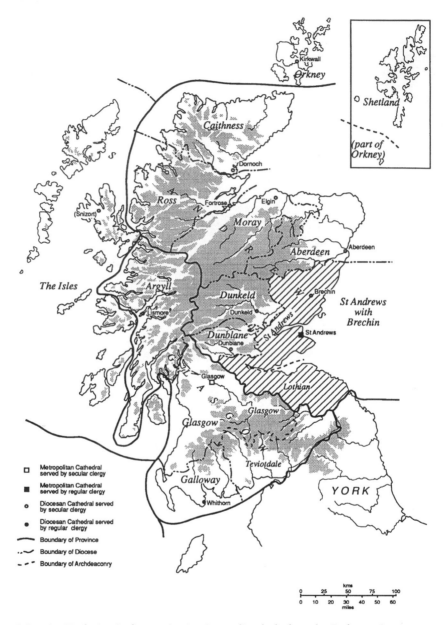

Map 1 Ecclesiastical organisation immediately before the Reformation
Note: Brechin, and to a lesser extent Dunblane and Dunkeld, were scattered
dioceses with detached portions embedded in other dioceses.

ROSS Dioceses of superintendents
  ●   Residences of superintendents

Map 2 Proposed dioceses of superintendents in 1560

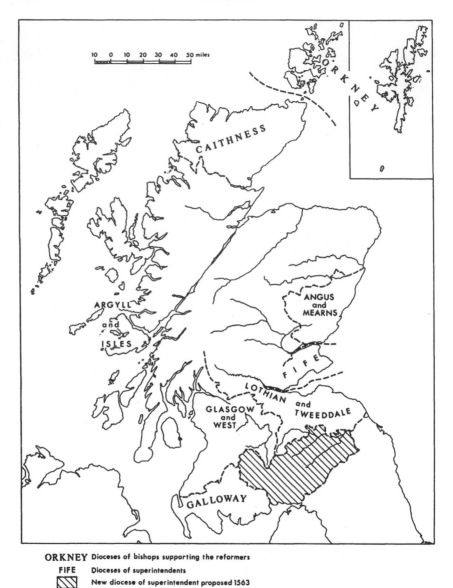

ORKNEY Dioceses of bishops supporting the reformers
FIFE   Dioceses of superintendents
 New diocese of superintendent proposed 1563

Map 3   Actual dioceses of superintendents and commissioners after 1560

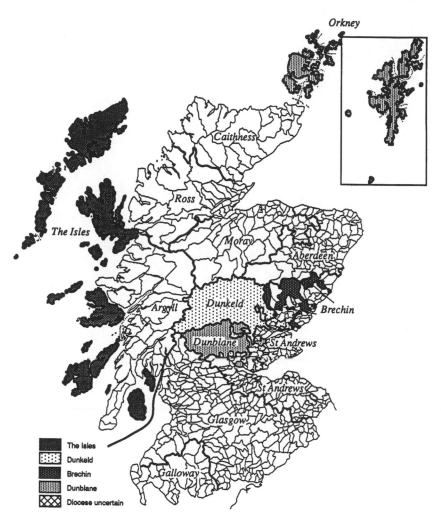

Map 4 Diocesan structure resulting from Concordat of Leith, 1572
Note: Brechin, and to a lesser extent Dunblane and Dunkeld, were scattered
dioceses with detached portions embedded in other dioceses.

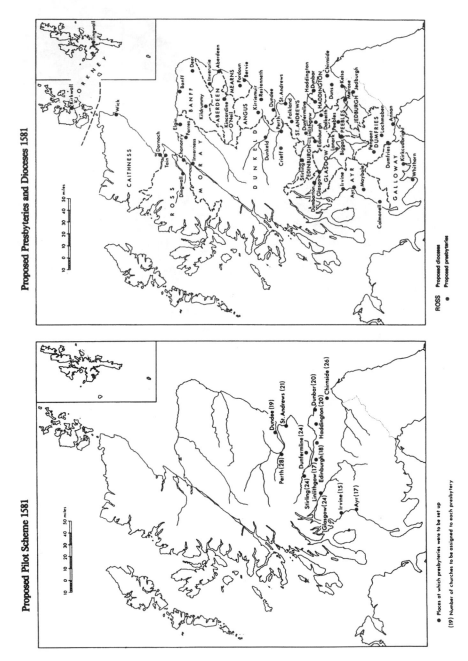

Proposed Pilot Scheme 1581

Dundee (19)
St.Andrews (21)
Perth (28)
Dunfermline (24)
Stirling (24)
Linlithgow (17)
Edinburgh (18)
Dunbar (20)
Haddington (20)
Chirnside (26)
Glasgow (24)
Irvine (15)
Ayr (17)

10 0 10 20 30 40 50 miles

● Places at which presbyteries were to be set up

(19) Number of churches to be assigned to each presbytery

Proposed Presbyteries and Dioceses 1581

ORKNEY
Kirkwall

CAITHNESS
Wick

ROSS
Dornoch
Tain
Dingwall
Chonony
Inverness

MORAY
Elgin
Forres

BANFF
Banff
Kildrummy
Kincardine
O'Neil

ABERDEEN
Inverurie
Aberdeen
Dee
MEARNS
Fordoun
Bervie

ANGUS
Kirriemuir
Rossinneth
Dundee

DUNKELD
Dunkeld
Crieff
Folkland
(St.Andrews)

ST.ANDREWS
Perth
Dunfermline
Falkirk
Haddington
Dunbar
HADDINGTON
Chirnside

EDINBURGH
Stirling
Edinburgh
Linlithgow
Dalkeith
Peebles
Duns

GLASGOW
Dumbarton
Glasgow
Lanark
PEEBLES
Kelso
Melrose
JEDBURGH
Jedburgh

AYR
Biggar
Irvine
Ayr
Maybole
Dumfries
DUMFRIES
Lochmaben
Annan

GALLOWAY
Colmonell
Kirkcudbright
Whithorn
Penpont

10 0 10 20 30 40 50 miles

ROSS Proposed dioceses

● Proposed presbyteries

Map 5 The 13 'model' presbyteries and the planned national system of presbyteries and synods of 1581

Note: In addition to the pilot 13 presbyteries, Dalkeith was operating from 1581

Map 6 Provinces of commissioners of visitation in 1586

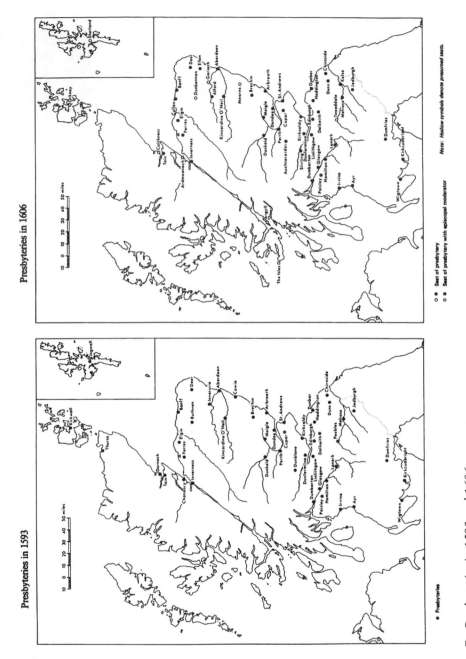

Presbyteries in 1593

Presbyteries in 1606

● Presbyteries

○ ● Seat of presbytery

□ ■ Seat of presbytery with episcopal moderator

Note: Hollow symbols denote presumed seats.

Map 7   Presbyteries in 1593 and 1606

Note: After 1593, Dunblane presbytery was split between Stirling and the newly-erected Auchterarder presbytery. It was

Bibliography

Primary sources

Manuscripts

National Library of Scotland
Advocates Manuscripts.
Wodrow Manuscripts, Folio and Quarto.

Public Record Office, London
State Papers Domestic, James I, SP 14.
State Papers Scottish, SP 52.

Scottish Record Office
Church records:

Synod:	Records of the Synod of Moray, CH2/271/1.
	Record of the Diocesan Synod of St Andrews benorth Forth from September 1610 to April 1636, CH 2/154/1.
Presbytcrics:	Aberdeen, CI I2/1/1.
	Dalkeith, CH2/424/1.
	Deer, CH2/89/1/1–2.
	Dunblane, CH2/723/1.
	Edinburgh, CH2/121/1–3.
	Ellon, CH2/146/1–2.
	Fordyce, CH2/158/1.
	Glasgow, CH2/171/1–2 (microfilm).
	Haddington, CH2/185/1–3.
	Jedburgh, CH2/198/1–2.
	Lanark, CH2/234/1.
	Linlithgow, CH2/242/1–2.
	Melrose (catalogued as Selkirk), CH2/327/1.
	Paisley, CH2/294/1.
	Peebles, CH2/295/1/1–2.
	Perth, CH2/299/1
	Stirling, CH2/722/1–4 (microfilm).
Miscellaneous:	'Copie to the presbiteries & uthers for sending & cumming to the generall assemblie', CH8/57.
	'Extract from the records of the synod of Cliddisdaill, accepting John, archbishop of Glasgow, as moderator', CH8/59.

State records:
  Parliamentary papers, supplementary, PA7.
  Register of Presentations to Benefices, CH4/1.
  Register of the Privy Seal, PS1.
  Treasurers' Accounts, E21/78–9.
Estate papers etc.:
  Balnagown Castle Manuscripts, GD129.
  Clerk of Penicuik Muniments, GD18.
  Cunningham of Caprington Papers, GD149.
  Elphinstone Muniments, GD156.
  Hamilton Manuscripts, GD406.
  Mar and Kellie Papers, GD124.
  Morton Papers, GD150.
  Ogilvie of Inverquharity Papers, GD205.
  Rattray of Craighall Rattray Muniments, RH4/126.
  Royal letters presented by Mr R.J. Bruce of Elmhurst Farm, Sussex, GD1/240.
  Earl of Stair Papers, GD135.

University of Glasgow Library
'The protestation drawn by Mr P. Simson, minister at Stirline, offered to the Estates convened in Parliament at Perth ... July 1606', MS Gen. 1216, Wodrow's Biographical Collections, appendix vol. ii.

University of St Andrews Library
Register of the Presbytery of St Andrews, MS 23.

Printed

Acts and Proceedings of the General Assembly of the Kirk of Scotland, ed. T. Thomson, 3 vols (Bannatyne Club, 1839–45).
Acts of the General Assemblies of the Church of Scotland, 1638–1842, ed. G. Peterkin (Edinburgh, 1843).
The Acts of the Parliaments of Scotland, eds T. Thomson and C. Innes, 12 vols (Edinburgh, 1815–75).
Botfield, B., ed., *Original Letters Relating to the Ecclesiastical Affairs of Scotland*, 2 vols (Bannatyne Club, 1851).
Calderwood, D., *History of the Kirk of Scotland by Mr David Calderwood*, ed. T. Thomson, 8 vols (Wodrow Society, 1842–49).
Calendar of State Papers Domestic Series of the Reign of James I, 1603–1610, ed. M.A.E. Green (London, 1857).
Calendar of State Papers Relating to Scotland and Mary, Queen of Scots, 1547–1603, eds J. Bain et al., 13 vols (Edinburgh, 1898–1969).

Craigie, J., ed., *The Basilikon Doron of King James VI*, 2 vols (Scottish Texts Society, 3rd series, 1944 and 1950).

Craigie, J., ed., *Minor Prose Works of James VI* (Scottish Texts Society, 4th series, 1982).

A Declaration of the Juste Causes of his Majesties proceiding against those ministers who are now lying in prison attainted of high treason (Edinburgh, 1606).

Extracts from the Records of the Burgh of Glasgow, 11 vols (Scottish Burgh Records Society/Corporation of Glasgow, 1876–1916).

The First Book of Discipline, ed. J.K. Cameron (Edinburgh, 1972).

Forbes, J., *Certaine Records Touching the Estate of the Kirk in the Years MDCV and MDCVI*, ed., D. Laing (Wodrow Society, 1846).

Fraser, W., ed., *The Red Book of Grandtully*, 2 vols (Edinburgh, 1868).

Galloway, B.R. and Levack, B.P., eds, *The Jacobean Union: Six Tracts of 1604* (Scottish History Society, 1985).

Haig, J., ed., *The Historical Works of Sir James Balfour*, 4 vols (Edinburgh 1824–25).

The Historie and Life of King James the Sext, ed. T. Thomson (Bannatyne Club, 1825).

Laing, D., ed., *The Miscellany of the Wodrow Society* (Wodrow Society, 1844).

Laing, D., ed., *Various Pieces of Fugitive Scottish Poetry Principally of the XVIIth Century* (Edinburgh, 1853).

Laing, D., ed., *The Works of John Knox* (6 vols, Wodrow Society, 1895).

Letters and State Papers During the Reign of James VI, ed. J. Maidment (Abbotsford Club, 1838).

Lippe, R., ed., *Selections from Wodrow's Biographical Collections* (New Spalding Club, 1890).

Melville, J., *The Autobiography and Diary of Mr James Melville*, ed., R. Pitcairn (Wodrow Society, 1843).

Miscellany of the Spalding Club, 5 vols (Spalding Club, 1844–52).

Moysie, D., *Memoirs of the Affairs of Scotland by David Moysie, MDLXXVII–MDCIII* (Bannatyne Club, 1830).

Pitcairn, R., ed., *Criminal Trials in Scotland from 1488 to 1624*, 3 vols (Edinburgh, 1833).

The Records of the Convention of the Royal Burghs of Scotland, ed. J.D. Marwick, 7 vols (Edinburgh, 1866–1918).

The Records of the Synod of Lothian and Tweeddale, 1589–1596, 1640–1649, ed. J. Kirk, (Stair Society, 1977).

The Register of the Privy Council of Scotland, eds J.H. Burton et al., 14 vols (Edinburgh, 1877–98).

Row, J., *History of the Kirk of Scotland from the Year 1558 to August 1637*, ed., D. Laing (Wodrow Society, 1842).

Scot, W., *An Apologetical Narration of the State and Government of the Kirk of Scotland since the Reformation*, ed., D. Laing (Wodrow Society, 1846).

The Second Book of Discipline, ed. J. Kirk (Edinburgh, 1980).

Spottiswoode, J., *History of the Church of Scotland ... by the Right Rev. John Spottiswoode*, eds. M. Russell and M. Napier, 3 vols (Spottiswoode Society, 1847–51).

State Papers and Miscellaneous Correspondence of Thomas, Earl of Melrose, ed. J. Maidment, 2 vols (Abbotsford Club, 1837).

Stirling Presbytery Records 1581–1587, ed. J. Kirk (Scottish History Society, 1981).

Tweedie, W.K., ed., *Select Biographies*, 2 vols (Wodrow Society, 1845–47).

Visitation of the Diocese of Dunblane and other Churches, 1586–9, ed. J. Kirk (Scottish Texts Society, 2nd series, 1984).

The Warrender Papers, ed. A.I. Cameron, 2 vols (Scottish History Society, 1931–32).

Reference works

Atlas of Scottish History to 1707, eds P.G.B. McNeill and H.L. MacQueen (Edinburgh, 1996).

Balfour Paul, J., ed., *The Scots Peerage*, 9 vols (Edinburgh, 1904–14).

Cameron, N.M. de S., Wright, D.F., Lachman, D.C. and Meek, D.E., eds, *Dictionary of Scottish Church History and Theology* (Edinburgh, 1993).

Cowan, I.B. and Easson, D.E., *Medieval Religious Houses: Scotland* (London, 1976).

Craigie, W.A. et al., eds, *Dictionary of the Older Scottish Tongue* (Oxford, Aberdeen and Edinburgh, 1937–).

Donaldson, G., *Scottish Historical Documents* (Edinburgh, 1974).

Robinson, M., ed., *The Concise Scots Dictionary* (Aberdeen, 1985).

Scott, H., ed., *Fasti Ecclesiae Scoticanae*, revised edn, 8 vols (Edinburgh, 1915–).

Watt, D.E.R., ed., *Fasti Ecclesiae Scoticanae Medii Aevi ad Annum 1638* (Scottish Record Society, 1969).

Secondary sources

Bradshaw, B. and Morrill, J., eds, *The British Problem c.1534–1707: State Formation in the Atlantic Archipelago* (London, 1996).
Brown, K.M., *Bloodfeud in Scotland, 1573–1625*, (Edinburgh, 1986).
Brown, K.M., 'In Search of the Godly Magistrate in Reformation Scotland', *Journal of Ecclesiastical History*, 40 (1989), 553–81.
Brown, K.M., *Kingdom or Province? Scotland and the Regal Union, 1603–1715* (London, 1992).
Burleigh, J.H.S., *A Church History of Scotland* (Edinburgh, 1960).
Burrel, S.A., 'The Covenant Idea as a Revolutionary Symbol: Scotland 1596–1637', *Church History*, 27 (1958), 338–50.
Cameron, E., *The European Reformation* (Oxford 1991).
Cargill Thomson, W.D., 'A Reconsideration of Richard Bancroft's Paul's Cross Sermon', *Journal of Ecclesiastical History*, 20 (1969), 233–66.
Collinson, P., *The Elizabethan Puritan Movement* (Oxford, 1967).
Cowan, I.B. and Shaw, D., eds., *The Renaissance and Reformation in Scotland: Essays in Honour of Gordon Donaldson* (Edinburgh, 1983).
Devine, T.M. and Lythe, S.G.E., 'The Economy of Scotland under James VI: a Revision Article', *SHR*, 50 (1971), 91–106.
Dickinson, W.C., *Scotland from the Earliest Times to 1603*, 3rd edn revised and updated by A.A.M. Duncan (Oxford, 1977).
Donaldson, G., 'The Relations between the English and Scottish Presbyterian Movements to 1604' (unpublished London PhD dissertation, 1938).
Donaldson, G., 'The Attitude of Whitgift and Bancroft to the Scottish Church', *Transactions of the Royal Historical Society*, 4th series, 24 (1942), 95–115.
Donaldson, G., *The Scottish Reformation* (Cambridge, 1960).
Donaldson, G., *Scotland: James V–James VII* (Edinburgh, 1971).
Donaldson, G., *Scottish Church History* (Edinburgh, 1985).
Donnachie, I. and Whatley, C., eds., *The Manufacture of Scottish History* (Edinburgh, 1992).
Durkan, J., 'Two Jesuits: Patrick Anderson and John Ogilvie', *Innes Review*, 21 (1970), 157–61.
Durston, C., *James I* (London, 1993).
Ellis, S.G. and Barber, S., eds, *Conquest and Union: Fashioning a British State, 1485–1725* (London, 1995).
Fincham, K., ed., *The Early Stuart Church, 1603–1642* (London, 1993).
Fincham, K. and Lake, P., 'The Ecclesiastical Policy of James I', *Journal of British Studies*, 24 (1985), 170–88.
Fletcher, A. and Roberts, P., eds, *Religion, Culture and Society in Early*

Modern Britain: Essays in Honour of Patrick Collinson (Cambridge, 1994).

Foster, W.R., 'The Operation of Presbyteries in Scotland, 1600–1638', *RSCHS*, 15 (1963), 21–33.

Foster, W.R., *The Church before the Covenants* (Edinburgh, 1975).

Galloway, B., *The Union of England and Scotland, 1603–1608* (Edinburgh, 1986).

Goodare, J., 'Parliamentary Taxation in Scotland, 1560–1603', *SHR*, 68 (1989), 23–52.

Goodare, J., 'Parliament and Society in Scotland, 1560–1603' (unpublished Edinburgh PhD dissertation, 1989).

Goodare, J., 'The Nobility and the Absolutist State in Scotland, 1584–1638', *History*, 78 (1993), 161–82.

Goodare, J., 'The Scottish Parliament of 1621', *The Historical Journal*, 38 (1995), 29–51.

Graham, M., *The Uses of Reform: 'Godly Discipline' and Popular Behavior in Scotland and Beyond, 1560–1610* (Leiden, 1996).

Henderson, G.D., 'The Exercise', *RSCHS*, 7 (1941), 13–29.

Hewitt, G.R., *Scotland under Morton, 1572–80* (Edinburgh, 1982).

Hill Burton, J., *The History of Scotland* (Edinburgh, 1873).

Hume, D., *The History of Great Britain*, 2 vols (London, 1757).

Hume Brown, P., *History of Scotland to the Present Time*, 3 vols (Cambridge, 1905).

Kidd, C., *Subverting Scotland's Past: Scottish Whig Historians and the Creation of an Anglo-British Identity, 1689–c.1830* (Cambridge, 1993).

Kirk, J., 'The Development of the Melvillian Movement in Late Sixteenth Century Scotland' (unpublished Edinburgh PhD dissertation, 1972).

Kirk, J., *Patterns of Reform: Continuity and Change in the Reformation Kirk* (Edinburgh, 1989).

Koenigsberger, H.G., Mosse, G.L. and Bower, G.Q., *Europe in the Sixteenth Century*, 2nd edn (London, 1989).

Lee, M., *John Maitland of Thirlestane and the Foundation of the Stewart Despotism in Scotland* (Princetown, 1959).

Lee, M., 'James VI and the Revival of Episcopacy in Scotland: 1596–1600', *Church History*, 43 (1974), 49–64.

Lee, M., 'James VI's Government of Scotland after 1603', *SHR*, 55 (1976), 41–54.

Lee, M., *Government by Pen: Scotland under James VI and I* (Urbana, 1980).

Lee, M., *Great Britain's Solomon: James VI and I in his Three Kingdoms* (Urbana, 1990).

Levack, B.P., *The Formation of the British State: England, Scotland and the Union, 1603–1707* (Oxford, 1987).

Lynch, M., *Edinburgh and the Reformation* (Edinburgh, 1981).

Lynch, M., ed., *The Early Modern Town in Scotland* (London, 1986).

Lynch, M., *Scotland: a New History* (London, 1991).

McCrie, T., *The Life of John Knox* (Edinburgh, 1811).

McCrie, T., *The Life of Andrew Melville*, 2nd edn, 2 vols (Edinburgh, 1824).

MacDonald, A.A., Lynch, M. and Cowan, I.B., eds, *The Renaissance in Scotland: Studies in Literature, Religion, History and Culture Offered to John Durkan* (Leiden, 1994).

MacDonald, A.R., 'The Subscription Crisis and Church–State Relations, 1584–1586', *RSCHS*, 25 (1994), 222–55.

MacDonald, A.R., 'Ecclesiastical Politics in Scotland, 1586–1610' (unpublished Edinburgh PhD dissertation, 1995).

MacDonald, A.R., 'A Fragment of a Copy of James Melville's *A True Narratioune of the Declyneing Aige of the Kirk of Scotland*', *Innes Review*, 47 (1996), 81–8.

Macinnes, A.I., *Charles I and the Making of the Covenanting Movement, 1625–1641* (Edinburgh, 1991).

Macinnes, A.I., 'Early Modern Scotland: the Current State of Play', *SHR*, 73 (1994), 30–46.

MacKay, P.H.R., 'The Reception Given to the Five Articles of Perth', *RSCHS*, 19 (1975–77), 185–201.

McMahon, G.I.R., 'The Scottish Courts of High Commission, 1610–1638', *RSCHS*, 15 (1966), 193–209.

MacQueen, E.E., 'The General Assembly of the Kirk as a Rival of Parliament' (unpublished St Andrews PhD dissertation, 1927).

Mason, R., ed., *Scots and Britons: Scottish Political Thought and the Union of 1603* (Cambridge, 1994).

Mitchison, R., *A History of Scotland* (London, 1970).

Moody, T.W., Martin, F.X. and Byrne, F.J., eds, *A New History of Ireland*, vol. iii, *Early Modern Ireland, 1534–1691* (Oxford, 1976).

Mullan, D.G., *Episcopacy in Scotland: the History of an Idea, 1560–1638* (Edinburgh, 1986).

Perry, J., 'John Spottiswoode, Archbishop and Chancellor as Churchman' (unpublished Edinburgh PhD dissertation, 1950).

Pettegree, A., Duke, A. and Lewis, G., et al., eds, *Calvinism in Europe, 1540–1620* (Cambridge, 1994).

Prestwich, M., ed., *International Calvinism, 1541–1715* (Oxford, 1985).

Quintrell, B.W., 'The Royal Hunt and the Puritans', *Journal of Ecclesiastical History*, 31 (1980), 41–57.

Robertson, W., *The History of Scotland during the Reigns of Queen Mary and King James VI* (London, 1794).

Sanderson, M.H.B., *Ayrshire and the Reformation: People and Change, 1490–1600* (East Linton, 1997).

Scribner, B., Porter, R. and Teich, M., eds, *The Reformation in National Context* (Cambridge, 1994).

Shaw, D., *The General Assemblies of the Church of Scotland 1560–1600* (Edinburgh, 1964).

Shaw, D., ed., *Reformation and Revolution* (Edinburgh, 1967).

Shriver, F., 'Hampton Court Revisited: James I and the Puritans', *Journal of Ecclesiastical History*, 33 (1982), 48–71.

Smith, A.G.R., ed., *The Reign of James VI and I* (Aylesbury, 1973).

Stevenson, D., 'Conventicles in the Kirk, 1619–1637: the Emergence of a Radical Party', *RSCHS*, 18 (1974), 99–114.

Stevenson, D., *Scotland's Last Royal Wedding: the Marriage of James VI and Anne of Denmark* (Edinburgh, 1997).

Torrance, J.B., 'The Covenant Concept in Scottish Theology and Politics – Its Legacy', *Scottish Journal of Theology*, 34 (1981).

Tyacke, N., 'Anglican Attitudes: Some Recent Writings on English Religious History, from the Reformation to the Civil War', *Journal of British Studies*, 35 (1996), 139–67.

Wadsworth, G.C., 'The General Assembly of 1610' (unpublished Edinburgh PhD dissertation, 1930).

Williams, G., *Recovery, Reorientation and Reformation: Wales c.1415–1642* (Oxford, 1987).

Williamson, A., *Scottish National Consciousness in the Age of James VI: the Apocalypse, the Union and the Shaping of Scotland's Public Culture* (Edinburgh, 1979).

Wormald, J., *Court, Kirk and Community: Scotland 1470–1625* (Edinburgh, 1981).

Wormald, J., 'No Bishop, no King: the Scottish Jacobean Episcopate, 1600–1625', in ed., B. Vogler, *Bibliotheque de la Revue d'Histoire Ecclesiastique: Miscellania Historiae Ecclesiasticae VIII* (Louvain, 1987).

Wormald, J., ed., *Scotland Revisited* (London, 1991).

Index

Those whose titles changed during the reign of James VI are found under the name by which they are either first described or most well known. Cross references are given to their other names and titles where appropriate. Ministers' names are given with the parishes and presbyteries relevant to the dates of citations in the text. Where the parish shares the name of the presbytery, no presbytery name is given. NB: the parish of Musselburgh was moved from the presbytery of Edinburgh to the presbytery of Dalkeith in 1591.

Abbot, George, Archbishop of
  Canterbury (1611–33), 139n.,
  149, 154, 158
Abercorn, James Hamilton, Earl of,
  132, 136, 145n.
Aberdeen, 41, 150, 151, 159
  bishops of, see Peter Blackburn,
    Patrick Forbes of Corse
  diocese of, 144
  university of, 6, 28
  presbytery of, 76, 96, 102, 107–8,
    109, 113, 126, 137, 140, 142
  synod of, 57, 63, 76, 102, 105,
    108, 109, 113, 118, 119, 133,
    140, 168
  General Assemblies at, 105, 108–
    12, 157
Abernethy, Thomas, minister of
  Eckford, Jedburgh presbytery
  (1610–40), 135–6
Act anent the restitutioun of the
  estate of bischoppis (1606), 120–
  21
Act of annexation (1587), 40, 47,
  121
Adamson, Patrick, minister of Paisley
  (1572–74), chaplain to Regent
  Morton (1574–76), Archbishop
  of St Andrews (1576–92), 19–
  20, 31, 32, 39, 41, 44
  appointed archbishop (1576), 17
  role in Arran regime, 24–8
Alford, presbytery of, 151
Anderson, James, minister of Stirling
  (1582–89), commissioner of
  visitation for Dunblane etc.
  (1586), 35

Angus, Archibald Douglas, 8th Earl
  of, Ruthven Raider, 24, 29, 57
Angus, William Douglas, 10th Earl
  of, 42, 51–5, 178
  forfeited by Parliament (1594), 57
  excommunicated (1593), 53,
    (1608), 141
  see also Catholic earls
Angus and the Mearns, 36
  superintendent of, see John Erskine
    of Dun
  synod of, 57, 76, 133
Annandale, Earl of, see Sir John
  Murray of Lochmaben
Anne, Queen of James VI, 66, 67
  coronation (1590), 42–3
  marriage to James VI (1590), 42
Argyll, Archibald 'the Grim'
  Campbell, 7th Earl of, 60
  Bishop of, see John Campbell
  diocese of, 31, 68n., 98n., 134,
    144, 145
  mounts military expedition against
    Catholic Earls (1594), 58
Arran, Captain James Stewart, Earl
  of, 20, 22, 23, 24, 64, 149
  role in government (1583–85), 25–
  9
  received at court (1593), 51
Arran regime, 24–9, 49, 149, 177,
  182
Auchterarder, presbytery of, 37, 92,
  130, 196
Aylmer, John, Bishop of London
  (1577–94), 25
Ayr, 29, 166
  presbytery of, 138, 164n.

Ayrshire, 37, 168

Balcanquhal, Walter, minister of
    Edinburgh (1574–1616), 19, 26,
    51, 69, 70, 80, 93–4, 96, 134
Balfour, James, minister of Edinburgh
    (1589–1610), 70, 80, 93–4, 96,
    119n., 124–5
Balmerino, James Elphinstone, 1st
    Lord, Comptroller (1596–97),
    one of the Octavians, Secretary
    (1598–1609), Lord President
    (1605–09), 70, 112, 129
Bancroft, Richard, Archbishop of
    Canterbury (1604–10), 107, 125
Basilikon Doron, 87–9, 103
Beaton, James, Catholic Archbishop
    of Glasgow (1550–1603), 18,
    31, 41, 87
Bellenden, Adam, minister of Falkirk
    (1593–1616), Bishop of
    Dunblane (1615–35), 79, 177
Berwick upon Tweed, 125, 148
Binning, Lord, see Hamilton, Thomas
bishops, 8, 9–10, 30, 103–4, 106–7,
    112, 118, 122–3, 124, 127, 129,
    134, 139, 142–5, 146–7, 150,
    161, 165, 180–82, 184
    status during 1570s, 11–12, 14, 15,
        16, 17, 19, 21
    retained in 1586 settlement, 31–2,
        34–7
    restoration of, 83, 87–9, 91, 94–5,
        97, 99–100, 119–21
    attitude to Catholicism, 153–5
    attitude to liturgical innovations,
        158, 162–5, 167–8, 169–170
    see also individual dioceses and
        bishops
Black, David, minister of St Andrews
    (1590–97), 75, 76, 78, 80, 81,
    82, 118
    trial of (1596), 66–8, 70, 176
Black Acts (1584), 26–8, 31, 37n.,
    47, 49, 66–7, 117, 118, 119,
    120, 174
Blackburn, Peter, minister of Aber-
    deen (1582–1616), Bishop of
    Aberdeen (1606–16), 58, 71, 94,
    99, 102, 108, 137, 140, 144,
    150, 170, 174, 177

Blackhall, Andrew, minister of
    Musselburgh (1574–1609), 28
Blackness Castle, 46, 113, 116, 130,
    133
Body, Gilbert, minister of Holm,
    Orkney (1590–1606), 85
Bothwell, Adam, Bishop of Orkney
    (1559–93), 9, 31, 43
Bothwell, James Hepburn, 4th Earl,
    6, 9
Bothwell, Francis Stewart, 5th Earl,
    56, 178
    governing during absence of king
        (1589–90), 42
    accused of consulting with witches,
        warded and rebels (1591), 46,
        47
    poses as ally of the Kirk (1592),
        47, 57
    joins with Catholic Earls (1594),
        57–8
    exiled (1595), 59
Bowes, Robert, English ambassador
    to Scotland, 18, 20, 43, 54, 79
Boyd, James, Bishop of Glasgow
    (1573–81), 12, 14, 16, 17, 19
Brand, John, minister of Canongate,
    Edinburgh (1564–1600), 28
Brechin
    Bishop of, see Andrew Lamb
    diocese of, 144, 190, 193
Brig of Dee, rising by Catholic earls
    (1589), 41
Bruce, Robert, minister of
    Edinburgh (1587–1605), 45, 51,
    54, 69, 70, 80, 87, 91, 93–4, 96,
    181
    role in government (1589–90), 42,
        177
    crowns and anoints Queen Anne
        (1590), 43
    on crown commission against
        witches (1591), 46
    refusal to accept official version of
        'Gowrie Conspiracy', 94, 97,
        101
    deposed from ministry and ban-
        ished to Inverness (1605), 108,
        120
Buchanan, George, humanist scholar
    and tutor to James VI, 30, 42, 47

Burntisland, General Assembly at (1601), 95
Byres, George, minister of Legerwood, Melrose presbytery (1593–1640), 135

Caithness
  bishops of, see Alexander Forbes, George Gledstanes, Robert Pont
  diocese of, 144, 145
Caithness, Jean Gordon, Countess of (sister of the Earl Huntly), 92
Calderwood, David, minister of Crailing, Jedburgh presbytery (1606–17) and historian, 2, 140, 151–2, 171, 186n.
  resists visitation by Bishop Law (1607), 135
  protests against royal ecclesiastical policy and banished (1617), 159
Campbell, Archibald, Earl of Argyll, see Argyll, Earl of
Campbell, John, Bishop of the Isles (1572–1605), 19
Campbell, John, Bishop of Argyll (1607–13), 120
Carmichael, James, minister of Haddington (1588–1628), 26n., 28, 137
Carmichael, John, minister of Newburn (1595–1603), Kilconquhar (1603–22), St Andrews presbytery, 94, 119n., 124–5, 151–2
Charles I, King of Scots (1625–49), 145, 165, 170, 187
Catholic earls, 39, 44, 50–60, 63–7, 71, 80, 97, 119, 142, 175–6, 178; see also Huntly, Angus, Errol
Catholicism
  ecclesiastical action against, 40, 79, 92–3, 101–2, 107–8, 109, 142, 152–5, 157
  ecclesiastical demands for state action against, 19, 23–4, 39, 40–42, 43, 45–6, 47, 51, 52, 54–5, 61, 63–7, 75, 79, 92–3, 107, 114, 118, 165, 176, 181

state action against, 41–2, 44, 46–7, 52–3, 55, 57–60, 97, 117–18, 139, 141, 143, 155–6, 157, 180
Chirnside, presbytery of, 136, 138
Chisholm, Sir James of Cromlix, 53
Chisholm, William, Catholic Bishop of Dunblane (1561–89), 40, 41
Crichton Castle, 46
Christison, John, minister of Logie, Dundee presbytery (1576–1608), 24n.
Clapperton, John, minister of Coldstream, Chirnside presbytery (1576–1617), 182n.
Civil War (1568–73), 6–7
Clydesdale, synod of, 54, 132, 133, 138
Colden, John, minister of Kinross, Dunfermline presbytery (1593–1640), 131n.
Colt, Adam, minister of Musselburgh, Edinburgh/Dalkeith presbytery (1597–1643), 119n., 124–5
commission of the General Assembly
  before 1597, 59, 63–9, 71
  after 1596, 80–82, 83, 84, 90, 94, 97, 102, 103, 104, 105–7, 108–9, 112, 118, 119–21, 122–3, 124, 127–8, 134, 139, 141, 142–3, 146–7, 180–81
commissioners of visitation, 8, 12, 14, 17, 192
  after 1586, 34–7, 195
Concordat of Leith (1572), 10–12, 14, 15, 17, 182, 193
constant moderators, see synods and presbyteries
conventicles, 169, 174, 186
Conventions of the Estates, 119
  Stirling, March 1578, 16;
  Holyrood, Feb. 1581, 20;
  Perth, 20 July 1582, 22;
  Holyrood, Oct. 1582, 23;
  Holyrood, June 1590, attended by 3 ministers, 43–4;
  Perth, Oct. 1593, 54;
  Holyrood, Nov. 1593, 54–5;
  Holyrood, March 1595, 59;
  Perth Feb./March 1597, 76,

78; Dundee, May 1597;
Edinburgh, Jan. 1609, 143
conventions of ministers and others,
unofficial
Edinburgh, Jan. 1588, 40–41;
Edinburgh, Jan. 1593, 51;
Edinburgh, Oct. 1593, 54
Convocation, 79, 156
Counter-Reformation, 176
Covenanting Revolution (1638), 1,
187
Cowper, William, Bishop of Gallo-
way (1612–19), 158, 161
Craig, John, minister of Edinburgh
(1563–73), Aberdeen (1573–79),
king's minister (1579–1600), 10,
19, 28
Cranston, William, minister of Kettle,
Cupar presbytery (1589–1620),
131 and n., 182n.
Cunningham, presbytery of, 37
Cupar, 64
presbytery of, 89, 131n., 149–50

Dalgleish, Nicol, minister of St
Cuthbert's, Edinburgh presbytery
(1581–88), 27
Dalkeith, 132
presbytery of, 35, 38, 52, 54, 113,
134, 137, 163, 164, 169, 194
Darnley, Henry Stewart, Lord,
husband of Mary Queen of
Scots, 6, 20
Davidson, John, regent at St
Leonard's College, St Andrews
(1570–74), minister of Liberton
(1579–84), Canongate (1590–
95) both Edinburgh presbytery,
Prestonpans, Haddington
presbytery (1595–1604), 13,
26n., 51, 86–7, 95
Deer, presbytery of, 102, 108, 110,
113, 126, 137, 140, 142, 150
Disruption (1843), 3
Douglas, Alexander, Bishop of
Moray (1602–23), 119, 151,
153, 154
Douglas, George, Bishop of Moray
(1575–89), 12
Douglas, John, principal of St Mary's
College St Andrews (1547–74),

Archbishop of St Andrews
(1572–74), 7, 9, 10, 11, 17
Doune Castle, 116
Dumbarton, 166
Castle, 20, 116, 150
presbytery of, 138
Dumfries, presbytery of, 137–8
Dunbar, 166
presbytery of, 113, 137, 138
George Hume of Spott, Earl of,
Lord High Treasurer (1601–
11), 5, 113, 117, 129, 139,
141, 142, 145n., 146, 147,
148, 149
George, minister of Ayr (1608–11),
150
Dunblane
bishops of, see Adam Bellenden,
William Chisholm, Andrew
Graham, George Graham
diocese of, 35, 144, 190, 193
presbytery of, 37, 40, 162, 166,
196
Duncan, Andrew, minister of Crail, St
Andrews presbytery (1597–
1620), 116–17n., 125–6
Duncanson, John, king's minister
(1567–1601), 19, 28
attends Convention of Estates
(1590), 44
on crown commission against
witches (1591), 46
Dundee, 81, 159
General Assemblies at, 18, 19, 52,
78, 79–81, 82, 84, 85–6
Dunfermline, 153
presbytery of, 126
Dunfermline, Alexander Seton, 1st
Earl of, Lord President (1593–
1605), Chancellor (1605–22)
one of the Octavians, 61, 65, 70,
106, 117, 122–3, 143, 148, 153
role in Aberdeen Assembly (1605),
110, 111–12, 113
Dunkeld
bishops of, see Alexander Lindsay,
James Paton
diocese of, 12, 144, 190, 193
Duns, presbytery of, 136, 138
Durie, John, minister of Edinburgh
(1573–85), Montrose, Brechin

presbytery (1585–1600), 14, 19, 22, 23, 24n., 25
Durie, Robert, minister of Anstruther, St Andrews presbytery (1592–1606), 116–17n., 125–6
Dykes, John, minister of Kilrenny, St Andrews presbytery (1596–1634), 131n.
Dysart, synod of Fife at (1607), 131

ecclesiastical finance, 7, 8–9, 10, 13, 40, 43, 47, 61, 62–3, 82–3, 84–5, 90, 96, 97, 107, 121, 128, 159, 178
ecclesiastical polity, 7–18, 34–7, 69, 75, 77, 85, 99, 101, 102–3, 114, 149, 174, 183
  see also bishops, superintendents, synods, presbyteries, Concordat of Leith, commissioners of visitation
Edinburgh, 9, 21, 28–9, 44, 52, 54, 65, 74, 81, 161, 163, 177
  Castle, 7, 19, 20, 41, 46, 95, 116
  ministers of, 19, 69, 72, 74–6, 78, 80, 81, 84, 93, 94, 97
  see also Walter Balcanquhal, James Balfour, Robert Bruce, John Craig, John Durie, Patrick Galloway, John Hall, Peter Hewatt, John Knox, James Lawson, William Watson
  college of, 28, 60, 80
  council of, 70, 168
  presbytery of, 22, 35, 42, 45–6, 51–3, 59, 63, 65, 67, 74–6, 78, 80, 86, 89, 92, 94, 95, 101, 134, 137
  'riot' in, (1596), 69–70, 72–3, 75, 80, 81, 84, 88, 176
  reaction to Five Articles of Perth, 167, 168–9, 170
Elizabeth, Queen of England, 27, 29, 30, 41, 50, 57, 66, 97, 179, 184
Elizabeth, Princess, daughter of James VI, 67, 79, 92
Ellon, presbytery of, 96, 108, 113, 120, 126, 137, 140, 142, 144, 153

Elphinstone, James, see Lord Balmerino
England, 6, 13, 14, 18, 20, 25, 26, 29, 79, 96, 99–100, 107, 115, 149, 156, 170, 174–5, 178, 183–4
  intervenes in Scottish affairs, 7, 20, 41, 50, 57, 158
episcopacy, see bishops
Errol, Francis Hay, 9th Earl of, 42, 50, 51–5, 58, 65, 77, 93, 119, 142, 152–4, 176, 178
  ordered to surrender his castle to the crown (1589), 41
  forfeited by parliament (1594), 57
  exiled (1595), 59
  returns to Scotland (1596), 64
  excommunicated (1593), 53, (1608), 141
  see also Catholic earls
Errol, Elizabeth Douglas, Countess of (wife of the above), 63, 65, 93, 153
Erskine of Dun, John, superintendent of Angus and the Mearns (1561–89), 9, 10, 11, 12, 36
exercise, Scottish, 18, 38, 71n., 114, 131, 135, 137, 149, 152; see also presbyteries, English

Falkland, 150
  Palace, 64
  ecclesiastical conferences at, 90, 134, 139
Ferguson, David, minister of Dunfermline, 24n., 84
Ferme, Charles, minister of Fraserburgh, Deer presbytery (1598–1617), 137, 151
Fife, 98, 167
  synod of, 32, 52–3, 54, 62, 63, 65, 76, 84, 85, 89, 94, 96–7, 105, 109, 112, 114, 115, 118, 131, 133, 138, 140
  reaction to constant moderation 131
  and Strathearn, superintendent of, see John Winram
  see also St Andrews, synod of 'benorth Forth'
First Book of Discipline (1560), 7, 10

Five Articles of Perth (1618), 29,
145, 181, 182, 186–7
introduction of, 157–8, 159–62
enforcement of, 164–70
lay reaction to, 166–9
see also liturgical innovations,
James VI, bishops
Forbes, Alexander, Bishop of Caithness (1604–16), Bishop of
Aberdeen (1616–17), 119, 157
Forbes, Arthur, 10th Lord, 69
Forbes, John, minister of Alford
(1593–1606), 109–10, 116–17n.,
125–6
Forbes of Corse, Patrick, Bishop of
Aberdeen (1618–35), 174, 177

Gaelic Scotland, 5 and n., 9, 37, 98,
184–6; see also Argyll, Isles
Galloway
bishops of, see Gavin Hamilton,
William Cowper
diocese of, 138, 144, 145
Galloway, Patrick, minister of Perth
(1581–84), king's minister
(1589–1626), minister of
Edinburgh (1607–26), 24n., 26,
41, 54, 58, 64, 71, 98, 103, 110,
118, 120, 127, 132, 139n., 177
attends Convention of Estates
(1590), 44
opinion of Five Articles of Perth,
159–60, 163, 186
General Assembly, 8–10, 26, 30, 34,
65, 67, 68–9, 74, 91, 103, 112,
115, 120, 121, 122, 128, 138,
144, 156, 159, 180
power of summons of, 32, 33–4,
56, 77, 78, 115, 138, 146
composition and election of, 15n.,
32, 38, 77, 79–80, 82, 85–6,
98–9 and n., 126–7, 139–140,
144–5, 157, 160, 162, 178
Meetings of (at Edinburgh unless
otherwise stated): July 1567,
6, 7; July, 1569, 8–9; March
1571, 34; Leith, Jan. 1572,
10; St Andrews, March 1572,
10–11; Perth, Aug. 1572, 11;
March 1574, 13; Aug. 1575,
14–15; Oct. 1576, 17; April

1577, 17; Oct. 1577, 15;
April 1578, 16–17; Stirling,
June 1578, 16–17; October
1578, 17; July 1579, 18;
Dundee, July 1580, 18, 19;
Glasgow, April 1581, 21; St
Andrews, April 1582, 22;
June, 1582, 22; Oct. 1582,
23; Oct. 1583, 24; May 1586,
31, 32–3; June 1587, 36, 39;
Feb. 1588; Aug. 1588, 41;
June 1589, 36; March 1590,
42; Aug. 1590, 36, 44–5; July
1591, 45; May 1592, 47;
Dundee, April 1593, 52; May
1594, 55–6, 57; Montrose,
June 1595, 59; March 1596,
60–62; Perth, Feb./March
1597, 72–3, 75–8, 80, 127,
172; St Andrews, April 1597
(abortive), 76, 77, 78;
Dundee, May 1597, 78, 79–
81; Dundee, March 1598, 83,
84–7; Montrose, March 1600,
91–2; Burntisland, May 1601,
94, 95–6; Holyrood, Nov.
1602, 96–8; Aberdeen, July
1604 (abortive), 104–5;
Aberdeen July 1605 (illegal),
108–12, 124–5, 146, 180,
state's reaction, 111–12,
kirk's reaction, 112–15, trials
and sentences of those
involved, 116–17, 122, 125–
6; Linlithgow, Dec. 1606, 71,
126–9; Linlithgow, July 1608,
139–43; Glasgow, June 1610,
71, 144–7, 148, 149; Aberdeen, Aug. 1616, 154, 157; St
Andrews, Nov. 1617, 160–61;
Perth, Aug. 1618, 162–3
Geneva, 12, 44, 176
Gibson, James, minister of
Pencaitland, (1580–97), 45
Glamis, Thomas Lyons, Master of,
Ruthven Raider, 24
Glamis, Patrick Lyon, Lord, later Earl
of Kinghorn, 102
Glasgow, 6, 21, 54, 151, 164
archbishops of, see James Beaton,
James Boyd, James Law,

Robert Montgomery, John Spottiswoode
council of, 140
diocese of, 12, 144
General Assemblies at, 21, 144–7
presbytery of, 21–2, 38, 52, 54, 65, 68, 79, 92, 96, 115, 126n., 136, 140, 141, 142, 162
university of, 22, 28
Gledstanes, George, minister of St Andrews (1597–1612), Bishop of Caithness (1600–04), Archbishop of St Andrews (1604–15), 94, 97, 103, 118, 119, 131, 133, 138, 140, 144–5, 149–50, 151, 153–4, 157, 175
Glenlivet, Battle of (1594), 58
Golden Act (1592), 37–8, 39, 47–9, 50–51, 60, 67, 115, 120
Gordon, James, Jesuit (uncle of Earl of Huntly), 45
Gordon, Sir Patrick of Auchindoun, 53, 58
Gowrie Conspiracy (1600), 93–4, 97, 101
Gowrie, William Ruthven, 1st Earl of, Lord High Treasurer (1571–84), 24
   leader of Ruthven Raid (1582), 23, 25
Gowrie, John Ruthven, 3rd Earl of, 93
Graham, Andrew, Bishop of Dunblane (1575–94), 14, 19
Graham, George, Bishop of Dunblane (1603–15), 151, 154
Graham of Fintry, David, 40
Gunpowder Plot (1605), 115

Haddington, 101
   Earl of, see Thomas Hamilton
   presbytery of, 38, 52, 54, 74, 110, 114, 118, 126, 127, 137, 138, 140, 152
Hailes Castle, 46
Hall, John, minister of Edinburgh (1598–1619), 93–4, 95, 101, 134
Hamilton
   Gavin, Bishop of Galloway (1605–12), 119, 141, 147
   of Bothwellhaugh, James, 7

John, Catholic Archbishop of St Andrews (1547–71), 9
John, Lord and 1st Marquis of, 70
   presbytery of, 138
Thomas, Lord Binning, 1st Earl of Melrose, 1st Earl of Haddington, Lord Advocate (1596–1612), Secretary (1612–27), Lord President (1616–26), one of the Octavians, 70, 132, 161, 169
Hampton Court
   conference at between king and English Puritan clergy (1604), 85, 102, 103, 107, 124, 179
   conference at between king and Scottish ministers (1606), 124–6, 180
Hay, Andrew, minister of Renfrew, Paisley presbytery (1560–91) and rector of Glasgow University (1569–86), 10, 24n., 27
Hay, John, minister of Renfrew (1593–1627), son of the above, 136
Henry, Prince, son and heir of James VI, (d. 1612), 57, 59, 88–9
Hepburn, Alexander, Bishop of Ross (1575–78), 14
Heriot, parish of, 35
Herries, John, minister of Newbattle, Dalkeith presbytery (1583–1620), 28
Hewatt, Peter, minister of Edinburgh (1594–1617), 159
High Commission, courts of, 144, 149, 150, 151, 153, 157, 159, 164, 181, 184
historiography, 1–4, 147, 171–5, 179, 183–4
Holyrood Palace, 46, 158, 161, 184
   conference of ministers and privy councillors at (1586), 30–32
   General Assembly at (1602), 96
   Conventions of Estates at, 52, 54
Howison, John, minister of Cambuslang, Glasgow presbytery (1580–1618), 22, 27
Hume, Alexander, minister of Logie, Dunblane presbytery (1597–1609), 72, 175

Hume, Alexander, Lord and 1st Earl
    of, 53, 56–7
Hume, George, of Spott, see Earl of
    Dunbar
Hunter, Andrew, minister of
    Newburn, St Andrews presbytery
    (1588–94), 56
Huntingtower, 23, 24
Huntly, George Gordon, 6th Earl and
    1st Marquis of, 39, 42, 44, 45–6,
    50, 58, 65, 69, 75–6, 77, 102,
    107–9, 115, 118, 119, 142, 152–
    4, 176, 178
    in correspondence with Philip of
        Spain (1589), 41, 51–5
    ordered to surrender his castle to
        the crown (1589), 41
    and murder of Earl of Moray
        (1592), 46–7
    forfeited by parliament (1594), 57
    exiled (1595), 59
    returns to Scotland (1596), 63
    excommunicated (1593), 53,
        (1608), 141
    absolved (1597), 76, 80, 102
        (1615–16), 154
Huntly, Henrietta Stewart, Countess
    of (sister of Ludovic, Duke of
    Lennox and wife of the above),
    45–6, 61, 63, 65, 67, 92, 118,
    153

Inverness, 108, 120, 150, 177, 185
Ireland, 24, 141, 162, 185–6
Irvine, presbytery of, 137
Irving, James, minister of Tough,
    Alford presbytery (1599–1607),
    151
Isles
    bishops of, see John Campbell,
        Andrew Knox
    diocese of, 31, 68n., 98n., 134,
        144, 145

James V, King of Scots (1513–42), 13
James VI, King of Scots (1567–1625),
    50, 68, 93
    coronation of (1567), 6
    nominal majority of (1578), 16
    and the Ruthven regime (1582–83),
        23–4

assumes government (1585), 29, 30
absence in Scandinavia (1589–90),
    42, 45, 46, 177
reaction to Huntly's return (1596),
    63–5
reaction to Edinburgh 'riot' (1596),
    69–70, 81, 88, 176
holds conferences on parliamentary
    representation (1598–1600),
    85, 90–91, 94–5, 178
accession to English throne (1603),
    101
reaction to Assembly at Aberdeen
    (1605), 112, 117
calls 8 ministers south (1606), 119,
    124–5
visits Scotland (1617), 158–9
absentee kingship, 5, 81, 101–2,
    106, 111–12, 122–3, 124,
    128–9, 139, 147, 153–4, 167,
    179–81
attitude to Anglo-Scottish union,
    107, 184, 186
attitude to enforcement of Five
    Articles of Perth, 165, 167,
    168, 170
attitude to Catholicism, 39, 41, 45,
    49, 50, 57–8, 65, 95, 115,
    142, 153–4, 165, 170
attitude to Church of England, 44,
    85, 88, 102–3, 156, 158, 183–
    4
confrontations with Andrew
    Melville, 64–5, 125
and the General Assembly, 33, 39,
    44, 47, 52, 55–6, 60–61, 72–
    3, 75–8, 79–81, 82, 84–7,
    91–2, 95–8, 104, 115, 126,
    139, 141, 146, 161, 162, 178
military action against Catholic
    Earls, 41, 52, 58
reaction to protests over inaction
    against Catholics, 39–41, 47,
    50, 54–6, 57
views on ecclesiastical jurisdiction
    and royal supremacy, 39–40,
    44–5, 67, 69, 70, 72–3, 74,
    79, 87–90, 115, 118, 180
views on ecclesiastical polity, 36–7,
    37n., 43, 87–9, 94, 102–3,
    118, 134, 156, 182–4

see also Basilikon Doron

Jesuits, Catholic missionaries etc., 24, 39, 43, 45, 92, 119, 153, 154–5

Jedburgh, 54
  presbytery of, 120, 126, 132, 134, 135–6, 139, 144, 151

Johnstone, George, minister of Ancrum, Melrose presbytery (1572–1622), 135, 151–2

Johnstone, John, regent at St Mary's College, St Andrews (1593–1611), 82, 84

Justice, Alexander, minister of Ashkirk, Melrose presbytery (1604–11), 135

Kilrenny, 151

King, George, Bishop of London (1611–18), 125, 139n.

Kinneil, 22, 24

Kirkcudbright, presbytery of, 110, 138

kirk sessions, 8, 18, 21

Knox, Andrew, minister of Paisley (1585–1607), Bishop of the Isles (1605–18), 71, 119

Knox, John, minister of Edinburgh (1560–72), 3, 6, 7, 9, 47
  views on episcopacy, 11

Knox, John, minister of Melrose (1584–1623), 134–5

Lamb, Andrew, minister of Burntisland, Kirkcaldy presbytery (1593–95), Bishop of Brechin (1607–19), Bishop of Galloway (1619–34), 53, 147, 153, 163, 168

Langside, Battle of (1568), 6

Lauriston, Sir Alexander Straiton of, 102, 105, 109–11, 122, 125

Law, James, minister of Kirkliston, Linlithgow presbytery (1585–1610), Bishop of Orkney (1605–15), Archbishop of Glasgow (1615–32), 99, 105, 119, 135–6, 139, 140, 142, 144, 157, 164
  reluctance to enforce Five Articles of Perth, 169

Lawson, James, minister of Edinburgh (1572–84), 19, 24n., 25, 26

Leith, 9, 30, 74, 126
  General Assembly at, 1572, 10
  see also Concordat of Leith, David Lindsay

Lennox, Matthew Stewart, 4th Earl of and Regent of Scotland (1570–71), 7, 13, 33

Lennox, Esmé Stewart, Lord d'Aubigny, 1st Duke of, favourite of James VI, 18, 19, 20, 21, 22, 23, 24, 51

Lennox, Ludovic Stewart, 2nd Duke of, son of Esmé, 58, 61

Leslie, John, Catholic Bishop of Ross (1566–89), 18, 41

Lindsay, Alexander, minister of St Madoes, Perth presbytery (1591–1638), Bishop of Dunkeld (1607–38), 130, 151, 153, 154

Lindsay, James, 7th Lord, 69

Lindsay, David, minister of Leith, Edinburgh presbytery (1560–1613), Bishop of Ross (1600–13), 10, 12n., 24n., 27, 33, 58, 71, 77, 97, 99, 103, 117, 122, 145, 151, 154, 174, 177
  commissioner of Lothian (1586–89), 35–6
  attends Convention of Estates (1590), 44
  made Bishop of Ross (1600), 94
  misgivings about royal ecclesiastical policy, 117, 122

Lindsay, David, minister of St Andrews (1597–1606), 117–18

Lindsay of Balcarres, John, Secretary (1596–98), one of the Octavians, 62, 81

Linlithgow, 54, 70, 116
  Countess of, *see* Lady Livingstone
  Earl of, *see* Lord Livingstone
  General Assemblies at, 126–9, 139–43
  Parliament at, December (1585), 30
  presbytery of, 92, 137, 152, 153, 166

liturgical innovations, 155–6, 158,
182, 184
see also Five Articles of Perth
Livingstone, Henry, minister of St
Ninians, Stirling presbytery
(1587–1624), 130–31
Livingstone, Helen Hay, Lady and
Countess of Linlithgow, 65, 67,
79, 92, 153
Livingstone, Alexander, 7th Lord and
1st Earl of Linlithgow (husband
of the above), 79, 145n.
Lochleven Castle, 6
Lothian, 36, 76, 98, 167
commissioner for, *see* David
Lindsay
superintendent of, *see* John
Spottiswoode snr
(and Tweeddale 1586–1610),
synod of, 19, 21, 42–4, 45, 65,
74–6, 84, 101, 105, 107, 114,
116, 119, 132, 133, 136–7,
138

Maitland of Thirlestane, John,
Secretary (1584–91), Chancellor
(1586–95), 30, 178
unhappy with royal failure to
avenge Moray's murder
(1592), 47
role in formulation of Golden Act
(1592), 47–9
Mar, John Erskine, 1st Earl of and
Regent of Scotland (1571–72), 7,
13
Mar, John Erskine, 2nd Earl of and
Ruthven Raider, 23, 24, 29, 60,
180n.
Mary, Queen of Scots (1542–67, d.
1587), 6, 9, 30, 39
Melrose
Earl of, *see* Thomas Hamilton
presbytery of, 126, 134–5, 139,
152
Melville, Andrew, principal of
Glasgow University (1574–80),
principal of St Mary's College, St
Andrews (1580–1606), 28, 32,
43, 58, 64, 80, 83, 98, 106, 173,
175
returns to Scotland (1574), 12–13

role in Kirk of 1570s, 13–14, 16
called before privy council and
flees to England (1584), 25
composes verses for Queen Anne's
coronation (1590), 42
confrontations with James VI, 64–
5, 125
loses rectorship of St Andrews
University and barred from
presbytery (1597), 82
excluded from General Assemblies,
84, 92, 96
summoned to England (1606),
119n.
imprisoned in England (1607), 125
Melville, James, regent at St Andrews
University (1580–86), minister of
Anstruther (1586–90), Kilrenny
(1590–1614) both St Andrews
presbytery, diarist, 2, 3, 32, 54,
56, 58, 64, 80, 87, 94, 106, 118,
151, 171–2, 177–8, 181
flees to England (1584), 26, 175
reaction to subscription of Black
Acts (1584), 28
opinions on parliamentary representation, 62–3, 83–5, 177–8
summoned to England (1606),
119n., 124–5
warded in Berwick (1607), 125,
148–9
Merse and Teviotdale, synod of, 132–
4, 138, 139, 165
Moffat, James, Jesuit, 155
Montbirneau, French ambassador to
Scotland, 19
Montgomery, Robert, minister of
Stirling (1572–82), Archbishop of
Glasgow (1580–85), 26, 39–40
appointed Archbishop (1581), 21
deprived and excommunicated
(1582), 21–2
Montrose, General Assemblies at, 59,
91
Moray
bishops of, *see* George Douglas,
Alexander Douglas
diocese of, 144
James Stewart, Earl of and Regent
of Scotland (1567–70), 6, 7,
13, 47

James Stewart, 'Bonnie' Earl of,
    murdered (1592), 46–7
synod of, 76, 102, 109, 118, 133
Morton, James Douglas, 4th Earl of
    and Regent of Scotland (1572–
    78), 7, 9, 10, 13, 16, 17, 18, 19,
    20, 23, 30
Murray of Lochmaben, Sir John
    (later Earl of Annandale), 154
Murray, Sir Patrick, gentleman of
    king's bedchamber, 75, 78, 80, 84
Musselburgh, 74

Negative Confession (1581), 21, 42,
    120
Nicolson, George, English ambassa-
    dor, 84, 87
Nicolson, James, minister of Meigle
    (1583–1607), Bishop of Dunkeld
    (1607), 58, 64, 68, 71, 130, 177

Octavians, 61, 62, 65, 70
Ogill, David, minister of Barra,
    Haddington presbytery (1594–
    1629), 74–5
Ogilvie, St John, trial and execution
    of (1614–15), 154–5
Orkney
    bishops of, see Adam Bothwell,
        James Law
    diocese of, 144, 145
Oswald, Archibald, minister of
    Pencatiland, Haddington
    presbytery (1598–1631), 152

Paisley, presbytery of, 115
Parliament, 3, 7, 14, 16, 119, 142,
    180n.
    ecclesiastical representation in, 9,
        31, 43–4, 47, 62–3, 82–5, 89–
        92, 94–5, 103–4, 106–7, 120,
        176–8
    meetings of (at Edinburgh unless
        otherwise stated): Aug. 1560,
        'Reformation Parliament', 6;
        Dec. 1567, 6–7; Stirling, June–
        July 1578, 17; May and Aug.
        1584, 26–7, 117; Linlithgow,
        Dec. 1585, 30; Holyrood, July
        1587, 40; April–June 1592,
        47–9; June 1594, 57; Dec.

1597, 83; July 1604, 103–4,
    180; Perth, July 1606, 120–22;
    Aug. 1607, 138–9; June 1609,
    143–4; Oct. 1612, 149; June
    1617, 159; June 1621, 145,
    165–6
Paton, James, Bishop of Dunkeld
    (1571–84), 12, 14
Peebles, 164
    presbytery of, 67, 79, 96, 136, 138
Perth, 23, 93, 105–7, 116
    Convention of the Estates at
        (1594), 54
    General Assemblies at, 11, 72–3,
        75–8, 80, 162–3
    parliament at (1606), 120–22
    presbytery of, 136, 141, 162, 169
    and Stirling, synod of, 53, 55, 62,
        130–31, 136, 138, 151
    see also Five Articles of Perth
Perthshire, 139
Philip II, King of Spain, 20n.
    in correspondence with the Earl of
        Huntly, 41, 51–5
Polwart, Andrew, minister of Cadder,
    Glasgow presbytery (1578–87),
    26n.
Pont, Robert, minister of St
    Cuthbert's, Edinburgh presbytery
    (1574–1606), Lord of Session,
    10, 12, 26 and n., 37, 78
presbyteries, 18, 21, 26, 31–2, 34,
    52, 62, 67–8, 83, 89, 109, 110,
    115, 120, 126, 142, 149, 150,
    166–7, 194
    absenteeism from, 152, 166, 187
    constant moderation of, 128, 134–
        8, 180
    co-operation with crown, 59–60
    development of after 1586, 35, 36,
        37–9, 60, 196
    English 18
    see also individual places
Privy Council, 10, 13, 24, 40, 42, 44,
    50, 59–60, 66–9, 102, 105, 108,
    111, 114, 115, 122, 130–34,
    136, 138, 144, 147, 153, 155,
    158, 161, 163–4

Rait, David, minister in St Andrews
    presbytery (1605), 114

Randolph, Thomas, English diplomat, 20
Reformation (1560), 1, 88, 158, 169, 182
regal union, see James VI, absentee kingship
Reid, John, minister of Logie-Buchan, Ellon presbytery (1594–1621), 137
religious houses, 10, 83 and n., 121,
Rig, William, bailie of Edinburgh, 169
Robertson, David, minister Inverugie, Deer presbytery (1599–1637), 137
Rollock, Robert, principal of college of Edinburgh (1585–99), 60, 80
Ross
  bishops of, see Alexander Hepburn, John Leslie, David Lindsay
  diocese of, 110, 144
Ross, John, minister in synod of Perth and Stirling, 55–6
Row, John, minister of Perth (1560–80), 7
Row, John, minister of Carnock, Dunfermline presbytery (1592–1646) and historian, 2, 171
Row, William, minister of Forgandenny, Perth presbytery (1589–1624), 130, 151
Roxburgh, Robert Kerr, 1st Lord and 1st Earl of, 134–5, 168
Rutherford, John, minister of Kilconquhar, St Andrews presbytery (1594–1603), 82
Ruthven
  John, see Earl of Gowrie
  William, see Earl of Gowrie
  Raid of (1582), 23
  Regime (1582–3), 23–4
    attempts to regain power (1584), 25

St Andrews, 29, 76, 81, 107, 166
  archbishops of, see Patrick Adamson, John Douglas, George Gledstanes, John Hamilton, John Spottiswoode
  diocese of, 11, 12, 27, 144

General Assemblies at, 10, 22, 76–8, 80, 160
presbytery of, 18, 39, 52, 54, 66, 67, 82, 86, 89, 96, 103, 105, 114, 131
provincial synod of (1614), 156
synod of 'benorth Forth', 151, 153, 156, 161, 162, 164, 166, 168, 175, 186
  see also Fife, synod of
university of, 9, 13, 53, 82, 84
  St Leonard's College, 91
  St Mary's College, 28, 64
Scone, Abbey of, 93
  David Murray, 1st Lord and 1st Viscount Stormont, 130, 170
Scot, William, minister of Kennoway, Kirkcaldy presbytery (1593–1604), Cupar (1604–42) and historian, 2, 68n., 71, 94, 151–2, 171
  summoned to England (1606), 119n., 124–5, 180n.
Scrimgeour, Alexander, minister of Kinghorn, Kirkcaldy presbytery (1620–39), 167
Scrimgeour, John, minister of Kinghorn (1606–20), 131n., 151–2
Second Book of Discipline, 14–16, 17, 18, 19, 21, 23, 34, 178
Seton, Alexander, see Earl of Dunfermline
Sharp, John, minister of Kilmany, Cupar presbytery (1601–06), 116–17n., 125–6
Sharp, Patrick, principal of Glasgow University (1585–1615), 136
Sibbald, Abraham, minister of Deer (1586–1621), 137
Simson, Archibald, minister of Dalkeith (1586–1628), 159
Simson, Patrick, minister of Stirling (1590–1618), 87, 95, 96, 136, 158
Skene of Curriehill, Sir James, Lord of Session, 168
Slains Castle, 58
Smeton, Thomas, principal of Glasgow University (1580–85), 24n.

Spain, 23, 40–41, 50–51, 53, 55, 59–60, 102, 141, 165, 170, 176, 178

Spanish Armada (1588), 40–41, 59

'Spanish Blanks' affair (1593), 51–2

Spottiswoode, John, minister of Calder, Linlithgow presbytery (1560–83), superintendent of Lothian (1560–85), 7, 11, 12

Spottiswoode, John (son of the above), minister of Calder (1583–1608), Archbishop of Glasgow (1603–15), Archbishop of St Andrews (1615–38), 2, 14, 71, 99, 105, 107, 114, 119, 120, 132–3, 136, 140, 144–5, 146, 147, 154–5, 157, 160, 162–3, 165, 171–2, 174, 177
  misgivings about royal policy, 109, 117, 122, 154, 162–3, 170
  attitude to the Five Articles of Perth, 163, 167, 169–70

Stewart, Captain James, see Earl of Arran

Stewart, Esmé, see Duke of Lennox

Stewart, Colonel William, captain of the king's guard, 24, 29

Stirling, 6, 7, 161
  Castle, 24, 116
  Convention of the Estates at (1578), 16
  General Assembly at (1578), 16–17
  Parliament at (1578), 17
  presbytery of, 21–2, 35, 37, 38, 40, 52, 53, 60, 67, 79, 92, 96, 136, 138, 139, 142, 152, 156, 196

Stirlingshire, 36, 139

Strachan, Alexander, minister of Creich, Cupar presbytery (1605–07), 116–17n.

Straiton of Lauriston, Sir Alexander, see Lauriston

Straiton, John, minister of Forres (1599–1613), 150

Strathbogie Castle, 58, 152

Subscription crisis (1584), 27–9

superintendents, 6, 8–12, 34, 36, 191, 192

Sutherland, Jean Gordon, Countess of (Huntly's aunt), 92

Sutherland, John Gordon, 12th Earl of, 154

Sutherland, presbytery of, 138

synods, 8, 31–2, 34, 52, 58, 59, 62, 63, 84, 89, 90, 94, 103, 104, 109, 112, 118–19, 159, 194
  absenteeism from, 166, 187
  constant moderation of, 129–34, 146, 180
  see also individual synods

Turriff, presbytery of, 144

union with England, attempted, 103–5, 107, 180, 184

Wales, 185

Wallace, Robert, minister of St Andrews (1593–97), 81, 118, 119n., 124–5

Walsingham, Francis, English statesman, 27

Watson, William, minister of Edinburgh (1585–1601), Burntisland, Kirkcaldy presbytery (1601–15), 69, 93–4, 96, 119n., 124–5, 151

Welsh, John, minister of Ayr (1600–06), 111, 116–17n., 125–6

Wemyss, David, minister of Glasgow (1562–1615), 22

Whitgift, John, Archbishop of Canterbury (1583–1604), 25, 27

Wigtown, presbytery of, 120, 138

Wilkie, Robert, minister of St Andrews (1586–90), principal of St Leonard's College, St Andrews (1570–91), 91

William the Lion, King of Scots (1165–1214), 1

Willock, John, superintendent of the West (1561–?), 7

Winram, John, superintendent of Fife (1561–82), 7, 9, 10, 11, 21

Winram, Robert, collector of thirds in Fife, 10n.

witchcraft, 46, 57

Young, Peter, tutor to James VI, 30

Youngson, Robert, minister of Clatt, Alford presbytery (1601–18), 116, 151